5-24-73

BURT FRANKLIN: RESEARCH & SOURCE WORKS SERIES
American Classics in History and Social Science 248

THE
TRADE UNION WOMAN

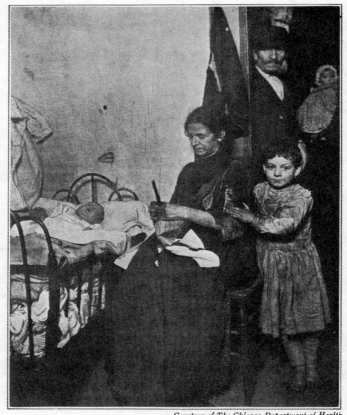

Courtesy of The Chicago Department of Health

A FACTORY OR A HOME?

THE
TRADE UNION WOMAN

BY

ALICE HENRY

MEMBER OF OFFICE EMPLOYÉS' ASSOCIATION OF CHICAGO, No. 12755,
AND FORMERLY EDITOR OF *LIFE AND LABOR*

BURT FRANKLIN
New York, N. Y.

Published by LENOX HILL Pub. & Dist. Co. (Burt Franklin)
235 East 44th St., New York, N.Y. 10017
Reprinted in the U.S.A.
Printed in the U.S.A.

Burt Franklin: Research and Source Works Series
American Classics in History and Social Science 248

Reprinted from the original edition in the University of Minnesota
    Library.

Library of Congress Cataloging in Publication Data

Henry, Alice, 1857-1943.
    The trade union woman.

    Bibliography: p.
    1. Women in trade-unions. 2. Women in trade-unions—United States.
I. Title.
HD6079.H46 1973   331.88   73-2799
ISBN 0-8337-5291-X

TO

THE TRADE UNION WOMEN
OF THE UNITED STATES AND CANADA

PREFACE

This brief account of trade unionism in relation to the working-women of the United States has been written to furnish a handbook of the subject, and to supply in convenient form answers to the questions that are daily put to the writer and to all others who feel the organization of women to be a vital issue.

To treat the subject exhaustively would be impossible without years of research, but meanwhile it seemed well to furnish this short popular account of an important movement, in order to satisfy the eager desire for information regarding the working-woman, and her attitude towards the modern labor movement, and towards the national industries in regard to which she plays so essential a part. Women are doing their share of their country's work under entirely novel conditions, and it therefore becomes a national responsibility to see that the human worker is not sacrificed to the material product.

Many of the difficulties and dangers surrounding the working-woman affect the workingman also, but on the other hand, there are special reasons, springing out of the ancestral claims which life makes upon woman, arising also out of her domestic and social environment, and again out of her special function as mother, why the condition of the wage-earning woman should be the subject of separate consideration. It is impossible to discuss intelligently wages, hours and sanitation in reference to women workers unless these facts are borne in mind.

What makes the whole matter of overwhelming importance is the wasteful way in which the health, the lives, and the capacity for future motherhood of our young girls are squandered during the few brief years they spend as human machines in our factories and stores. Youth, joy and the possibility of future happiness lost forever, in order that we may have cheap (or dear), waists or shoes or watches.

Further, since the young girl is the future mother of the race, it is she who chooses the father of her children. Every condition, either economic or social, whether of training or of environment, which in any degree tends to limit her power of choice, or to narrow its range, or to lower her standards of selection, works out in a national and racial deprivation. And surely no one will deny that the degrading industrial conditions under which such a large number of our young girls live and work do all of these, do limit and narrow the range of selection and do lower the standards of the working-girl in making her marriage choice.

Give her fairer wages, shorten her hours of toil, let her have the chance of a good time, of a happy girlhood, and an independent, normal woman will be free to make a real choice of the best man. She will not be tempted to passively accept any man who offers himself, just in order to escape from a life of unbearable toil, monotony and deprivation.

So far, women and girls, exploited themselves, have been used as an instrument yet further to cheapen and exploit men. In this direction things could hardly reach a lower level than they have done.

Now the national conscience has at length been touched regarding women, and we venture to hope that in proportion as women have been used to debase industrial standards, so in like degree as the nation insists upon better treatment being accorded her, the results may so re-

act upon the whole field of industry that men too may
be sharers in the benefits.

But there is a mightier force at work, a force more
significant and more characteristic of our age than even
the awakened civic conscience, showing itself in just
and humane legislation. That is the spirit of independence expressed in many different forms, markedly in the
new desire and therefore in the new capacity for collective action which women are discovering in themselves
to a degree never known before.

As regards wage-earning working-women, the two
main channels through which this new spirit is manifest-
ing itself are first, their increasing efforts after industrial organization, and next in the more general realization by them of the need of the vote as a means of
self-expression, whether individual or collective.

Thus the trade union on the one hand, offering to
the working-woman protection in the earning of her living, links up her interests with those of her working
brother; while on the other hand, in the demand for the
vote women of all classes are recognizing common disabilities, a common sisterhood and a common hope.

This book was almost completed when the sound of the
war of the nations broke upon our ears. It would be
vain to deny that to all idealists, of every shade of
thought, the catastrophe came as a stupefying blow. "It
is unbelievable, impossible," said one. "It can't last,"
added another. Reaction from that extreme of incre-
dulity led many to take refuge in hopeless, inactive despair and cynicism.

Even the few months that have elapsed have enabled
both the over-hopeful and the despairing to recover their
lost balance, and to take up again their little share of
the immemorial task of humanity, to struggle onward,
ever onward and upward.

What had become of the movement of the workers, that they could have permitted a war of so many nations, in which the workers of every country involved must be the chief sufferers?

The labor movement, like every other idealist movement, contains a sprinkling of unpopular pessimistic souls, who drive home, in season and out of season, a few unpopular truths. One of these unwelcome truths is to the effect that the world is not following after the idealists half as fast as they think it is. Reformers of every kind make an amount of noise in the world these days out of all proportion to their numbers. They deceive themselves, and to a certain extent they deceive others. The wish to see their splendid visions a reality leads to the belief that they are already on the point of being victors over the hard-to-move and well-intrenched powers that be. As to the quality of his thinking and the soundness of his reasoning, the idealist is ahead of the world all the time, and just as surely the world pays him the compliment of following in his trail. But only in its own time and at its own good pleasure. It is in quantity that he is short. There is never enough of him to do all the tasks, to be in every place at once. Rarely has he converts enough to assure a majority of votes or voices on his side.

So the supreme crises of the world come, and he has for the time to step aside; to be a mere onlooker; to wait in awe-struck patience until the pessimist beholds the realization of his worst fears; until the optimist can take heart again, and reviving his crushed and withered hopes once more set their fulfillment forward in the future.

In spite of all, the idealist is ever justified. He is justified today in Europe no less than in America; justified by the ruin and waste that have come in the train of following outworn political creeds, and yielding to animosities inherited from past centuries; justified by the disastrous results of unchecked national economic competition, when the age of international coöperation is already upon us; justified by the utter contempt shown by masculine rulers and statesmen for the constructive and the fostering side of life, typified and embodied in the woman half of society.

No! our ideals are not changed, nor are they in aught belittled by what has occurred. It is for us to cherish and guard them more faithfully, to serve them more devotedly than ever. Even if we must from now on walk softly all the days of our life, and prepare to accept unresentfully disappointment and heart-sickening delay, we can still draw comfort from this:

Hope thou not much, and fear thou not at all.

Meanwhile we sit, as it were, facing a vast stage, in front of us a dropped curtain. From behind that veil there reaches our strained ears now and then a cry of agony unspeakable, and again a faint whisper of hope.

But until that curtain is raised, after the hand of the war-fiend is stayed; until we can again communicate, each with the other as human beings and not as untamed, primitive savages, we can know in detail little that has happened, and foresee nothing that may hereafter happen.

That some of America's industrial and social problems will be affected radically by the results of the European war goes without saying; how, and in what degree, it is impossible to foretell.

Meanwhile our work is here, and we have to pursue it. Whatever will strengthen the labor movement, or the woman movement, goes to strengthen the world forces of peace. Let us hold fast to that. And conversely,

whatever economic or ethical changes will help to insure
a permanent basis for world peace will grant to both
the labor movement and the woman movement enlarged
opportunity to come into their own.

ALICE HENRY,

Chicago, July, 1915.

CONTENTS

LIST OF ILLUSTRATIONS

INTRODUCTION

It was a revolutionary change in our ways of thinking when the idea of development, social as well as physical, really took hold of mankind. But our minds are curiously stiff and slow to move, and we still mostly think of development as a process that has taken place, and that is going to take place—in the future. And that change is the very stuff of which life consists (not that change is taking place at this moment, but that this moment is change), that means another revolution in the world of thought, and it gives to life a fresh meaning. No one has, as it appears to me, placed such emphasis upon this as has Henri Bergson. It is not that he emphasizes the mere fact of the evolution of society and of all human relations. That, he, and we, may well take for granted. It has surely been amply demonstrated and illustrated by writers as widely separated in their interpretation of social evolution as Herbert Spencer and Karl Marx. But with the further thought in mind that, alike in the lowliest physical organism or in the most complex social organism, life itself is change, we view every problem of life from another angle. To see life steadily and see it whole is one stage. Bergson bids us see life on the move, ever changing, growing, evolving, a creation new every moment.

For students of society this means that we are to aim at the understanding of social processes, rather than stop short with the consideration of facts; facts are to be studied because they go to make up processes. We are not to stop short with the study of conditions, but go on to find out what tendencies certain conditions encourage. All social and industrial questions therefore are to be interpreted in their dynamic rather than in their static aspects.

In the Labor Museum of Hull House is shown a very ingenious diagram, representing the development on the mechanical side of the process of spinning, one of the oldest of the arts. It consists of a strip of cardboard, about a yard long, marked off into centuries and decades. From 2000 B. C. up to A. D. 1500 the hand spindle was the only instrument used. From 1500 up to the middle of the eighteenth century the spinning-wheel was used as well. From the middle of the eighteenth century up till today has been the period of the application of steam to spinning machinery.

The profound symbolism expressed by the little chart goes beyond the interesting fact in the history of applied physics and mechanics which it tells, on to the tremendous changes which it sums up. The textile industries were primarily women's work, and with the mechanical changes in this group of primitive industries were inextricably bound up changes far more momentous in the social environment and the individual development of the worker.

Yet, if a profoundly impressive story, it is also a simple and plain one. It is so easy to understand because we have the help of history to interpret it to us, a help that fails us completely when, instead of being able to look from a distance and see events in their due proportions and in their right order, we are driven to extract as best we can a meaning from occurrences that happen and conditions that lie before our very eyes. That we cannot see the wood for the trees was never more painfully true than when we first try to tell a clear story amid the clatter and din of our industrial life. Past history is of little assistance in interpreting the social and industrial development, in which we ourselves are atoms. Much information is to be obtained, though piecemeal and with difficulty, but especially as relates to women, it has not yet been classified and ordered and placed ready to hand.

The industrial group activities of women are the inevitable, though belated result of the entry of women into the modern industrial system, and are called forth by the new demands which life is making upon women's faculties. We cannot stop short here, and consider these activities mainly in regard to what has led up to them, nor yet as to what is their extent and effect today. Far more important is it to try to discover what are the tendencies, which they as yet faintly and imperfectly, often confusedly, express.

In the labor movement of this country woman has played and is playing an important part. But in its completeness no one knows the story, and those who know sections of it most intimately are too busy living their own parts in that story, to pause long enough to be its chroniclers. For to be part of a movement is more absorbing than to write about it. Whom then shall we ask? To whom shall we turn for even an imperfect knowledge of the story, at once noble and sordid, tragic and commonplace, of woman's side of the labor movement? To whom, you would say, but to the worker herself? And where does the worker speak with such clearness, with such unfaltering steadiness, as through her union, the organization of her trade?

In the industrial maze the individual worker cannot interpret her own life story from her knowledge of the little patch of life which is all her hurried fingers ever touch. Only an organization can be an interpreter here.

Fortunately for the student, the organization does act as interpreter, both for the organized women who have been drawn into the labor movement and for those less fortunate who are still struggling on single-handed and alone. The organized workers in one way or another come into fairly close relations with their unorganized sisters. Besides, the movement in its modern form is still so young that there is scarcely a woman worker in the unions who did not begin her trade life as an unorganized toiler.

Speaking broadly, the points upon which the trade-union movement concentrates are the raising of wages, the shortening of hours, the diminution of seasonal work, the abolition or regulation of piece-work, with its resultant speeding up, the maintaining of sanitary conditions, and the guarding of unsafe machinery, the enforcement of laws against child-labor, the abolition of taxes for power and working materials such as thread and needles, and of unfair fines for petty or unproved offenses—and with these, the recognition of the union to insure the obtaining and the keeping of all the rest.

A single case taken from a non-union trade (a textile trade, too) must serve to suggest the reasons that make organization a necessity. Twenty-one years ago in the bag and hemp factories of St. Louis, girl experts turned out 460 yards of material in a twelve-hour day, the pay being 24 cents per bolt (of from 60 to 66 yards). These girls earned $1.84 per day (on the bolt of from 60 to 66 yards). Four years ago a girl could not hold her job under 1,000 yards in a ten-hour day. "The fastest possible worker can turn out only 1,200 yards, and the price has dropped to 15 cents per hundred yards. The old rate of 24 cents per bolt used to net $1.80 to a very quick worker. The new rate to one equally competent is but $1.50. Workers have to fill a shuttle every minute and a half or two minutes. This necessitates the strain of constant vigilance, as the breaking of the thread causes unevenness, and for this operators are laid off for two or three days. The operators are at such a tension that they not only stand all day, but may not even bend their knees. The air is thick with lint, which the workers inhale. The throat and eyes are terribly affected, and it is necessary to work with the head bound up, and to comb the lint from the eyebrows. The proprietors have to retain a physician to attend the workers every morning, and medicine is supplied free, as an accepted need for everyone so engaged. One year is spent in learning the trade, and the girls last at it only from three to four years afterwards. Some of them enter marriage, but many of them are thrown on the human waste-heap. One company employs nearly 1,000 women, so that a large number are affected by these vile and inhuman conditions. The girls in the trade are mostly Slovaks, Poles and Bohemians, who have not long been in this country. In their inexperience they count $1.50 as good wages, although gained at ever so great a physical cost."

These are intolerable conditions, and that tens of thousands are enduring similar hardships in the course of earning a living and contributing their share towards the commercial output of the country only aggravates the cruelty and the injustice to the helpless and defrauded girls. It is not an individual problem merely. It is a national responsibility shared by every citizen to see that such cruelty and such injustice shall cease. No system of commercial production can be permanently maintained which ignores the primitive rights of the human workers to such returns for labor as shall provide decent food, clothing, shelter, education and recreation for the worker and for those dependent upon him or her, as well as steadiness of employment, and the guarantee of such working conditions as shall not be prejudicial to health.

If the community is not to be moved either by pity or by a sense of justice then perhaps it will awake to a realization of the national danger involved when so many of the workers, and especially when so many of the girls and women work under circumstances ruinous to health, and affording, besides, small chance for all-round normal development on either the individual or the social side. These are evils whose results do not die out with the generation primarily involved, but must as well through inheritance as through environment injure the children of the workers, and their offspring yet unborn.

The passing away from the individual worker of personal control over the raw material and the instruments of production, which has accompanied the advent of the factory system, means that some degree of control corresponding to that formerly possessed by the individual should be assured to the group of workers in the factory or the trade. Such control is assured through the collective power of the workers, acting in coöperation in their trade union. One reason why the woman worker is in so many respects worse off than the man is because she has so far enjoyed so little of the protection of the trade union in her work. Why she has not had it, and why more and more she desires it, is what I will try to show in the following pages.

There is one criticism, to which almost every writer dealing with a present-day topic, lies exposed. That is, why certain aspects of the subject, or certain closely related questions, have either not been dealt with at all, or touched on only lightly. For instance, the subject of the organization of wage-earning women is indeed bound up with the industrial history of the United States, with the legal and social position of women, with the handicaps under which the colored races suffer, and with the entire labor problem.

In answer I can but plead that there had to be some limits. These are all matters which have been treated by many others, and I intentionally confined myself to a section of the field not hitherto covered.

Though the greatest care has been taken to avoid errors, some mistakes have doubtless crept in and the author would be glad to have these pointed out. I acknowledge gratefully what I owe to others, whether that help has come to me through books and periodical literature or through personal information from those possessing special expert knowledge. No one can ever begin to repay such a debt, but such thanks as are possible, I offer here.

The brief historical sketch of the early trade unions is based almost entirely upon the "History of Women in Trade Unions," Volume X, of the "Report on the Condition of Women and Child Wage-Earners in the United States," issued by the Commissioner of Labor, then Mr. Charles P. Neill. Dr. John B. Andrews deals with the earlier period, and he shows how persistent have been the efforts of working-women to benefit themselves through collective action.

"Organization," he writes, "among working-women, contrary to the general impression, is not new. Women, from the beginning of the trade-union movement in this country have occupied an important place in the ranks of organized labor. For eighty years and over, women wage-earners in America have formed trade unions and gone on strike for shorter hours, better pay, and improved conditions. The American labor movement had its real beginning about the year 1825. In that year the tailoresses of New York formed a union."

The history of women in trade unions he divides into four periods: (1) the beginnings of organization, extending from 1825 to about 1840; (2) the development of associations interested in labor reform, including the beginnings of legislative activity, 1840 to 1860; (3) the sustained development of pure trade unions, and the rise of the struggle over the suffrage, 1860 to 1880; and (4) the impress and educative influence of the Knights of Labor, 1881 to date, and the present development under the predominant leadership of the American Federation of Labor.

THE
TRADE UNION WOMAN

THE TRADE UNION WOMAN

I

EARLY TRADE UNIONS AMONG WOMEN
1825–1840

The earliest factory employment to engage large numbers of women was the cotton industry of New England, and the mill hands of that day seem to have been entirely native-born Americans. The first power loom was set up in Waltham, Massachusetts, in 1814, and the name of the young woman weaver who operated it was Deborah Skinner. In 1817 there were three power looms in Fall River, Massachusetts; the weavers were Sallie Winters, Hannah Borden and Mary Healy.

The first form of trade-union activity among wage-earning women in the United States was the local strike. The earliest of these of which there is any record was but a short-lived affair. It was typical, nevertheless, of the sudden, impulsive uprising of the unorganized everywhere. It would hardly be worth recording, except that in such hasty outbursts of indignation against the so unequal distribution of the burdens of industry lies the germ of the whole labor movement. This small strike took place in July, 1828, in the cotton mills of Paterson, New Jersey, among the boy and girl helpers over the apparently trifling detail of a change of the dinner hour from twelve o'clock to one. Presently there were involved the carpenters, masons and machinists in a general demand for a ten-hour day. In a week the strike had collapsed, and the leaders found themselves out of work, although the point on which the young workers had gone out was conceded.

It was among the mill operatives of Dover, New Hampshire, that the first really important strike involving women occurred. This was in December of the same year (1828). On this occasion between three hundred and four hundred women went out. The next we hear of the Dover girls is six years later, when eight hundred went out in resistance to a cut in wages. These women and girls were practically all the daughters of farmers and small professional men. For their day they were well educated, often teaching school during a part of the year. They prided themselves on being the "daughters of freemen," and while adapting themselves for the sake of earning a living to the novel conditions of factory employment, they were not made of the stuff to submit tamely to irritating rules of discipline, to petty despotism, and to what they felt was a breach of tacit agreement, involved in periodical cutting of wages. Although most of them may have but dimly understood that factory employment required the protection of a permanent organization for the operatives, and looked to the temporary combination provided by the strike for the remedy of their ills, still there was more in the air, and more in the minds of some of the girl leaders than just strikes undertaken for the purpose of abolishing single definite wrongs.

That employers recognized this, and were prepared to stifle in the birth any efforts that their women employés might make towards maintaining permanent organizations, is evident by the allusions in the press of the day to the "ironclad oath" by which the employé had to agree, on entering the factory, to accept whatever wage the employer might see fit to pay, and had to promise not to join any combination "whereby the work may be impeded or the company's interest in any work injured."

Also we find that no general gathering of organized workingmen could take place without the question of the inroad of women into the factories being hotly debated. All the speakers would be agreed that the poorly paid and overworked woman was bringing a very dangerous element into the labor world, but there was not the same unanimity when it came to proposing a remedy. Advice that women should go back into the home was then as now the readiest cure for the evil, for even so early as this the men realized that the underpayment of women meant the underpayment of men, while the employment of women too often meant the dis-employment of men. But it was not long before the more intelligent understood that there was some great general force at work here, which was not to be dealt with nor the resultant evils cured by a resort to primitive conditions. Soon there were bodies of workingmen publicly advocating the organization of women into trade unions as the only rational plan of coping with a thoroughly vicious situation.

Meanwhile such a powerful organ as the *Boston Courier* went so far as to say that the girls ought to be thankful to be employed at all. If it were not for the poor labor papers of that day we should have little chance of knowing the workers' side of the story at all.

During the next few years many women's strikes are recorded among cotton operatives, but most of them, though conducted with spirit and intelligence, seemed to have ended none too happily for the workers. It is nevertheless probable that the possibility that these rebellious ones might strike often acted as a check upon the cotton lords and their mill managers. Indeed the strikes at Lowell, Massachusetts, of 1834 and 1836 involved so large a number of operatives (up to 2,500 girls at one time), and these were so brave and daring in their public demands for the right of personal liberty and just treatment that the entire press of the country gave publicity to the matter, although the orthodox newspapers were mostly shocked at the "wicked misrepresentations" of the ringleaders in this industrial rebellion.

The 1836 strike at the Lowell mills throws a curious light upon the habits of those days. Something analogous to the "living-in" system was in force. In 1825 when the Lowell mills were first opened, the companies who owned the mills provided boarding-houses for their girl operatives, and the boarding-house keepers had in their lease to agree to charge them not more than $1.25 per week. (Their wages are said to have rarely exceeded $2.50 per week.) But in these thirteen years the cost of living had risen, and at this rate for board the boarding-house keepers could no longer make ends meet, and many were ruined. The mill-owners, seeing what desperate plight these women were in, agreed to deduct from the weekly rent a sum equivalent to twelve cents per boarder, and they also authorized the housekeepers to charge each girl twelve cents more. This raised the total income of the housekeepers to practically one dollar and fifty cents per head. As there was no talk of raising wages in proportion, this arrangement was equivalent to a cut of twelve cents per week and the girls rebelled and went out on strike to the number of twenty-five hundred. In all probability, however, it was not only the enforced lessening of their wages, but some of the many irritating conditions as well that always attend any plan of living-in, whether the employé be a mill girl, a department-store clerk or a domestic servant, that goaded the girls on, for we hear of "dictation not only as to what they shall eat and drink and wherewithal they shall be clothed, but when they shall eat, drink and sleep."

The strikers paraded through the streets of Lowell, singing,

> Oh, isn't it a pity that such a pretty girl as I
> Should be sent to the factory to pine away and die?
> Oh! I cannot be a slave,
> For I'm so fond of liberty
> That I cannot be a slave.

The girls appealed to the memories, still green, of the War of Independence.

"As our fathers resisted unto blood the lordly avarice of the British ministry, so we, their daughters, never will wear the yoke which has been prepared for us."

With this and many similar appeals they heartened one another. But before the close of October, 1836, the strike was broken and the girls were back at work on the employers' terms. Still an echo of the struggle is heard in the following month at the Annual Convention of the National Trades Union, where the Committee on Female Labor recommended that "they [the women operatives] should immediately adopt energetic measures, in the construction of societies to support each other."

Almost every difficulty that the working-woman has to face today had its analogue then. For instance, speeding up: "The factory girls of Amesbury have had a flare-up and turned out because they were told they must tend two looms in future without any advance of wages."

A pitiful account comes from eastern Pennsylvania, where the cotton industry had by this time a footing. Whole families would be in the mill "save only one small girl to take care of the house and provide the meals."

Yet the wages of all the members were needed to supply bare wants. The hours in the mills were cruelly long. In the summer, "from five o'clock in the morning until sunset, being fourteen hours and a half, with an intermission of half an hour for breakfast and an hour for dinner, leaving thirteen hours of hard labor." Out of repeated and vain protests and repeated strikes, perhaps not always in vain, were developed the beginnings of the trade-union movement of Pennsylvania, the men taking the lead. The women, even where admitted to membership in the unions, seem to have taken little part in the ordinary work of the union, as we only hear of them in times of stress and strike.

The women who worked in the cotton mills were massed together by the conditions of their calling, in great groups, and a sense of community of interest would thus, one would think, be more easily established. Women engaged in various branches of sewing were, on the other hand, in much smaller groups, but they were far more widely distributed. One result of this was that meeting together and comparing notes was always difficult and often impossible. Even within the same town, with the imperfect means of transit, with badly made and worst lit streets, one group of workers had little means of knowing whether they were receiving the same or different rates of pay for the same work, or for the same number of work hours. So much sewing has always been done in the homes of the workers that it is a matter of surprise to learn that the very first women's trade union of which we have any knowledge was formed, probably in some very loose organization, among the tailoresses of New York in the year 1825. Six years later the tailoresses of New York were again clubbed together for self-protection against the inevitable consequences of reduced and inadequate wages. Their secretary, Mrs. Lavinia Waight, must have been a very new woman. She, unreasonable person, was not content with asking better wages for her trade and her sex, but she even wanted the vote for herself and her sisters. Indeed, from the expression she uses, "the duties of legislation," she perhaps even desired that women should be qualified to sit in the legislature. In this same year, 1831, there was a strike of tailoresses reported to include sixteen hundred women, and they must have remained out several weeks. This was not, like so many, an unorganized strike, but was authorized and managed by the United Tailoresses' Society, of which we now hear for the first time. We hear of the beginning of many of these short-lived societies, but rarely is there any record of when they went under, or how.

Innumerable organizations of a temporary character existed from time to time in the other large cities, Baltimore and Philadelphia. Philadelphia has the distinguished honor of being the home of Matthew Carey, who was instrumental in starting the first public inquiry into the conditions of working-women, as he was also the first in America to make public protest against the insufficient pay and wretched conditions imposed upon women, who were now entering the wage-earning occupations in considerable numbers. He assisted the sewing-women of all branches to form what was practically a city federation of women's unions, the first of its kind. One committee was authorized to send to the Secretary of War a protest against the disgracefully low prices paid for army clothing. Matthew Carey was also held responsible, rightly or wrongly, for an uprising in the book-binding establishments of New York.

All this agitation among workers and the general public was having some effect upon the ethical standards of employers, for a meeting of master book-binders of New

York disowned those of their number who paid "less than $3 a week." An occasional word of support and sympathy, too, filters through the daily press. The *Commercial Bulletin* severely criticized the rates the Secretary of War was paying for his army clothing orders, while the *Public Ledger* of Philadelphia, speaking of a strike among the women umbrella sewers of New York, commented thus: "In this case we decidedly approve the turn-out. Turning out, if peaceably conducted, is perfectly legal, and often necessary, especially among female laborers."

The next year we again find Matthew Carey helping the oppressed women. This time it is with a letter and money to support the ladies' Association of Shoe Binders and Corders of Philadelphia, then on strike. Shoe-binding was a home industry, existing in many of the towns, and open to all the abuses of home-work.

Lynn, Massachusetts, was then and for long after the center of the shoe trade, and the scene of some of the earliest attempts of home-workers to organize.

1840–1860

Nothing in the history of women's organizations in the last century leaves a more disheartening impression than the want of continuity in the struggle, although there was never a break nor a let-up in the conditions of low wages, interminably long hours, and general poverty of existence which year in and year out were the lot of the wage-earning women in the manufacturing districts.

Although based in every instance upon a common and crying need, the successive attempts of women at organization as a means of improving their industrial condition are absolutely unrelated to one another. Not only so, but it is pathetic to note that the brave women leaders of women in one generation cannot even have known of the existence of their predecessors in the self-same fight. They were not always too well informed as to the conditions of their sister workers in other cities or states, where distance alone severed them. But where time made the gap, where they were separated by the distance of but one lifetime, sometimes by a much shorter period, the severance seems to have been to our way of thinking, strangely complete, and disastrously so. Students had not begun to be interested in the troubles of everyday folk, so there were no records of past occurrences of the same sort that the workers could read. To hunt up in old files of newspapers allusions to former strikes and former agreements is a hard, slow task for the trained student of today; for those girls it was impossible. We have no reason to believe that the names of Lavinia Waight and Louisa Mitchell, the leaders of New York tailoresses in 1831, were known to Sarah Bagley or Huldah Stone, when in 1845 they stirred Lowell. Each of the leaders whose names have come down to us, and all of their unknown and unnamed followers had to take their courage in their hands, think out for themselves the meaning of intolerable conditions, and as best they could feel after the readiest remedies. To these women the very meaning of international or even interstate trade competition must have been unknown. They had every one of them to learn by bitter experience how very useless the best meant laws might be to insure just and humane treatment, if the ideal of an out-of-date, and therefore fictitious, individual personal liberty were allowed to overrule and annul the greatest good of the greatest number.

This second period was essentially a seedtime, a time of lofty ideals and of very idealist philosophy. The writers of that day saw clearly that there was much that was rotten in the State of Denmark, and they wrought hard to find a way out, but they did not realize the complexity of society any more than they recognized the economic basis upon which all our social activities are built. They unquestionably placed overmuch stress upon clearing the ground in patches, literally as well as metaphorically. Hence it was that so many plans for general reform produced so little definite result, except on the one hand setting before the then rising generation a higher standard of social responsibility which was destined deeply to tinge the after conduct and social activities of that generation, and on the other hand much social experimenting upon a small scale which stored up information and experience for the future. For instance the work done in trying out small coöperative experiments like that of Brook Farm has taught the successors of the first community builders much that could only be learned by practical experience, and not the least important of those lessons has been how not to do it.

The land question, which could have troubled no American when in earlier days he felt himself part proprietor in a new world, was beginning to be a problem to try the mettle of the keenest thinkers and the most eager reformers. And even so early as the beginning of this second period there was to be seen on the social horizon a small cloud, no bigger than a man's hand, which was to grow and grow till in a few years it was to blot out of sight all other matters of public concern. This was the movement for the abolition of slavery. Till that national anachronism was at least politically and legally cleared out of the way, there was no great amount of public interest or public effort to be spared for any other subject. And yet were there any, on either side of that great question, who guessed that the passing of that even then belated institution was to give rise to and leave in its train problems quite as momentous as the abolition of slavery, and far more tremendous in their scope and range? By these problems we have been faced ever since, and continue to be faced by them today. To grant to any set of people nominal freedom, and deny them economic freedom is only half solving the difficulty. To deny economic freedom to the colored person is in the end to deny it to the white person, too.

The immediate cause which seems to have brought about the downfall of the labor organizations of the first period (1825-1840) was the panic of 1837, and the long financial depression which succeeded. We read, on the other side of the water, of the "Hungry Forties," and although no such period of famine and profound misery fell to the lot of the people of the United States, as Great Britain and Ireland suffered, the influence of the depression was long and widely felt in the manufacturing districts of the Eastern states. Secondarily the workers were to know of its effects still later, through the invasion of their industrial field by Irish immigrants, starved out by that same depression, and by the potato famine that followed it. These newcomers brought with them very un-American standards of living, and flooded the labor market with labor unskilled and therefore cheaper than the normal native supply. When the year 1845 came it is to be inferred that the worst immediate effects of the financial distress had passed, for from then on the working-women made repeated efforts to improve their condition. Baffled in one direction they would turn in another.

As earlier, there is a long series of local strikes, and another long succession of short-lived local organizations. It is principally in the textile trade that we hear of both strikes and unions, but also among seamstresses and tailoresses, shoemakers and capmakers. New York, Philadelphia, Pittsburgh, Boston, Fall River and Lowell all contributed their quota of industrial uprisings among the exasperated and sorely pressed workers, with a sad similarity in the stories.

In a class by themselves, however, were the female labor reform associations, which for some years did excellent work in widely separated cities. These were strictly trade unions, in spite of their somewhat vague name. They seem to have drawn their membership from the workers in the local trades. That of Lowell, perhaps the best known, originated among the mill girls, but admitted other workers. Lowell, as usual, was to the fore in the quality of its women leaders. The first president of the Association was the brilliant and able Sarah G. Bagley. She and other delegates went before the Massachusetts legislative committee in 1845, and gave evidence as to the conditions in the textile mills. This, the first American governmental investigation, was brought about almost solely in response to the petitions of the working-women, who had already secured thousands of signatures of factory operatives to a petition asking for a ten-hour law.

The Lowell Association had their correspondent to the *Voice of Industry,* and also a press committee to take note of and contradict false statements appearing in the papers concerning factory operatives. They had most modern ideas on the value of publicity, and neglected no opportunity of keeping the workers' cause well in evidence, whether through "factory tracts," letters to the papers, speeches or personal correspondence. They boldly attacked legislators who were false to their trust, and in one case, at least, succeeded in influencing an election, helping to secure the defeat of William Schouler, chairman of that legislative committee before which the women delegates had appeared, which they charged with dishonesty in withholding from the legislature all the most important facts brought forward by the trade-union witnesses.

Other female labor reform associations existed about this period in Manchester and Dover, New Hampshire. The first-named was particularly active in securing the passage of the too soon wrecked ten-hour law. In New York a similar body of women workers was organized in 1845 as the Female Industrial Association. The sewing trades in many branches, cap-makers, straw-workers, book-folders and stitchers and lace-makers were among the trades represented. In Philadelphia the tailoresses in 1850 formed an industrial union. It maintained a coöperative tailoring shop, backed by the support of such coöperative advocates as George Lippard, John Shedden, Lucretia Mott and Elizabeth Oakes Smith. In 1853 the Industrial Union published a report of its activities, showing that in two years the business had paid away in wages to tailoresses more than four thousand dollars.

In the men's conventions of this time a number of women besides the redoubtable Sarah Bagley took an active part, being seated as delegates from their own labor reform associations. At the meeting in 1846 of the New England Workingmen's Association, for instance, Miss Huldah J. Stone, of Lowell, was elected recording secretary, and Mrs. C. N. M. Quimby was appointed one of the board of six directors. At all the meetings of the New England Congress, which met several times a year, the women's point of view was well presented by the delegates from the various trades.

The National Industrial Congress, organized first in New York in 1845, and which met yearly for the next ten years, was supposed to stand for all the interests of the workingman and woman, but gave most of its attention to the land question and other subjects of general reform. This scattered the energies of the organizations and weakened their power as trade unions. But in the long anti-slavery agitation, which was just then rising to its height on the eve of the Civil War, even the land question was forgotten, and the voice of the trade unionists, speaking for man or woman, was utterly unheeded.

Imperfect as are the accounts that have come down to us, it is clear that this second generation of trade unionists were educating themselves to more competent methods of handling the industrial problem. The women workers of Pittsburgh coöperated with the women of New England in trying to obtain from the manufacturers of their respective centers a promise that neither group would work their establishments longer than ten hours a day—this, to meet the ready objection so familiar in our ears still, that the competition of other mills would make the concession in one center ruinous to the manufacturers who should grant it. This was the crowning effort of the Pittsburgh mill-workers to obtain improvement. Strikes for higher wages had failed. Strikes for a ten-hour day had failed. And now it is pitiful to write that even this interstate coöperation on the part of the girls for relief by a peaceful trade agreement failed, too, the employers falling back upon their "undoubted right" to run their factories as many hours as they pleased.

The women then appealed to the legislatures, and between 1847 and 1851, New Hampshire, New Jersey and Pennsylvania all passed ten-hour laws.[1] But they were not passed simultaneously, which gave the employers in the particular state dealt with, the excuse that under such legislation they could not face interstate competition in their business, and since every law contained a saving

[1] In the same year, 1847, a ten-hour law was passed in New Hampshire and in Great Britain, with, however, very different outcome, for in Great Britain the law was enforced, there being no complication of state and national control there.

clause permitting contracting out by individual employers and employés, all these beneficial acts were so much waste paper. The manufacturers expressed themselves as willing enough to stand for the shorter work-day, but absolutely declined to risk the loss of their business in competing with those rival manufacturers who might take advantage of the "saving clause."

For nearly fifty years after this period, the right 'to overwork and the "right" to be overworked remained untouched by legislative interference. And yet the need for labor legislation, restricting hours, and for uniform federal legislation was as clearly evident then as it is to us today, to meet the industrial needs and to satisfy the undoubted rights of the working folk of the twentieth century.

1860–1880

The organization of labor upon a national basis really began during this period. During the ten years from 1863 to 1873 there existed more than thirty national trade unions. Of these only two, the printers and the cigar-makers, admitted women to their membership. But in addition the women shoemakers had their own national union, the Daughters of St. Crispin. Women's unions of all sorts were represented in the National Labor Union.

From this body women's local unions received every possible encouragement. As far as I can understand, the National Labor Union carried on little active work between conventions, but at these gatherings it stood for equal pay for equal work, although, as it appears to us, inconsistently and short-sightedly the delegates refused to incorporate into their resolutions the demand for the ballot as a needful weapon in the hands of women in their strivings after industrial equality. The need for industrial equality had been forced upon the apprehension of men unionists after they had themselves suffered for

long years from the undercutting competition of women.
That women needed to be strong politically in order that
they might be strong industrially was a step beyond these
good brothers.

There were also two state labor unions, composed
solely of women, the Massachusetts Working-Women's
League, and the Working-Women's Labor Union for the
state of New York.

But most of the organization work among women was
still local in character. The New England girl was now
practically out of the business, driven out by the still
more hardly pushed immigrant. With her departure
were lost to the trades she had practiced the remnants
of the experience and the education several generations
of workers had acquired in trade unionism and trade-
union policy and methods.

Still, at intervals and under sore disadvantages the
poor newcomers did some fighting on their own account.
Although they were immigrants they were of flesh and
blood like their predecessors, and they naturally rebelled
against the ever-increasing amount of work that was demanded of them. The two looms, formerly complained
of, had now increased to six and seven. The piece of
cloth that used to be thirty yards long was now forty-two
yards, though the price per piece remained the same.
But strike after strike was lost. A notable exception
was the strike of the Fall River weavers in 1875. It was
led by the women weavers, who refused to accept a ten
per cent. cut in wages to which the men of the organization (for they were organized) had agreed. The women
went out in strike in the bitter month of January, taking the men with them. The leaders selected three mills,
and struck against those, keeping the rest of their members at work, in order to have sufficient funds for their
purposes. Even so, 3,500 looms and 156,000 spindles

were thrown idle, and 3,125 strikers were out. The strike lasted more than two months and was successful.

Progress must have seemed at the time, may even seem to us looking back, to be tantalizingly slow, but far oftener than in earlier days do the annals of trade unionism report, "The strikers won." Another feature is the ever-increasing interest and sympathy shown in such industrial risings of the oppressed by a certain few among the more fortunate members of society. One strike of cap-makers (men and women), was helped to a successful issue by rich German bankers and German societies.

The account of the condition of women in the sewing trades during the sixties makes appalling reading. The wonder is not that the organizations of seamstresses during those years were few, short-lived, and attended with little success, but that among women so crushed and working at starvation wages any attempt at organization should have been possible at all. A number of circumstances combined to bring their earnings below, far below, the margin of subsistence. It was still the day of pocket-money wages, when girls living at home would take in sewing at prices which afforded them small luxuries, but which cut the remuneration of the woman who had to live by her needle to starvation point.

It was still the period of transition in the introduction of the sewing-machine. The wages earned under these circumstances were incredibly low. The true sweating system with all its dire effects upon the health of the worker, and threatening the very existence of the home, was in full force. The enormous amount of work which was given out in army contracts to supply the needs of the soldiers then on active service in the Civil War, was sublet by contractors at the following rates. The price paid by the Government for the making of a shirt might be eighteen cents. Out of that all the worker would receive would be seven cents. And cases are cited of old women, presumably slow workers, who at these rates could earn but a dollar and a half per week. Even young and strong workers were but little better off. From innumerable cases brought to light $2 and $3 a week seem to have been a common income for a woman. Some even "supported" (Heaven save the mark!) others out of such wretched pittances.

Aurora Phelps, of Boston, a born leader, in 1869, gave evidence that there were then in Boston eight thousand sewing-women, who did not earn over twenty-five cents a day, and that she herself had seen the time when she could not afford to pay for soap and firing to wash her own clothes. She said that she had known a girl to live for a week on a five-cent loaf of bread a day, going from shop to shop in search of the one bit of work she was able to do. For by this time division of work had come in, and the average machine operator was paid as badly as the hand needlewoman.

The circumstance that probably more than any other accentuated this terrible state of affairs was the addition to the ranks of the wage-earners of thousands of "war widows." With homes broken up and the breadwinner gone, these untrained women took up sewing as the only thing they could do, and so overstocked the labor market that a new "Song of the Shirt" rose from attic to basement in the poorer districts of all the larger cities.

As early as 1864 meetings were held in order to bring pressure upon the officials who had the giving out of the army contracts, to have the work given out direct, and therefore at advanced prices to the worker. Only three months before his death, in January, 1865, these facts reached President Lincoln, and were referred by him to the quartermaster with a request that "he should hereafter manage the supplies of contract work for the Government, made up by women, so as to give them remunerative wages for labor."

During these years a number of small unions were formed, some as far west as Detroit and Chicago, but in almost every case the union later became a coöperative society. Some of them, we know, ceased to exist after a few months. Of others the forming of the organization is recorded in some labor paper, and after a while the name drops out, and nothing more is heard of it.

Ten years later, in New York, there was formed a large, and for several years very active association of umbrella-sewers. This organization so impressed Mrs. Patterson, a visiting Englishwoman, that when she returned home, she exerted herself to form unions among working-women and encouraged others to do the same. It was through her persistence that the British Women's Trade Union League came into existence.

If the conditions in the sewing trades were at this period the very worst that it is possible to imagine, so low that organization from within was impossible, while as yet the public mind was unprepared to accept the alternative of legislative interference with either hours or wages, there were other trades wherein conditions were far more satisfactory, and in which organization had made considerable progress.

The Collar Laundry Workers of Troy, New York, had in 1866 about as bad wages as the sewing-women everywhere, but they were spared the curse of homework, as it was essentially a factory trade. The collars, cuffs and shirts were made and laundered by workers of the same factories. How early the workers organized is not known, but in the year 1866 they had a union so prosperous that they were able to give one thousand dollars from their treasury towards the assistance of the striking iron-molders of Troy, and later on five hundred dollars to help the striking bricklayers of New York. They had in course of time succeeded in raising their own wages from the very low average of two dollars and three dollars per week to a scale ranging from eight dollars to fourteen dollars for different classes of work, although their hours appear to have been very long, from twelve to fourteen hours per day. But the laundresses wanted still more pay, and in May, 1869, they went on strike to the number of four hundred, but after a desperate struggle, in which they were supported by the sympathy of the townspeople, they were beaten, and their splendid union put out of existence.

Miss Kate Mullaney, their leader, was so highly thought of that in 1868 she had been made national organizer of women for the National Labor Union, the first appointment of the kind of which there is any record. She tried to save what she could out of the wreck of the union by forming the Coöperative Linen, Collar and Cuff Factory, and obtained for it the patronage of the great department store of A. T. Stewart, in Broadway.

The experiences of the women printers have been typical of the difficulties which women have had to face in what is called a man's trade of the highly organized class. The tragic alternative that is too often offered to women, just as it is offered to any race or class placed at an economic disadvantage, of being kept outside a skilled trade, through the short-sighted policy of the workers in possession, or of entering it by some back door, whether as mere undersellers or as actual strike-breakers, is illustrated in all its phases in the printing trade.

As early as 1856 the Boston Typographical Union seriously considered discharging any member found working with female compositors. This feeling, though not always so bluntly expressed, lasted for many years. It was not singular, therefore, that under these circumstances, employers took advantage of such a situation, and whenever it suited them, employed women. These were not even non-unionists, seeing that as women they were by the men of their own trade judged ineligible for admission to the union. It is believed that women were thus the means of the printers losing many strikes. In 1864 the proprietor of one of the Chicago daily papers boasted that he "placed materials in remote rooms in the city and there secretly instructed girls to set type, and kept them there till they were sufficiently proficient to enter the office, and thus enabled the employer to take a 'snap judgment' on his journeymen."

After this a wiser policy was adopted by the typographical unions. The keener-sighted among their members began not only to adopt a softer tone towards their hardly pressed sisters in toil, but made it clear that what they were really objecting to was the low wage for which women worked.

The first sign of the great change of heart was the action of the "Big Six," of New York, which undertook all the initial expenses of starting a women's union. On October 12, 1868, the Women's Typographical Union No. 1 was organized, with Miss Augusta Lewis as president. Within the next three years women were admitted into the printers' unions of Chicago, Washington, Philadelphia, Pittsburgh and Boston. Meantime, the Women's Typographical No. 1 was growing in numbers and influence, and was evidently backed by the New York men's union. It obtained national recognition on June 11, 1869, by receiving a charter from the International Typographical Union of North America. It was represented by two delegates at the International Convention

held in Cincinnati in 1870. One of these delegates was
Miss Lewis herself. She was elected corresponding secretary of the International Union, and served, we are
told, with unusual ability and tact. It is less encouraging to have to add, that since her day, no woman has
held an international office.

The two contrary views prevailing among men unionists: that of the man who said, "Keep women out at all
hazards—out of the union, and therefore out of the best
of the trade, but out of the trade, altogether, if possible," and that of the man who resigned himself to the
inevitable and contented himself with urging equal pay,
and with insisting upon the women joining the union,
were never more sharply contrasted than in the cigar-
making trade. We actually find the International Union,
which after 1867 by its constitution admitted women,
being openly defied in this vital matter by some of its
own largest city locals. These were the years during
which the trade was undergoing very radical changes.
From being a home occupation, or an occupation carried
on in quite small establishments, requiring very little
capital, it was becoming more and more a factory trade.
The levying by the government of an internal revenue
tax on cigars, and the introduction of the molding machine, which could be operated by unskilled girl labor,
seem to have been the two principal influences tending
towards the creation of the big cigar-manufacturing
plant.

The national leaders recognized the full gravity of the
problem, and met it in a tolerant, rational spirit. Not so
many of the local bodies. Baltimore and Cincinnati
cigar-makers were particularly bitter, and the "Cincinnati Cigar-makers' Protective Union was for a time denied affiliation with the International Union on account
of its attitude of absolute exclusion towards women."

In 1887 the Cincinnati secretary (judging from his impatience we wonder if he was a very young man) wrote: "We first used every endeavor to get women into the union, but no one would join, therefore we passed the resolution that if they would not work with us we would work against them; but I think we have taught them a lesson that will serve them another time." This unhappy spirit Cincinnati maintained for several years. The men were but building up future difficulties for themselves, as is evident from the fact that in Cincinnati itself there were by 1880 several hundred women cigar-makers, and not one of them in a union.

As the Civil War had so profoundly affected the sewing trades, so it was war, although not upon this continent, that added to the difficulties of American cigarmakers. In the Austro-Prussian War, the invading army entered Bohemia and destroyed the Bohemian cigar factories. The workers, who, as far as we know, were mostly women, and skilled women at that, emigrated in thousands to the United States, and landing in New York either took up their trade there or went further afield to other Eastern cities. This happened just about the time that the processes of cigar-making were being subdivided and specialized, so presently a very complicated situation resulted. Finding the control of their trade slipping away from them, the skilled men workers in the New York factories went out on strike, and many of the Bohemian women, being also skilled, followed them, and so it came about that it was American girls upon whom the manufacturers had to depend as strike-breakers. Their reliance was justified. With the aid of these girls, as well as that of men strike-breakers, the employers gained the day.

To what extent even the more intelligent trade-union leaders felt true comradeship for their women co-workers it is difficult to say. The underlying thought may often have been that safety for the man lay in his insisting upon just and even favorable conditions for women. Even under conditions of nominal equality the woman was so often handicapped by her physique, by the difficulty she experienced in obtaining thorough training, and by the additional claims of her home, that the men must have felt they were likely to keep their hold on the best positions anyhow, and perhaps all the more readily with the union exacting identical standards of accomplishment from all workers, while at the same time claiming for all identical standards of wages.

There is certainly something of this idea in the plan outlined by President Strasser of the International Cigarmakers, and he represented the advance guard of his generation, in his annual report in the year 1879.

"We cannot drive the females out of the trade but we can restrict this daily quota of labor through factory laws. No girl under eighteen should be employed more than eight hours per day; all overwork should be prohibited; while married women should be kept out of factories at least six weeks before and six weeks after confinement."

But it is a man's way out, after all, and it is the man's way still. There is the same readiness shown today to save the woman from overwork before and after confinement, although she may be thereby at the same time deprived of the means of support, while there is no hint of any provision for either herself or the baby, not to speak of other children who may be dependent upon her. In many quarters today there is the same willingness to stand for equal pay, but very little anxiety to see that the young girl worker be as well trained as the boy, in order that the girl may be able with reason and justice to demand the same wage from an employer.

II

WOMEN IN THE KNIGHTS OF LABOR

So little trace is left in the world of organized labor today of that short-lived body, the Knights of Labor, that it might be thought worthy of but slight notice in any general review.

But women have peculiar reason to remember the Knights, and to be grateful to them, for they were the first large national organization to which women were admitted on terms of equality with men, and in the work of the organization itself, they played an active and a notable part.

From the year 1869 till 1878 the Knights of Labor existed as a secret order, having for its aim the improvement of living conditions. Its philosophy and its policy were well expressed in the motto, taken from the maxims of Solon, the Greek lawgiver: "That is the most perfect government in which an injury to one is the concern of all."

The career of the Knights of Labor, however, as an active force in the community, began with the National Convention of 1878, from which time it made efforts to cover the wage-earning and farming classes, which had to constitute three-fourths of the membership. The organization was formed distinctly upon the industrial and not upon the craft plan. That is, instead of a local branch being confined to members of one trade, the plan was to include representatives of different trades and callings. That the fundamental interests of the wage-earner and the farmer were identical, was not so much stated as taken for granted. In defining eligibility for membership there were certain significant exceptions made; the following, being considered as pursuing distinctly antisocial occupations, were pointedly excluded: dealers in intoxicants, lawyers, bankers, stock-brokers and professional gamblers.

Women were first formally admitted to the order in September, 1881. It is said that Mrs. Terence V. Powderly, wife of the then Grand Master Workman, was the first to join. It is not known that any figures exist showing the number of women who at any one time belonged to the Knights of Labor, but Dr. Andrews estimates the number, about the year 1886, when the order was most influential, at about 50,000. Among this 50,000 were a great variety of trades, but shoe-workers must have predominated, and many of these had received their training in trade unionism among the Daughters of St. Crispin.

The Knights evidently took the view that the woman's industrial problem must to a certain extent be handled apart from that of the men, and more important still, that it must be handled as a whole. This broad treatment of the subject was shown when at the convention of 1885 it was voted, on the motion of Miss Mary Hannafin, a saleswoman of Philadelphia, that a committee to collect statistics on women's work be appointed. This committee consisted of Miss Hannafin and Miss Mary Stirling, also of Philadelphia, and Mrs. Lizzie H. Shute, of Haverhill, Massachusetts, who were the only women delegates to the Convention.

At the next convention, held in 1886 in Richmond, Virginia, there were sixteen women delegates, out of a total of six hundred. Mr. Terence V. Powderly, Grand Master Workman, appointed the sixteen women as a committee to receive and consider the report of this previously appointed special committee of three. The result of their deliberations was sufficiently remarkable. They set an example to their sex in taking the free and independent stand they did. For they announced that they had "formed a permanent organization, the object of which will be to investigate the abuses to which our sex is subjected by unscrupulous employers, to agitate the principle which our order teaches of equal pay for equal work and abolition of child labor." They also recommended that the expenses of this new woman's department and the expenses of a woman investigator should be borne by the order. The report was adopted and the memorable Woman's Department of the Knights of Labor was created. Memorable for the purpose and the plan that underlay its foundation, it was also memorable for the character and achievements of the brilliant, able and devoted woman who was chosen as general investigator.

Mrs. Leonora Barry was a young widow with three children. She had tried to earn a living for them in a hosiery mill at Amsterdam, New York. For herself her endeavor to work as a mill hand was singularly unfortunate, for during her first week she earned but sixty-five cents. But if she did not during that week master any of the processes concerned in the making of machinemade stockings, she learned a good deal more than this, a good deal more than she set out to learn. She learned of the insults young girls were obliged to submit to on pain of losing their jobs, and a righteous wrath grew within her at the knowledge. During this hard time also she heard first of the Knights of Labor, and having heard of them, she promptly joined. As she was classified at the 1886 convention as a "machine hand," it is probable that she had by this time taken up her original trade.

For four years Mrs. Barry did fine work. She combined in a remarkable degree qualities rarely found in the same individual. She followed in no one's tracks, but planned out her own methods, and carried out a campaign in which she fulfilled the duties of investigator, organizer and public lecturer. This at a time when the means of traveling were far more primitive than they are today; and not in one state alone, for she covered almost all the Eastern half of the country. We know that she went as far west as Leadville, Colorado, because of the touching little story that is told of her visit there. In that town she had founded the Martha Washington Assembly of the Knights of Labor, and when she left she was given a small parcel with the request that she would not open it until she reached home. But, as she tells it herself,

My woman's curiosity got the better of me, and I opened the package, and found therein a purse which had been carried for fifteen years by Brother Horgan, who was with us last year, and inside of that a little souvenir in the shape of five twenty-dollar gold pieces. You say that I was the instrument through whose means the Martha Washington Assembly was organized. This is partially true, but it is also true that the good and true Knights of Leadville are as much the founder as I am.

She possessed a social vision, and saw the problems of the wrongs of women in relation to the general industrial question, so that in her organizing work she was many-sided. The disputes that she was forever settling, the apathy that she was forever encountering, she dealt with in the tolerant spirit of one to whom these were but incidents in the growth of the labor movement. In dealing with the "little ones" in that movement we hear of her as only patient and helpful and offering words of encouragement, however small the visible results of her efforts might be.

But towards those set in high places she could be intensely scornful, as for instance when she is found appealing to the order itself, asking that "more consideration be given, and more thorough educational measures be adopted on behalf of the working-women of our land, the majority of whom are entirely ignorant of the economic and industrial question, which is to them of vital importance, and they must ever remain so while the selfishness of their brothers in toil is carried to such an extent as I find it to be among those who have sworn to demand equal pay for equal work. Thus far in the history of our order that part of our platform has been but a mockery of the principle intended."

Mrs. Barry started out to make regular investigations of different trades in which women were employed, in order that she might accurately inform herself and others as to what actual conditions were. But here she received her first serious check. She had no legal authority to enter any establishment where the proprietor objected, and even in other cases, where permission had been given, she discovered afterwards to her dismay that her visits had led to the dismissal of those who had in all innocence given her information, as in the case quoted of Sister Annie Conboy, a worker in a mill, in Auburn, New York. But little was gained by shutting out such a bright and observant woman. Mrs. Barry's practical knowledge of factory conditions was already wide and her relations with workers of the poorest and most oppressed class so intimate that little that she wanted to know seems to have escaped her, and she was often the channel through which information was furnished to the then newly established state bureaus of labor.

Baffled, however, in the further carrying out of her

plans for a thorough, and for that day, nation-wide investigation, she turned her attention mainly to education and organizing, establishing new local unions, helping those already in existence, and trying everywhere to strengthen the spirit of the workers in striving to procure for themselves improved standards.

In her second year of work Mrs. Barry had the assistance of a most able headquarters secretary, Mary O'Reilly, a cotton mill hand from Providence, Rhode Island. During eleven months there were no fewer than three hundred and thirty-seven applications for the presence of the organizer. Out of these Mrs. Barry filled two hundred and thirteen, traveling to nearly a hundred cities and towns, and delivering one hundred public addresses. She was in great demand as a speaker before women's organizations outside the labor movement, for it was just about that time that women more fortunately placed were beginning to be generally aroused to a shamefaced sense of their responsibility for the hard lot of their poorer sisters. Thus she spoke before the aristocratic Century Club of Philadelphia, and attended the session of the International Women's Congress held in Washington, D. C., in March and April, 1887.

The wages of but two dollars and fifty cents or three dollars for a week of eighty-four hours; the intolerable sufferings of the women and child wage-earners recorded in her reports make heart-rending reading today, especially when we realize how great in amount and how continuous has been the suffering in all the intervening years. So much publicity, however, and the undaunted spirit and unbroken determination of a certain number of the workers have assuredly had their effect, and some improvements there have been.

Speeding up is, in all probability, worse today than ever. It is difficult to compare wages without making a close investigation in different localities and in many trades, and testing, by a comparison with the cost of living, the real and not merely the money value of wages, but there is a general agreement among authorities that wages on the whole have not kept pace with the workers' necessary expenditures. But in one respect the worker today is much better off. At the time we are speaking of, the facts of the wrong conditions, the low wages, the long hours, and the many irritating tyrannies the workers had to bear, only rarely reached the public ear. Let us thank God for our muck-rakers. Their stories and their pictures are all the while making people realize that there is such a thing as a common responsibility for the wrongs of individuals.

Here is a managerial economy for you. The girls in a corset factory in Newark, New Jersey, if not inside when the whistle stopped blowing (at seven o'clock apparently) were locked out till half-past seven, and then they were docked two hours for waste power.

In a linen mill in Paterson, New Jersey, we are told how in one branch the women stood on a stone floor with water from a revolving cylinder flying constantly against the breast. They had in the coldest weather to go home with underclothing dripping because they were allowed neither space nor a few moments of time in which to change their clothing.

Mrs. Barry's work, educating, organizing, and latterly pushing forward protective legislation continued up till her marriage with O. R. Lake, a union printer, in 1890, when she finally withdrew from active participation in the labor movement.

Mrs. Barry could never have been afforded the opportunity even to set out on her mission, had it not been for the support and coöperation of other women delegates. The leaders in the Knights of Labor were ahead of their time in so freely inviting women to take part in their deliberations. It was at the seventh convention, in 1883, that the first woman delegate appeared. She was Miss Mary Stirling, a shoe-worker from Philadelphia. Miss Kate Dowling, of Rochester, New York, had also been elected, but did not attend. Next year saw two women, Miss Mary Hannafin, saleswoman, also from Philadelphia, and Miss Louisa M. Eaton, of Lynn, probably a shoe-worker. During the preceding year Miss Hannafin had taken an active part in protecting the girls discharged in a lock-out in a Philadelphia shoe factory, not only against the employer, but even against the weakness of some of the men of her own assembly who were practically taking the side of the strike-breakers, by organizing them into a rival assembly. The question came up in the convention for settlement, and the delegates voted for Miss Hannafin in the stand she had taken.

It was upon her initiative, likewise, at the convention in the following year, that the committee was formed to collect statistics of women's work, and in the year after (1886), it was again Miss Hannafin, the indefatigable, backed by the splendid force of sixteen women delegates, who succeeded in having Mrs. Barry appointed general investigator.

One of the most active and devoted women in the Knights of Labor was Mrs. George Rodgers, then and still of Chicago. For a good many years she had been in a quiet way educating and organizing among the girls in her own neighborhood, and had organized a working-women's union there. For seven years she attended the state assembly of the Knights of Labor, and was judge of the district court of the organization. But it is by her attendance as one of the sixteen women at the 1886 National Convention, which was held in Richmond, Virginia, that she is best remembered. She registered as "housekeeper" and a housekeeper she must indeed have been, with all her outside interests a busy housemother. There accompanied her to the gathering her baby of two weeks old, the youngest of her twelve children. To this youthful trade unionist, a little girl, the convention voted the highest numbered badge (800), and also presented her with a valuable watch and chain, for use in future years.

One cannot help suspecting that such an unusual representation of women must have been the reward of some special effort, for it was never repeated. Subsequent conventions saw but two or three seated to plead women's cause. At the 1890 convention, the occasion on which Mrs. Barry sent in her letter of resignation, there was but one woman delegate. She was the remarkable Alzina P. Stevens, originally a mill hand, but at this time a journalist of Toledo, Ohio. The men offered the now vacant post of general investigator to her, but she declined. However, between this period and her too early death, Mrs. Stevens was yet to do notable work for the labor movement.

During the years that the Knights of Labor were active, the women members were not only to be found in the mixed assemblies, but between 1881 and 1886 there are recorded the chartering of no fewer than one hundred and ninety local assemblies composed entirely of women. Even distant centers like Memphis, Little Rock and San Francisco were drawn upon, as well as the manufacturing towns in Ontario, Canada. Besides those formed of workers in separate trades, such as shoe-workers, mill operatives, and garment-workers, there were locals, like the federal labor unions of today, in which those engaged in various occupations would unite together. Some of the women's locals existed for a good many years, but a large proportion are recorded as having lapsed or suspended after one or two years. Apart from the usual difficulties in holding women's organizations together, there is no doubt that many locals, both of men and of women, were organized far too hastily, without the members having the least understanding of the first principles of trade unionism, or indeed of any side of the industrial question.

The organizers attempted far too much, and neglected the slow, solid work of preparation, and the no less important follow-up work; this had much to do with the early decline of the entire organization. The women's end of the movement suffered first and most quickly. From 1890 on, the women's membership became smaller and smaller, until practical interest by women and for women in the body wholly died out.

But the genuine workers had sown seed of which another movement was to reap the results. The year 1886 was the year of the first meeting of the American Federation of Labor as we know it. With its gradual development, the growth of the modern trade-union movement among women is inextricably bound up.

III

THE BEGINNINGS OF MODERN ORGANIZATION

As the Knights of Labor declined, the American Federation of Labor was rising to power and influence. It was at first known as the Federation of Organized Trades and Labor Unions of the United States and Canada, and organized under its present name in 1886. For some time the Knights of Labor and the younger organization exchanged greetings and counsel, and some of the leaders cherished the expectation that the field of effort was large enough to give scope to both. The American Federation of Labor, being a federation of trade unions, kept well in view the strengthening of strictly trade organizations. The Knights, as we have seen, were on the other hand, far more loosely organized, containing many members, both men and women, and even whole assemblies, outside of any trade, and they were therefore inclined to give a large share of their attention to matters of general reform, outside of purely trade-union or labor questions. It was the very largeness of their program which proved in the end a source of weakness, while latterly the activities of the organization became clogged by the burden of a membership with no intelligent understanding of the platform and aims.

But although the absence of adequate restrictions on admission to membership, and the ease of affiliation, not to speak of other reasons, had led to the acceptance of numbers of those who were only nominally interested in trade unionism, it had also permitted the entry of a band of women, not all qualified as wage-workers, but in faith and deed devoted trade unionists, and keenly alive to the necessity of bringing the wage-earning woman into the labor movement. The energies of this group were evidently sadly missed during the early years of the American Federation of Labor.

The present national organization came into existence in 1881, under the style and title of the Federation of Trades and Labor Unions of the United States and Canada. It reorganized at the convention of 1886, and adopted the present name, the American Federation of Labor. It was built up by trade-union members of the skilled trades, and to them trade qualifications and trade autonomy were essential articles of faith. This was a much more solid groundwork upon which to raise a labor movement. But at first it worked none too well for the women, although as the national organizations with women members joined the Federation the women were necessarily taken in, too. Likewise they shared in some, at least, of the benefits and advantages accruing from the linking together of the organized workers in one strong body. But the unions of which the new organization was composed in these early days were principally unions in what were exclusively men's trades, such as the building and iron trades, mining and so on. In the trades, again, in which women were engaged, they were not in any great numbers to be found in the union of the trade. So the inferior position held by women in the industrial world was therefore inevitably reflected in the Federation. It is true that time after time, in the very earliest conventions, resolutions would be passed recommending the organization of women. But matters went no further.

In 1882 Mrs. Charlotte Smith, president and representative of an organization styled variously the Women's National Labor League, and the Women's National Industrial League, presented a memorial to the Convention of the Federation of Organized Trades and Labor Unions (the Federation's name at that time), asking for the advice, assistance and coöperation of labor organizations. She mentioned that in 1880, there were recorded 2,647,157 women as employed in gainful occupations. A favorable resolution followed. At the convention of 1885, she was again present, and was accorded a seat without a vote. On her request again the delegates committed themselves to a resolution favoring the organization of women.

In 1890 Delegate T. J. Morgan, of Chicago, introduced, and the convention passed, a resolution, favoring the submission to Congress of an amendment extending the right of suffrage to women. At this convention appeared the first fully accredited woman delegate, Mrs. Mary Burke, of the Retail Clerks, from Findlay, Ohio. A resolution was introduced and received endorsement, but no action followed. It asked for the placing in the field of a sufficient number of women organizers to labor in behalf of the emancipation of women of the wage-working class.

In 1891 there were present at the annual convention of the American Federation of Labor Mrs. Eva McDonald Valesh and Miss Ida Van Etten. A committee was appointed with Mrs. Valesh as chairman and Miss Van Etten as secretary. They brought in a report that the convention create the office of national organizer, the organizer to be a woman at a salary of twelve hundred dollars a year and expenses, to be appointed the following January, and that the constitution be so amended that the woman organizer have a seat on the Executive Board. The latter suggestion was not acted upon. But Miss Mary

E. Kenney of the Bindery Women (now Mrs. Mary Kenney O'Sullivan) was appointed organizer, and held the position for five months. She attended the 1892 convention as a fully accredited delegate. Naturally she could produce no very marked results in that brief period, and the remark is made that her work was of necessity of a pioneer and missionary character rather than one of immediate results—a self-evident commentary. Later women were organizers for brief periods, one being Miss Anna Fitzgerald, of the National Women's Label League.

As years passed on, and the American Federation of Labor grew by the affiliation of almost all the national trade unions, it became the one acknowledged central national body. Along with the men, such women as were in the organizations came in, too. But it was only as a rare exception that we heard of women delegates, and no woman has ever yet had a seat upon the Executive Board, although women delegates have been appointed upon both special and standing committees.

The responsibility for this must be shared by all. It is partly an outgrowth of the backward state of the women themselves. They are at a disadvantage in their lack of training, their lower wages and their unconsciousness of the benefits of organization; also owing to the fact that such a large number of women are engaged in the unskilled trades that are hardest to organize. On the other hand, neither the national unions, the state and central bodies, nor the local unions have ever realized the value of the women membership they actually have, nor the urgent necessity that exists for organizing all working-women. To their own trade gatherings even, they have rarely admitted women delegates in proportion to the number of women workers. Only now and then, even today, do we find a woman upon the executive board of a national trade union, and when it comes to electing delegates to labor's yearly national gathering, it is men who are chosen, even in a trade like the garment-workers, in which there is a great preponderance of women.

Of the important international unions with women members there are but two which have a continuous, unbroken history of over fifty years. These are the Typographical Union, dating back to 1850, and the Cigar Makers' International Union, which was founded in 1864.

Other international bodies, founded since, are:

Boot and Shoe Workers' Union	1889
Hotel and Restaurant Employés Union	1890
Retail Clerks' International Protective Association	1890
United Garment Workers of America	1891
International Brotherhood of Bookbinders	1892
Tobacco Workers' International Union	1895
International Ladies' Garment Workers' Union	1900
Shirt, Waist and Laundry Workers International U'n	1900
United Textile Workers' Union	1901
International Glove Workers' Union of N. America	1902

One group of unions, older than any of these, dating back to 1885, are the locals of the hat trimmers. These workers belong to no national organization, and it is only recently that they have been affiliated with the American Federation of Labor. They are not, as might be judged from the title, milliners; they trim and bind men's hats. They coöperate with the Panama and Straw Hat Trimmers and Operators. In New York the hat-trimmers and the workers in straw are combined into one organization, under the name of the United Felt, Panama and Straw Hat Trimmers' and Operators' Union of Greater New York. The Hat Trimmers are almost wholly a women's organization, and their affairs are controlled almost entirely by women. The various locals coöperate with and support one another. But in their stage of organization this group of unions closely resembles the local unions, whether of men or women, which existed in so many trades before the day of nation-wide organizations set in. Eventually it must come about that they join the national organization. Outside of New York there are locals in New Jersey, Massachusetts and Connecticut. The parent union is that of Danbury, Connecticut.

The girl hat-trimmers, under the leadership of Melinda Scott, of Newark and New York, have during the last ten years improved both wages and conditions and have besides increased their numbers and aided in forming new locals in other centers. They are known in the annals of organized labor chiefly for the loyalty and devotion they showed during the strike of the Danbury hatters in 1909. They not only refused, to a girl, to go back to work, when that would have broken the strike, but time after time, when money was collected and sent to them, even as large a sum as one thousand dollars, they handed it over to the men's organizations, feeling that the men, with wives and children dependent upon them, were in even greater need than themselves. "Seeing the larger vision and recognizing the greater need, these young women gave to the mother and the child of their working brothers. Although a small group, there is none whose members have shown a more complete understanding of the inner meaning of trade unionism, or a finer spirit of self-sacrifice in the service of their fellows."

When we try to estimate the power of a movement, we judge it by its numbers, by its activities, and by its influence upon other movements.

As to the numbers of women trade unionists, we have

very imperfect statistics upon which to base any finding. If the statistics kept by the Labor Bureau of the
state of New York can be taken as typical of conditions
in other parts of the country, and they probably can, the
proportion of women unionists has not at all kept pace
with the increasing numbers of men organized. In 1894
there were in that state 149,709 men trade unionists,
and 7,488 women. In 1902 both had about doubled their
numbers—these read: men, 313,592; women, 15,509. By
1908, however, while there were then of men, 363,761, the
women had diminished to 10,698. Since then, we have
to note a marked change, beginning with 1910, and
continuing ever since. In 1913 the unionized men reached
568,726, and the women 78,522. The increase of men
in the organized trades of the state during the twelve-
month preceding September 30, 1913, was twenty per
cent., while of women it was one hundred and eleven
per cent. This enormous increase, more than doubling
the entire union strength among women, is mainly due to
the successful organization in the garment trades in
New York City.

So far there has been no adequate investigation covering the activities of women in the labor world during
the last or modern period. We know that after the panic
of 1893, which dealt a blow to trade unionism among
men, the movement among women was almost at a
standstill. We may feel that the international unions
have failed to see the light, and have mostly fallen
far short of what they might have done in promoting
the organization of women workers; but we must acknowledge with thankfulness the fact that they have
at least kept alive the tradition of trade unionism among
women, and have thus prepared the way for the education and the organization of the women workers by the
women workers themselves.

As to legislation, the steady improvement brought
about through the limitation of hours, through modern
sanitary regulations, and through child-labor laws, has
all along been supported by a handful of trade-union
women, working especially through the national organizations, in which, as members, they made their influence
felt.

There were always brave souls among the women, and
chivalrous souls, here and there among the men, and the
struggles made to form and keep alive tiny local unions
we shall probably never know, for no complete records
exist. The only way in which the ground can be even
partially covered is by a series of studies in each locality,
such as the one made by Miss Lillian Matthews, through
her work in San Francisco.

In this connection it must be remembered that those
uprisings among women of the last century, were after
all local and limited in their effects and range. Most of
them bore no relation to national organization of even
the trade involved, still less to an all-embracing, national
labor organization, such as the American Federation of
Labor. In these earlier stages, when organization of
both men and women was mainly local, women's influence, when felt at all, was felt strongly within the
locality affected, and it is therefore only there that we
hear about it.

Still, twenty-five years ago, the day of national organization had already dawned. To organize a trade
on a national scale is at best a slow process, and it
naturally takes a much longer time for women to influence and enter into the administrative work of a
national union, than of a separate local union, which
perhaps they have helped to found. They are therefore
too apt to lose touch with the big national union, and
even with its local branch in their own city. It is almost

like the difference between the small home kitchen, with whose possibilities a woman is familiar, and the great food-producing factory, run on a business scale, whose management seems to her something far-removed and unfamiliar. It was not until 1904, when the National Women's Trade Union League was formed out of unions with women members, that women workers, as women, can be said to have begun national organization at all. The account of that body is reserved for another chapter.

Meanwhile as instances of the many determined localized efforts among women to raise wages and better conditions, there follow here outlines of the formation of the Working Women's Society in New York, the successful organization of the Laundry Workers in San Francisco, and of the splendid but defeated struggle of the girls in the packing plants of Chicago.

In 1886 a small body of working-women, of whom Leonora O'Reilly was one, began holding meetings on the East Side of New York City, to inquire into and talk over bad conditions, and see how they could be remedied. They were shortly joined by some women of position, who saw in this spontaneous effort one promising remedy, at least for some of the gross evils of underpayment, overwork and humiliation suffered by the working-women and girls of New York, in common with those in every industrial center. Among those other women who thus gave their support, and gave it in the truly democratic spirit, were the famous Josephine Shaw Lowell, Mrs. Robert Abbé, Miss Arria Huntingdon and Miss L. S. Perkins, who was the first treasurer of the little group. Mrs. Lowell's long experience in public work, and her unusual executive ability were of much value at first. The result of the meetings was the formation of the Working Women's Society. They held their first public meeting on February 2, 1888. In their an-

nouncement of principles they declared "the need of a
central society, which shall gather together those already
devoted to the cause of organization among women,
shall collect statistics and publish facts, shall be ready
to furnish information and advice, and, above all, shall
continue and increase agitation on this subject." Among
their specific objects were "to found trade organizations,
where they do not exist, and to encourage and assist
existing labor organizations, to the end of increasing
wages and shortening hours." Another object was to
promote the passing and the enforcement of laws for the
protection of women and children in factories, and yet
another the following up of cases of injustice in the
shops.

The Working Women's Society gave very valuable
aid in the feather-workers' strike. Without the Society's
backing the women could never have had their case put
before the public as it was. Again, it was through their
efforts, chiefly, that the law was passed in 1890, providing for women factory inspectors in the state of New
York. It is stated that this was the first law of the
kind in the world, and that the British law, passed shortly
afterwards, was founded upon its provisions.

Not limiting itself to helping in direct labor organization, and legislation, the Working Women's Society
undertook among the more fortunate classes a campaign
of sorely needed education, and made upon them, at the
same time, a claim for full and active coöperation in the
battle for industrial justice.

This was done through the foundation of the Consumers' League of New York, now a branch of the
National Consumers' League, which has done good and
faithful service in bringing home to many some sense
of the moral responsibility of the purchaser in maintaining oppressive industrial conditions, while, on the other

hand it has persistently striven for better standards of labor legislation. It was through the Consumers' League, and especially through the ability and industry of its notable officer, Josephine Goldmark, that the remarkable mass of information on the toxic effects of fatigue, and the legislation to check overwork already in force in other countries was brought together in such complete form, as to enable Louis Brandeis to successfully defend the ten-hour law for women, first for Oregon, and afterwards for Illinois. The Working Women's Society did its work at a time when organization for women was even more unpopular than today. It did much to lessen that unpopularity, and to hearten its members for the never-ending struggle. All its agitation told, and prepared the way for the Women's Trade Union League, which, a decade later, took up the very same task.

In the year 1900, the status of the steam-laundry-workers of San Francisco was about as low as could possibly be imagined. White men and girls had come into the trade about 1888, taking the place of the Chinese, who had been the first laundrymen on the West Coast. Regarding their treatment, Miss Lillian Ruth Matthews writes:

The conditions surrounding the employment of these first white workers were among those survivals from the eighteenth century, which still linger incongruously in our modern industrial organization. The "living-in" system was the order, each laundry providing board and lodging for its employés. The dormitories were wretched places, with four beds in each small room. The food was poor and scanty, and even though the girls worked till midnight or after, no food was allowed after the evening meal at six o'clock. Half-an-hour only was allowed for lunch. Early in the morning, the women were routed out in no gentle manner and by six o'clock the unwholesome breakfast was over, and every one hard at work. * * * * The girls were physically depleted from their hard work and poor nourishment. Their hands were "blistered and puffed, their feet swollen, calloused, and sore." One girl said, "Many a time I've been so tired that I hadn't the courage to take my clothes off. I've thrown myself on the bed and slept like dead until I got so cold and cramped that at two or three in the morning I'd rouse up and undress and crawl into bed, only to crawl out again at half-past five."

As to wages, under the wretched "living-in" system the girls received but eight dollars and ten dollars a month in money. But even those who lived at home in no instance received more than twenty-five dollars a month, and in many cases widows with children to support would be trying to do their duty by their little ones on seventeen dollars and fifty cents a month.

In the summer of 1900, letters many of them anonymous, were received both by the State Labor Commissioner and by the newspapers. A reporter from the *San Francisco Examiner* took a job as a laundry-worker, and published appalling accounts of miserable wages, utter slavery as to hours and degrading conditions generally. Even the city ordinance forbidding work after ten at night (!) was found to be flagrantly violated, the girls continually working till midnight, and sometimes till two in the morning.

The first measure of improvement was the passing of a new ordinance, forbidding work after seven in the evening. The workers, however, promptly realized that the more humane regulation was likely to be as ill enforced as the former one had been unless there was a union to see that it was carried out.

About three hundred of the men organized, and applied to the Laundry Workers' International Union for a charter. The men did not wish to take the women in, but the executive board of the national organization, to their everlasting credit, refused the charter unless the women were taken in as well. Even so, a great many of the women were too frightened to take any steps themselves, as the employers were already threatening with dismissal any who dared to join a union, but the most courageous of the girls, with the help of some of the best of the men resolved to go on. Hannah Mahony, now Mrs. Hannah Nolan, Labor Inspector, took up the difficult task of organizing. So energetic and successful was she, that in sixteen weeks the majority of the girls, as well as the men, had joined the new union. It was all carried out secretly, and only when they felt themselves strong enough did they come out into the open with a demand for a higher wage-scale and shorter hours.

By April 1, 1901, the conditions in the laundry industry were effectually revolutionized. The boarding system was abolished, wages were substantially increased and the working day was shortened; girls who had been receiving $8 and $10 a month were now paid $6 and $10 a week; ten hours was declared to constitute the working day and nine holidays a year were allowed. For overtime the employés were to be paid at the rate of time and a half. An hour was to be taken at noon, and any employé violating this rule was to be fined. The fine was devised as an educative reminder of the new obligation the laborers were under to protect one another, and to raise the standard of the industry upon which they must depend for a living, so fearful was the union that old conditions might creep insidiously back upon workers unaccustomed to independence.

The next step was the nine-hour day, and this in good time was obtained too, but only as the result of the power of the strong, well-managed union.

The union was just five years old, when unheard-of

disaster fell on San Francisco, the earthquake and fire. Well indeed did the members stand the test. Like their fellow-unionists, the waitresses, they made such good use of their trade-union solidarity, and showed such courage, wisdom and resource, that the union became even more to the laundry-workers than it had been before this severe trial of its worth. Two-thirds of the steam laundries had been destroyed, likewise the union headquarters. Yet within a week all the camps and bread lines had been visited, and members requested to register at the secretary's home, and called together to a meeting.

Temporary headquarters were found and opened as a relief station, where members were supplied with clothing and shoes. Within another week the nine laundries that had escaped the fire resumed work, the employés going back under the old agreement.

By the time the next April came round nine of the burnt laundries were rebuilt, all on the most modern scale as to design and fittings, and equipped with the very newest machinery. But still there were only eighteen steam laundries to meet all San Francisco's needs, and therefore business was very brisk. So in April, 1907, it seemed good to the union leaders to try for better terms when renewing their agreement. When they made their demand for the eight-hour day as well as for increased wages, the proprietors refused, and eleven hundred workers went out, the entire working force of fourteen laundries. The other four laundries, with but two hundred workers altogether, had the old agreement signed up, and kept on working. The strike lasted eleven weeks, and cost the union over $24,000. Meanwhile the Conciliation Committee of the Labor Council, after many conferences and much effort succeeded in arranging a compromise, the working week to be fifty-one hours, with a sliding scale under which the eight-hour day would be reached in April, 1910. Work before seven in the morning was prohibited, all time after five o'clock was considered overtime, and must be paid for at time-and-a-half rate. The passing of the eight-hour law in May, 1911, suggested to some ingenious employers a method of getting behind their own agreement, at least to the extent of utilizing their plant to the utmost. They accordingly proposed to free themselves from any obligation to pay overtime, as long as the eight consecutive hours were not exceeded. The leaders of the union saw the danger lurking under this suggestion, in that it might mean all sorts of irregular hours, or even a two-shift system, involving perpetual night work, and going home from work long distances in the middle of the night. After many months of haggling, the union won its point. All work after five o'clock was to be paid at overtime rate, with the exception of Monday, when the closing time was made six. This because in all laundries there is apt to be delay in starting work on Monday, as hardly any work can be done until the drivers have come in from their first round, with bundles of soiled linen. This arrangement remained in force at time of writing.

As regards wages, Miss Matthews estimates the average increase in the twelve years since the Steam Laundry Workers' Union was first formed at about thirty per cent. With the exception of the head marker, and the head washer at the one end, each at twenty-two dollars and fifty cents per week, and the little shaker girl on the mangle at seven dollars per week at the other, wages range from eighteen dollars down to eight dollars, more than the scale, however, being paid, it is said, to every worker with some skill and experience. Apprentices are allowed for in the union agreement.

The union does not permit its members to work at

unguarded machinery, hence accidents are rare, and for such as do happen, usually slight ones, like burns, the union officials are inclined to hold the workers themselves responsible.

All of the steam laundries in San Francisco, now thirty-two in number, are unionized, including the laundries operated in one of the largest hotels. The union regards with just pride and satisfaction the fine conditions, short hours and comparatively high wages which its trade enjoys, as well as the improved social standards and the spirit of independence and coöperation which are the fruit of these many years of union activity.

But outside the labor organization, and at once a sad contrast and a possible menace, lie two groups of businesses, the French laundries and the Japanese laundries. The former are mostly conducted on the old, out-of-date lines of a passing domestic industry, housed in made-over washrooms and ironing rooms, equipped with little modern machinery, most of the work being done by hand, and the employés being often the family or at least the relatives of the proprietor. In their present stage it is quite difficult to unionize these establishments and they do cut prices for the proprietors of the steam laundries.

But both steam laundries and French laundries, both employers and workers, both unionists and non-unionists are at least found in agreement in their united opposition to the Japanese laundries, from whose competition all parties suffer, and in this they are backed by the whole of organized labor. The possibility of unionizing the Japanese laundries is not even considered.

The story of the Steam Laundry Workers' Union of San Francisco is an encouraging lesson to those toilers in any craft who go on strike. But it also holds for them a warning. A successful strike is a good thing, for the most part, but its gains can be made permanent only if, when the excitement of the strike is over, the workers act up to their principles and keep their union together. The leaders must remember that numbers alone do not make strength, that most of the rank and file, and not unfrequently the leaders too, need the apprenticeship of long experience before any union can be a strong organization. The union's choicest gift to its membership lies in the opportunity thus offered to the whole of the members to grow into the spirit of fellowship.

A few words should be said here of another strike among laundry-workers, this time almost entirely women, which although as bravely contested, ended in complete failure. This was the strike of the starchers in the Troy, New York, shirt and collar trade. In the Federal Report on the Condition of Women and Child Wage Earners, Mr. W. P. D. Bliss gives a brief account of it. In 1905 the starchers had their wages cut, and at the same time some heavy machinery was introduced. The starchers went out, and organized a union, which over one thousand women joined. They kept up the struggle from June, 1905, throughout a whole summer, autumn and winter till March, 1906. It was up till that time, probably the largest women's strike that had ever taken place in this country and was conducted with uncommon persistence and steadiness of purpose. They were backed by the international union, and appointing a committee visited various cities, and obtained, it is said, about twenty-five thousand dollars in this way for the support of their members. Many meetings and street demonstrations were held in Troy, and much bitter feeling existed between the strikers and the non-union help brought in. The strike at length collapsed; the firms continued to introduce more machinery, and the girls had to submit. Mr. Bliss concludes: "The Troy union was broken up and since then has had little more than a nominal existence."

During the nineties there were a number of efforts made to organize working-women in Chicago. Some unions were organized at Hull House, where Mrs. Alzina P. Stevens and Mrs. Florence Kelley were then residents. Mrs. George Rodgers (K. of L.), Mrs. Robert Howe, Dr. Fannie Dickenson, Mrs. Corinne Brown, Mrs. T. J. Morgan, Mrs. Frank J. Pearson, Mrs. Fannie Kavanagh and Miss Lizzie Ford were active workers. Miss Mary E. Kenney (Mrs. O'Sullivan), afterwards the first woman organizer under the American Federation of Labor, was another. She was successful in reaching the girls in her own trade (book-binding), besides those in the garment trades and in the shoe factories, also in bringing the need for collective bargaining strongly before social and settlement workers.

Chicago has long been the largest and the most important among the centers of the meat-packing industry. None of the food trades have received more investigation and publicity, and the need for yet more publicity, and for stricter and yet stricter supervision is perpetually being emphasized. But most of the efforts that have been made to awake and keep alive a sense of public rights and responsibility in the conducting of huge institutions like the Chicago packing-plants, have centered on the danger to the health of the consumer through eating diseased or decomposed meat. The public cares little, and has not troubled to learn much about the conditions of the workers, without whom there could be no stockyards and no meat-packing industry. Not that some of the investigators have not tried to bring this point forward. It was the chief aim of Upton Sinclair, when he wrote "The Jungle," and yet even he discovered to his dismay that, as he bitterly phrased it, he had hoped to strike at the heart of the American people, and he had only hit them in their stomach.

But that is a story by itself. Let us go back to the brave struggle begun by the women in the packing-plants in the year 1902 to improve their conditions by organizing.

For a great many years prior to this, women had been employed in certain branches of the work, such as painting cans and pasting on labels. But towards the close of the nineties the packers began to put women into departments that had always been staffed by men. So it was when girls began to wield the knife that the men workers first began to fear the competition of the "petticoat butchers." The idea of organizing the girls, were they painters or butchers, as a way of meeting this new menace, did not occur to them.

At this time, in the fall of 1902, the oldest and best workers were Irish girls, with all the wit and quickness of their race. Especially was Maggie Condon a favorite and a leader. She was an extremely quick worker. With the temperament of an idealist, she took a pride in her work, liked to do it well, and was especially successful in turning out a great amount of work. Quicker and quicker she became till, on the basis of the good wages she was making, she built up dreams of comfort for herself and her family. One of her choicest ambitions was to be able to afford a room of her own. But just so surely as she reached the point where such a luxury would be possible, just so surely would come the cut in wages, and she had to begin this driving of herself all over again. Three times this happened. When her well and hardly earned twenty-two dollars was cut the third time Maggie realized that this was no way to mend matters. The harder she worked, the worse she was paid! And not only was she paid worse, she who as one of the best workers could stand a reduction better than most, but the cut went all down the line, and affected the poorest paid and the slowest workers as well.

Hannah O'Day was not one of the quick ones. Her strength had been too early sapped. There was no child-labor law in Illinois when she should have been at school, and at eleven she was already a wage-earner. Along with the rest she also had suffered from the repeated cuts that the pace-making of the ones at the top had brought about. It was evident that something must be done. Maggie Condon, Hannah O'Day and some of the others, began, first to think, and then to talk over the matter with one another. They knew about the Haymarket trouble. There were rumors of a strike the men had once had. They had heard of the Knights of Labor, and wrote to someone, but nothing came of it. So one day, when there was more than usual cause for irritation and discouragement, what did Hannah O'Day do but tie a red silk handkerchief to the end of a stick. With this for their banner and the two leaders at their head, a whole troop of girls marched out into Packingtown.

The strike ended as most such strikes of the unorganized, unprepared for, and unfinanced sort, must end, in failure, in the return to work on no better terms of the rank and file, and in the black-listing of the leaders. But the idea of organization had taken root, and this group of Irish girls still clung together. "We can't have a union," said one, "but we must have something. Let us have a club, and we'll call it the Maud Gonne Club." This is touching remembrance of the Irish woman patriot.

Time passed on, and one evening during the winter of 1903 Miss Mary McDowell, of the University of

Chicago Settlement, was talking at a Union Label League meeting, and she brought out some facts from what she knew of the condition of the women workers in the packing-houses, showing what a menace to the whole of the working world was the underpaid woman. This got into the papers, and Maggie Condon and her sister read it, and felt that here was a woman who understood. And she was in their own district, too.

So it came about that the Maud Gonne Club became slowly transformed into a real union. This took quite a while. The girls interested used to come over once a week to the Settlement, where Michael Donnelly was their tutor and helper. Miss McDowell carefully absented herself, feeling that she wanted the girls to manage their own affairs, until it transpired that they wished her to be there, and thought it strange that she should be so punctilious. After that she attended almost every meeting. When they felt ready, they obtained the charter with eight charter members and were known as Local 183 of the Amalgamated Meat Cutters and Butcher Workmen of North America. Little by little the local grew in numbers. One July night the meeting was particularly well attended and particularly lively, none the less so that the discussion was carried on to the accompaniment of a violent thunderstorm, the remarks of the excitable speakers being punctuated by flashes of lightning and crashes of thunder. The matter under consideration was to parade or not to parade on the coming Labor Day. The anxious question to decide was whether they could by their numbers make an impression great enough to balance the dangers of the individual and risky publicity.

The vote was cast in favor of parading. When the day came the affair was an entire success. Two wagons gaily trimmed were filled with girls in white dresses, carrying banners and singing labor songs. The happy results were seen at subsequent meetings of the union, for after that other girls from other than the Irish group came in fast, peasant girls, wearing their shawls, and colored girls, till, when the union was six months old, it had five hundred members. The initiation of the first colored girl was a touching occasion. Hannah O'Day had been present at one of the men's meetings, on an evening when it had been a colored man who at the ceremony of initiation had presented white candidates for membership, and the sense of universal brotherhood had then come over her as a sort of revelation. And there were others who felt with her. One night, Hannah being doorkeeper at her own union meeting, a colored girl applied to be admitted. Hannah called out: "A colored sister is at the door; what'll I do with her." It was the young president herself, Mollie Daley, though she had been brought up to think of colored folks as "trash," who, with a disregard of strict parliamentary law, but with a beautiful cordiality, broke in with: "I say, admit her at once, and let yez give her a hearty welcome." The girl who was very dark, but extremely handsome, had been not a little nervous over the reception that might await her. She was quite overcome when she found herself greeted with hearty applause.

On another occasion, on the question being asked from the ritual: "Any grievances?" a sensitive colored girl arose, and said a Polish girl had called her names. The Polish girl defended herself by saying: "Well, she called me Polak, and I won't stand for that." The president summoned them both to the front. "Ain't you ashamed of yourselves?" She proceeded: "Now shake and make up, and don't bring your grievances here, unless they're from the whole shop."

The girls had good training in union principles from

the first, so that if their phrases were sometimes a trifle crude, they were none the less the expression of genuine good sense. For instance, some complaint would be brought forward, and in the early days the question would come: "Is this your own kick, or is it all of our kick?" A sound distinction to make, quite as sound as when later on, the officers having learned the formal phrases, they would put it in another way, and say: "Is this a private grievance or is it a collective grievance?"

Instead of the old hysterical getting mad, and laying down their tools and walking out, when things did not go right, grievances were now taken to the union, and discussed, and if supported by the body, taken to the foreman and managers by the business agent, Maud Sutter.

From the beginning the women delegates from Local 183 to the Packing Trades Council of Chicago were on an equality with the men, and girl delegates attended the convention of the National Association at Cincinnati and also at St. Louis.

It is sad to record that through no fault of their own, the girls' organization met an early downfall. It passed out of existence after the stockyards' strike of 1904, being inevitably involved in the defeat of the men, and going down with them to disaster.

The Irish leadership that produced such splendid results, is now, in any case, not there to be called upon, as the girls now employed in the packing-plants of Chicago are practically all immigrant girls from eastern Europe. When the present system of unorganized labor in the trade is abolished, as some day it must be, it will only be through a fresh beginning among an altogether different group, that it will be possible to reach the women.

But the spirit that permeated Local 183 has never wholly died in the hearts of those who belonged to it, and it springs up now and then in quarters little expected, calling to remembrance Maggie Condon's reason for pushing the union of which she was a charter member and the first vice-president. "Girls, we ought to organize for them that comes after us."

IV

THE WOMEN'S TRADE UNION LEAGUE

One of the least encouraging features of trade unionism among women in the United States has been the
small meed of success which has attended efforts after
organization in the past, especially the lack of permanence in such organizations as have been formed. In
the brief historical review it has been shown how fitful
were women's first attempts in this direction, how limited
the success, and how temporary the organizations themselves.

It is true there is an essential difference between
the loose and momentary coöperation of unorganized
workers aiming at the remedying of special grievances,
and disbanding their association whenever that particular struggle is over, and a permanent organization representing the workers' side all the time and holding them
in a bond of mutual helpfulness. Most of the strikes
of women during the first half of the last century, like
many today, sprang from impatience with intolerable
burdens, and the "temporary union," often led by some
men's organization, merely dissolved away with the ending of the strike, whether successful or not. But altogether apart from such sporadic risings as these, there
were, as we have seen, from a very early period, genuine
trade unions composed of working-women.

The Women's Trade Union League is the first organization which has attempted to deal with the whole
of the problems of the woman in industry on a national

scale. As we have seen, there have been, besides the many women's unions, and the men's unions to which women have been and are admitted, the large body, the Women's National Union Label League, and a number of women's auxiliaries in connection with such unions as the Switchmen, the Machinists, and the Typographical Union. The Women's Union Label League has, however, devoted most of its energies to encouraging the purchase and use of union-made products. The women's auxiliaries have been formed from the wives of men from that particular union. They have often maintained a fund for sick and out-of-work members and their families, and have besides furnished a social environment in which all could become better acquainted, and they would besides take an active part in the entertainment of a national convention, whenever it came to their city. But except indirectly, none of these associations have aided in the organization of women wage-earners, still less have taken it for their allotted task. Perhaps earlier, the formation of such a body as the National Women's Trade would have been impracticable. But it certainly responds to the urgent needs of today, and is, after all, but a natural development of the trade-union movement, with especial reference to the crying needs of women and children in the highly specialized industries.

The individual worker, restless under the miseries of her lot, and awakening also, it may be, to a sense of the meaning of our industrial system, learns to see the need of the union of her trade. When she does so, she has taken a distinct step forward. If an extensive trade, the local is affiliated with the international, but neither local nor international, as we shall see, as yet grant to the woman worker the same attention as they give to the man, because to men trade unionists the men's problems are the chief and most absorbing. So what more natural than that women belonging to various unions should come together to discuss the problems that are common to them all as women workers, whatever their trade, and aid one another in their difficulties, coöperate in their various activities, and thus, also, be able to present to their brothers the collective expression of their needs? Upon this simple basis is the local Women's Trade Union League formed. Linking together the organized women of the same city, it brings them, through the National League, into touch and communication with the trade-union women in other cities.

While it is true that organization can neither be imposed nor forced upon any group, it is no less true that when girls are ready such a compact body, founded upon so broad a basis, can bring about results both in the line of education and organization which no other branch of the labor movement is equipped or fitted to do. And many labor leaders, who have sadly enough acknowledged that the labor movement that did not embrace women was like a giant carrying one arm in a sling, have already gratefully admitted that such a league of women's unions can produce results under circumstances where men, unaided, would have been helpless.

For the origin of the Women's Trade Union League, we must go back to 1874, when Mrs. Emma Patterson, the wife of an English trade unionist and herself deeply impressed with the deplorable condition of women wage-earners everywhere, was on a visit to the United States. The importance of combination as a remedy was freshly brought home to her through what she saw of the women's organizations then most prominent and flourishing in New York, the Parasol and Umbrella Makers' Union, the Women's Typographical Union, and the Women's Protective Union. She returned to England with a plan for helping women workers to help themselves. Shortly afterwards she and others whom she interested formed the Women's Protective and Provident League, the title later on being changed to the bolder and more radical British Women's Trade Union League, a federation of women's unions, with an individual membership as well. It is known to the public on this side of the water through the visits of Mary Macarthur, its very able secretary.

This body had been in existence nearly thirty years before the corresponding organization was formed in this country. About 1902 Mr. William English Walling had his attention drawn to what the British Women's Trade Union League was accomplishing among some of the poorest working-women in England.

He mentioned what he had learned to others. Among the earliest to welcome the idea of forming such a league was Mrs. Mary Kenney O'Sullivan, a bindery-worker of Boston, long in touch with the labor movement. In the fall of 1903 the American Federation of Labor was holding its annual convention in that city. The presence of so many labor leaders seemed to make the moment a favorable one. A meeting of those interested was called in Faneuil Hall on November 14. Mr. John O'Brien, president of the Retail Clerks' International Protective Union, presided. Among the trades represented were the Ladies' Garment Workers, the United Garment Workers, the Amalgamated Meat Cutters and Butcher Workmen, Clerks, Shoe Workers and Textile Workers. The National Women's Trade Union League was organized and the following officers elected: president, Mrs. Mary Morton Kehew, Boston; vice-president, Miss Jane Addams, Chicago; secretary, Mrs. Mary Kenney O'Sullivan, Boston; treasurer, Miss Mary Donovan, Boot and Shoe Workers; board mem-

bers, Miss Mary McDowell, Chicago; Miss Lillian D.
Wald, New York; Miss Ellen Lindstrom, United Gar-
ment Workers; Miss Mary Trites, Textile Workers;
Miss Leonora O'Reilly, Ladies' Garment Workers.

The one main purpose of the new league, as of its
British prototype, was from the first the organization
of women into trade unions, to be affiliated with the
regular labor movement, in this case with the American
Federation of Labor, and the strengthening of all such organizations as already existed. While, as in England,
the backbone of the League was to consist of a federation of women's unions, provision was made for taking
into individual membership not only trade unionists, but
those women, and men too, who, although not wage-
earners themselves, believed that the workers should be
organized and were unwilling that those who toil should
suffer from unjust conditions.

A branch of the National Women's Trade Union
League was formed in Chicago in January, 1904; another in New York in March of the same year, and a
third in Boston in June of the same year. With these
three industrial centers in line, the new campaign was
fairly begun.

The first three years were occupied mainly with preparatory work, becoming known to the unions and the
workers, and developing activities both through the office
and in the field.

Early in 1907 Mrs. Raymond Robins, of Chicago,
became National President, a position which she has
held ever since. To the tremendous task of aiding the
young organization till it was at least out of its swaddling
clothes she brought boundless energy and a single-minded
devotion which admitted of attention to no rival cause.
Being a woman of independent means, she was able to
give her time entirely to the work of the League. She

would be on the road for weeks at a time, speaking, interviewing working-women, manufacturers or legislators, all the while holding the threads, organization here, legislation there.

But the first opportunity for the Women's Trade Union League to do work on a large scale, work truly national in its results, came with the huge strikes in the sewing trades of 1909-1911. To these a separate chapter is devoted. It is sufficient here to say that the backing given by the National League and its branches in New York, in Philadelphia and in Chicago was in great part responsible for the very considerable measure of success which has been the outcome of these fierce industrial struggles. On the whole, the strikers gained much better terms than they could possibly have done unassisted. Almost entirely foreigners, they had no adequate means of reaching with their story the English-speaking and reading public of their city. The Leagues made it their particular business to see that the strikers' side of the dispute was brought out in the press and in meetings and gatherings of different groups. It is related of one manufacturer, whose house was strike-bound, that he was heard one day expressing to a friend in their club his bewilderment over the never-ending publicity given to this strike in the daily newspapers, adding that it was a pity; these affairs were always better settled quietly.

To win even from failure success, to win for success permanence, was the next aim of the League, and nowhere has this constructive policy of theirs brought about more significant results than in the aid which they were able to give to the workers in the sewing trades. In New York it was the League which made possible the large organizations which exist today among the cloak-makers, the waist-makers and other white-goods-workers.

The League support during the great strikes, and its continued quiet work after the strikes were over, first showed the public that there was power and meaning in this new development, this new spirit among the most oppressed women workers. The attitude of the League also convinced labor men that this was no dilettante welfare society, but absolutely fair and square with the labor movement. The Chicago League, after helping in the same way in the garment-workers' strike which is now in its fifth year, contributed towards bringing about the agreement between the firm of Hart, Schaffner and Marx, Chicago, and their employés, an agreement controlling the wages and the working conditions of between 7,000 and 10,000 men and women, the number varying with the season and the state of trade. The plan of preference to unionists, which gives to this form of contract the name of the "Preferential Shop," had its origin in Australia, where it is embodied in arbitration acts, but in no single trade had it been applied on such a huge scale. The Protocol of Peace, which is a trade agreement similar to that of the Hart, Schaffner and Marx employés, and which came into force first in the cloak and suit industry in New York after the strike of 1913, affects, it is stated, the enormous number of 300,000 workers.[1]

Just as sound and important work is being done all the time with many smaller groups. For instance, the straw- and panama-hat-makers of New York tried to organize and were met by a number of the manufacturers with a black list. A general strike was declared

---

[1] In May, 1915, the Protocol was set aside by the cloak and suit manufacturers. A strike impended. Mayor Mitchel called a Council of Conciliation, Dr. Felix Adler as chairman. Their report was accepted by the union and finally by the employers, and industrial peace was restored.

on February 14, 1913. The League members were able to give very valuable aid to the strikers by assisting in picketing and by attending the courts when the pickets were arrested. This strike had to be called off, and was apparently lost, but the union remains and is far stronger than before the strike took place.

But better results even than this were gained in the strike in the potteries in Trenton, New Jersey. The Central Labor Union of Trenton and all the trade-union men in the city gave splendid coöperation to the strikers. They handed over the girls to the care of Miss Melinda Scott, the League organizer, and under her directions the inexperienced unionists did fine work and helped to bring about a satisfactory settlement. This success gave heart of grace to the girls in certain woolen and silk mills of Trenton. Wages there were appalling. They varied from two dollars and fifty cents to eleven dollars. Many children, nominally fourteen, but looking very young, were employed. The owner of the factory at length consented to meet tne workers with the League organizer in conference at the New York headquarters, and after several weeks the strike was settled on the workers' terms.

The New York organizer also helped the Boston League in the strike of the paper factories of Holyoke, Massachusetts. The cause of the strike here was an arrangement under which eight girls could be got to do the work of twelve. Here the workers actually stood up for a share of the profits under the new arrangement, or else that the discharged girls should be reinstated. The manufacturers chose the latter alternative.

The Candy Workers' Union in Boston was also formed through the Women's Trade Union League. The girls had walked all over Boston for two days asking policemen, carmen and anyone else who would listen to them how to form a union. They had no umbrellas, and their shoes were dripping with the wet. They were Jewish, Italian and American girls. As a result of the organization formed they obtained a very material raise in wages, the better allotment of work in the slack season and the taking up of all disputed questions between the manufacturers and the union.

From experience gained during these gigantic industrial wars, the National League has laid down definite conditions under which its locals may coöperate with unions in time of strike. These take part only in strikes in which women are involved, and then only after having been formally invited to assist, and on the understanding that two League representatives may attend all executive meetings of the strikers' union. It has been found that the lines in which the aid of the Women's Trade Union League is of most value to any exploited group are these: (1) organization and direction of public opinion; (2) patrolling the streets; (3) fair play in the courts; (4) help in the raising of funds through unions and allies; (5) where workers are unorganized, help in the formation of trade-union organization.

The League workers thus make it their business to open up channels of publicity, at least giving the papers something to talk about, and reaching with the strikers' side of the story, churches, clubs, and other associations of well-meaning citizens, who are not at all in touch with organized labor. Allies, in particular, can do much to preserve traditions of fair play, in regard to the use of the streets for peaceful picketing. By providing bonds for girls arrested, lawfully or unlawfully, and by attending in person such cases when these come up in court, they are standing for the principles of democracy.

In addition, the local leagues are willing to take charge

of the arrangements under which girls are sent to other unions, asking for moral and financial aid. Men trade unionists long ago discovered how irresistible a pleader the young girl can be, but they are not always equally impressed with the need of safeguarding the girls, often little more than children, chosen for these trying expeditions, and sent off alone, or at best, two together, to distant industrial centers. The working-girl needs no chaperon, but equally with her wealthier sister, she does require and ought to receive motherly care and oversight. She is perhaps leaving home for the first time, and there should be someone to see to it that when she arrives in a strange city a comfortable and convenient lodging-place has been found for her. She should be shown how to conserve her strength in finding her way from one locality to another in following up the evening meetings of unions, and she should have some woman to turn to if she should become sick. Points, all of these, the busy secretaries of central labor bodies may very easily overlook, accustomed as they are to deal with mature men, in the habit of traveling about the country, who may surely be left to take care of themselves.

The activities of the local leagues vary in detail in the different cities. In all there are monthly business meetings, the business run by the girls, with perhaps a speaker to follow, and sometimes a program of entertainment. Lectures on week evenings, classes and amusements are provided as far as workers and funds permit. The first important work among newly arrived women immigrants in the Middle West was done by the Chicago League, and this laid the groundwork for the present Immigrants' Protective League. Headquarters are a center for organizing, open all the time to receive word of struggling unions, helping out in difficulties, counseling the impulsive, and encouraging the timid. When a group of workers see for themselves the need of organization, a body of experienced women standing, ready to mother a new little union, the hospitable room standing open, literally night and day, can afford the most powerful aid in extending organization among timid girls. If courage and daring are needed in this work, courage to stand by the weak, daring to go out and picket in freezing weather with unfriendly policemen around, patience is if possible more essential in the organizer's make-up. It often takes months of gentle persistence before the girls, be they human-hair-workers or cracker-packers, or domestic workers or stenographers, see how greatly it is to their own interest to join or to form a labor organization. Many locals formed with so much thought and after so much pains, drop to pieces after a few months or a year or two. That is a universal experience in the labor movement everywhere. But it does not therefore follow that nothing has been gained. Even a group so loosely held together that it melts away after the first impulse of indignation has died out is often successful in procuring shorter hours or better wages or improved conditions for the trade or shops of their city. Besides each individual girl has had a little bit of education in what coöperation means, and what collective bargaining can do. The League itself is a reminder, too, that all working-girls have many interests in common, whatever their trade.

But besides aiding in the forming of new locals, the Women's Trade Union League can be a force strengthening the unions already established. Each of the leagues has an organization committee, whose meetings are attended by delegates from the different women's trades. These begin mostly as experience meetings, but end generally in either massing the effort of all on one particular union's struggle, or in planning legislative action by which all women workers can be benefited.

In New York and Boston, Chicago and St. Louis and Kansas City the local leagues have in every case had a marked effect upon industrial legislation for women. They have been prime movers in the campaigns for better fire protection in the factories in both New York and Chicago, and for the limitation of hours of working-women in the states of New York, Massachusetts, Illinois and Missouri, and for minimum-wage legislation in Massachusetts and Illinois.

In every one of these states the Women's Trade Union League has first of all provided an opportunity for the organized women of different trades to come together and decide upon a common policy; next, to coöperate with other bodies, such as the State Federation of Labor, and the city centrals, the Consumers' League, the American Association for Labor Legislation, and the women's clubs, in support of such humane legislation. Much of the actual lobbying necessary has been done by the girls themselves, and they have exercised a power out of all proportion to their numbers or the tiny treasury at their disposal. No arguments of sociologists were half so convincing to legislators or so enlightening to the public as those of the girls who had themselves been through the mill. "Every hour I carry my trays I walk a mile," said Elizabeth Maloney of the Waitresses' Union. "Don't you think that eight hours a day is enough for any girl to walk?"

When we turn to the National League itself, if there is less to record of actual achievement, there are possibilities untold. Never before have all the working-women of this country had an organization, open to all, with which to express themselves on a national scale.

Early in 1905 the Executive Board of the League appointed a committee with Mary McDowell chairman to secure the coöperation of all organizations interested in the welfare of woman in demanding a federal investigation and report upon the conditions of working-women and girls in all the principal industrial centers. Miss McDowell called to her aid all the forces of organized labor, the General Federation of Women's Clubs and other women's associations, the social settlements and church workers. So strengthened and supported, the committee then went to Washington, and consulted with President Roosevelt and the then Commissioner of Labor, Dr. Charles P. Neill.

Miss McDowell, more than any other one person, was responsible for the passing in 1907 of the measure which authorized and the appropriation which made possible the investigation which during the next four years the Department of Commerce and Labor made. The result of that investigation is contained in the nineteen volumes of the report.

The first gatherings of any size at which League members met and conferred together were the interstate conferences, held simultaneously in Boston, New York and Chicago, the first in the summer of 1907 and the second in 1908. The former was the first interstate conference of women unionists ever held in the United States, and it was therefore a most notable event. Especially was it interesting because of the number of women delegates who came from other states, and from quite distant points, Boston drawing them from the New England states, New York from its own extensive industrial territory, and Chicago from the Middle West. Inspired by what she heard in Chicago, Hannah Hennessy went back to found the St. Louis Women's Trade Union League. It was at the first interstate conference, also, that a committee was appointed to wait upon the American Federation of Labor Executive Board, during the

Norfolk Convention in November, 1907. The Illinois State Committee of the Women's Trade Union League, whose fine legislative work helped to secure the passage of the present ten-hour law for women, also grew out of the discussion which came up in the Chicago conference.

The lines on which the League is developing can be observed through the work done and reported upon at the biennial conventions of which five have been held. The first, at Norfolk, Virginia, in 1907, was an informal gathering of but seven delegates, women who had been attending the convention of the American Federation of Labor of that year. Subsequent conventions have taken place every two years since then. These have been held in Chicago, Boston and St. Louis and New York respectively. On each occasion about seventy delegates have reported. They are certainly a picked lot of girls. They are trained, trained not in fancy debate, but in practical discussion. They have met with employers in trade conferences where an error in statement or a hasty word might mean a cut in wages or an increase in hours for two years to come. They have met with their fellow-workers in union meetings, where, if a girl aspires to lead her sisters or brothers, she has to show both readiness of wit and good-humored patience in differing from the others.

These women are growing too, as all must grow who live on life's firing line, and shrink not from meeting the very hardest problems of today. The working-woman, in her daily struggle comes up against every one of them, and not one can be evaded.

Industrial legislation, judicial decisions, the right to organize, the power to vote, are to the awakened working-woman not just academic questions, but something that affects her wages, her hours. They may mean enough to eat, time to rest, and beyond these home happiness and social freedom.

In two directions especially can the growing importance of the women's trade-union movement be observed: on the one hand in the incessant appeals, coming from all over the continent, to the National League, for advice and assistance in organizing women into the local unions of their trade; on the other in the degree in which it is gradually coming to be recognized by public men, by politicians, by business men, as well as by students and thinkers, that it is to organized women they must turn, whenever they want an authoritative expression as to the working-women's needs and desires.

Two sets of resolutions discussed and passed by the fourth biennial convention of the National Women's Trade Union League, held in 1913, were afterwards published broadcast over the country, and have been of marked educational value. The one pleaded for the speedy enfranchisement of women for these reasons: because the most costly production and the most valuable asset of any nation is its output of men and women; because the industrial conditions under which more than six million girls and women are forced to work is an individual and social menace; and because working-women as an unenfranchised class are continually used to lower the standards of men. The League in particular protested against the ill-judged activities of the anti-suffrage women, "a group of women of leisure, who by accident of birth have led sheltered and protected lives, and who never through experience have had to face the misery that low wages and long hours produce."

This stirring appeal made a profound impression on suffragists and anti-suffragists alike, in the labor world, and amid the general public. It was of course hotly resented by that small group of women of privilege, who think they know better than working-women what are the needs of working-women. Its deep significance lay in that it was a voice from the voiceless millions. It gave many pause to think and catch, as they had never caught before, the vital meaning underlying the demand for the vote.

The other series of resolutions expressed no less forcefully the women's consciousness of the intimate connection between education and labor, and pressed home the fact that organized laboring-women are watchful of the work being done in our public schools, and are anxious that it should be brought and kept up to the level of present-day needs. As is mentioned elsewhere, these resolutions laid special stress upon the necessity of making all courses of industrial training coeducational, of including in them the history of the evolution of industry, and the philosophy of collective bargaining, and of insuring that all boys and girls, before they leave school to go to work, have a knowledge of the state and federal laws that exist for their protection. These resolutions were sent to 1,075 boards of education in the United States. Replies have been received from twenty-six boards in fifteen states. Of these fourteen already have vocational training in their schools, two are planning such training, and six referred the resolutions to committees. Of those having training in the schools, thirteen have courses open to both boys and girls, and one has courses for girls exclusively, but is planning to open a school for boys.

The National League for four years published its own magazine, *Life and Labor*, with a double function; on the one hand as the organ of the League activities, and the expression of the members' views; on the other as a running diary of what was happening in the world of working-women, for the information of students and of all interested in sociological matters.

In the chapter on The Woman Organizer allusion is made to the efforts of the League to train women as trade-union organizers. Miss Louisa Mittelstadt, of Kansas City, and Miss Myrtle Whitehead, of Baltimore, belonging to different branches of the Brewery Workers, came to Chicago to be trained in office and field work, and are now making good use of their experience. One was sent by the central labor body, and the other by the local league. Miss Fannie Cohn was a third pupil, a member of the International Ladies' Garment Workers, from New York City.

A word in conclusion regarding some of the typical leaders who are largely responsible for the policy of the League, and are to be credited in no small measure with its successes.

After Mrs. Raymond Robins, the national president, already spoken of, and standing beside her as a national figure comes Agnes Nestor, of Irish descent, and a native of Grand Rapids, Michigan, upon whose slight shoulders rest alike burdens and honors. Both she bears calmly. She is a glove-worker, and the only woman president of an international union. She is both a member of the National Executive Board of the Women's Trade Union League, and the president of the Chicago League, and she has served as one of the two women members of the Federal Commission on Industrial Education. She has done fine work as a leader in her own city of Chicago, but neither Chicago, nor even Illinois, can claim her when the nation calls.

Melinda Scott is English by birth, belongs to New York, and has achieved remarkable results in her own union of the hat-trimmers. It is not during the exciting stage of a perhaps spectacular strike that Miss Scott shines; it is during the weary time when only patience and endurance can hold the girls together, and afterwards, when, whether the strike is lost or won, enthusiasm is apt to flag, and when disputes bid fair to break down the hardly won agreement.

Initiated at sixteen into the Knights of Labor, Leonora O'Reilly took the vows that she has ever since kept in the spirit and in the letter. After many years spent as a garment-worker, she became a teacher in the Manhattan Trade School for Girls. She was one of the charter members of the New York Women's Trade Union League and has always been one of its most effective speakers. Leonora and her Celtic idealism have made many converts.

Russia in America is embodied in Rose Schneidermann. She is the living representative of the gifts that the Slavic races, and especially the Russian Jew, have contributed to American life. Coming here in childhood, her life has been spent in New York.

As an example of her achievements, for four years she worked untiringly among the white-goods-workers of New York, until they were strong enough to call a general strike, a strike which was so successful that they won a great part of their demands, and ever since have held their union together, seven thousand strong. Penetrated with the profound sadness of her people, and passionately alive to the workers' wrongs, Rose Schneidermann can stir immense audiences, and move them to tears as readily as to indignation. For her all the hope of the world's future is embodied in two movements, trade unionism on the one hand and socialism on the other.

The New York League owes much of its success to Mary Dreier, the sister of Mrs. Raymond Robins. She was its president for several years, and by her persever-

IN A BASEMENT SWEATSHOP

Women picking rags collected from households.   These rags have neither been cleaned nor disinfected and give off dust at every handling

GIRL GAS BLOWERS.   KANSAS CITY

ance and devotion, did much to build up the organization in its early days.

The rest of the League leaders must be summed up even more briefly. Mary Anderson, a member of the Boot and Shoe Workers' International Board, is of Scandinavian origin, and has all the steadfastness of the Swedes. Another very excellent organizer and much-loved trade unionist is Emma Steghagen, also of the Boot and Shoe Workers, and for seven years secretary of the Chicago League. She may be called the League veteran, for her association with trade unionism began, with the Knights of Labor. Others are Mary McEnerney, Mary Haney, Hilda Svenson.

Elizabeth Maloney, she of the snapping eyes and fervent heart, marshals her waitresses through strike after strike against grinding employers, or she eloquently pleads their cause, whether in the state legislature, or with her own International, at the convention of the Hotel and Restaurant Employés, if the men show themselves a bit forgetful, as they sometimes do, of the girls' interest.

Nelle Quick, bindery woman, has been transferred from her trade-union activities in St. Louis to the Bureau of Labor Statistics of the state of Missouri.

From among clerical workers came into the League women who have left their mark, Helen Marot and Alice Bean, of New York, and Mabel Gillespie, of Boston, while Stella Franklin, the Australian, for long held the reins of the national office in Chicago.

Gertrude Barnum, who graduated into trade unionism from settlement work, and Josephine Casey, of the Elevated Railroad Clerks, are two who were long actively associated with the Woman's Trade Union League, but of late years both have been organizers under the International of the Ladies' Garment Workers.

Among the allies, the non-wage-earners, are Mary Dreier, president of the New York League, who was also the only woman member of the New York State Factory Investigating Commission; Mrs. Glendower Evans, notable for her service in advancing legislation for the minimum wage; Mary McDowell, of the University of Chicago Settlement, mother of the stockyards folk, beloved of the Poles and the Bohemians and the Ruthenians, who cross the ocean to settle on the desolate banks of Bubbly Creek. Mrs. D. W. Knefler, of St. Louis, did pioneering work for girlish trade unionism in that conservative city.

Miss Gillespie, the Secretary of the Boston Women's Trade Union League, has been for years its main standby. Working in coöperation with the young president, Miss Julia O'Connor, of the Telephone Operators, her influence in the labor movement is an important factor in the Massachusetts situation. She is a member of the State Minimum Wage Commission.

Young as is the League, some most heroic members have already passed into the unseen. Adelaide Samuels was a teacher in the public schools who, in the day of very small things for the New York League, acted as treasurer and chairman of the label committee. In her scant leisure she worked patiently towards the end that girls in the poorest trades should win for themselves the power of making the collective bargain. She died before she could have seen any tangible results from her efforts.

Hannah Hennessy, who carried away from the first interstate conference in Chicago a vision in her heart of a Women's Trade Union League in every large city, a few years later laid down her life as the result of the hardships endured while picketing on behalf of the Marx and Haas strikers. Her youth had slipped away, and her strength had been sapped by weary years as an ill-paid garment-worker, so that exposure to cold and wet found her power of resistance gone, and a few weeks later she was no more.

At the other end of the social scale, but thrilled with the same unselfish desire to better the conditions of the girl toilers, stood Carola Woerishofer, the rich college girl, who, once she was committed to the cause, never spared herself, picketing today, giving bonds tomorrow for the latest prisoner of the strike, spending a whole hot summer in a laundry, that she might know first-hand what the toiler pays that we may wear clean clothes. And so on, until the last sad scene of all, when on duty as inspector of the New York State Immigration Bureau, her car capsized, and Carola Woerishofer's brief, strenuous service to humanity was ended.

From yet another group came Frances Squire Potter, formerly professor of English Literature in the University of Minnesota, who a few years ago became profoundly impressed with the unfair and oppressive conditions under which working-women live and toil. Thus was she led far away from academic fields, first into suffrage work, and later into the National Women's Trade Union League. Until her health gave way, about a year before her death, she acted as official lecturer for the League. Through her unique gifts as a speaker, and her beautiful personality, she interpreted the cause of the working-woman to many thousands of hearers. She was also departmental editor of *Life and Labor*, the League's magazine.

Great have been the vicissitudes of the labor movement among men, but for many years now, the tendency towards national cohesion has been growing. This tendency has been greatly strengthened by the rapid development, and at the same time, the cheapening of the means of transport and communication between distant regions of the country.

In the advantages arising from this general growth of the labor movement, both in its local activities and on its national side, women workers have indeed shared. This is true, both on account of the direct benefits accruing to them through joining mixed organizations, or being aided by men to form separate organizations of their own, and also through the vast assistance rendered by organized labor in obtaining protective legislation for the most utterly helpless and exploited toilers, for example, the child-labor laws which state after state has placed upon the statute book, sanitary regulations, and laws for the safeguarding of machinery dangerous to workers.

Still, compared with the extensive movement among men, in which the women have been more or less a side issue, feminine trade unionism has been but fitful in its manifestations, and far indeed from keeping pace with the rate at which women have poured into the industrial field. The youth of a large number of the girl workers, and the fact that, as they grow up, so many of them pass out of the wage-earning occupations, marriage, and the expectation of marriage, the main obstacles that stand in the way today in getting women to organize and to hold their unions together, furnish also the underlying causes of the want of continuity of the trade-union movement among women since it first began in the United States in the early part of the last century. The too frequent change in the personnel of the members, and therefore in the composition of the union itself, means an absence of the permanence of spirit which is an essential condition for the handing on in unbroken succession of standards of loyalty and esprit de corps.

It is continuity that has rendered possible all human progress, through the passing on from all of us to our successors, of each small acquirement, of each elevation of standard. Where, but for such continuity would be the college spirit, that descends upon and baptizes the newcomer as he enters the college gates? Where, but for continuity would be the constantly rising standards of morality and social responsibility? Where, but for continuity would be national life and all that makes patriotism worthy? Where, indeed, would be humanity itself?

The average man is a wage-earner, and as such a fit subject for organization. If extensive groups of men remain unorganized, the responsibility lies partly on the trade unions, and is partly conditioned by our social and political environment. But either way, a man is a trade unionist or he is not. The line is clear cut, and trade unions therefore admit no one not actually a worker in their own trade.

But it is not so with women. Outside the wage-earning groups there is the great bulk of married women, and a still considerable, though ever-lessening number of single women, who, although productive laborers, are yet, owing to the primitive and antiquated status of home industry, not acknowledged as such in the labor market. Not being remunerated in money, they are not considered as wage-earners. (Witness the census report, which, in omitting those performing unpaid domestic duties from the statistics of gainful occupations, does but reflect the tragic fact that woman's home work has no money value and confirms the popular impression that "mother doesn't work.")

Yet another force to be reckoned with in estimating the difficulties which stand in the way of unionizing women is the widespread hostility to trade unionism, as expressed through newspaper and magazine articles, and through public speakers, both religious and secular. The average girl, even more than the average man, is sensitive to public opinion, as expressed through such accepted channels of authority. The standards of public opinion have been her safeguard in the past, and she still looks to them for guidance, not realizing how often such commonly accepted views are misinterpretations of the problems she herself has to face today. In the middle of the last century, a period that was most critical for men's unions in England, a number of leaders of public thought, men of influence and standing in the community, such as Charles Kingsley, Frederick Denison Maurice and others, came to the help of the men by maintaining their right to organize. In the United States, during the corresponding stage of extreme unpopularity, Horace Greeley, Charles A. Dana and Wendell Phillips extended similar support to workingmen. We today are apt to forget that women's unions with us are just now in the very same immature stage of development, as men's unions passed through half a century ago. The labor men of that day had their position immensely strengthened by just such help afforded from outside their immediate circle. It is therefore not strange that women's unions, at their present stage of growth, should be in need of just such help.

To sum up, in addition to all the difficulties which have to be met by men in the labor movement, women are at a disadvantage through the comparative youth and inexperience of many female workers, through their want of trade training, through the assumption, almost universal among young girls, that they will one day marry and leave the trade, and through their unconscious response to the public opinion which disapproves of women joining trade unions.

It is then the lack of permanence, of continuity in spirit and in concerted action, produced by all these causes, working together, and the difficulties in the way of remedying this lack of permanence, which this young organization, the National Women's Trade Union League of America, has fully and fairly recognized, and which, with a courage matched to its high purpose, it is facing and trying to conquer.

The Women's Trade Union League, while essentially a part of the labor movement, has yet its own definite rôle to play, and at this point it is well to note the response made by organized labor in supporting the League's efforts. It works under the endorsement of both the American Federation of Labor and the Trades and Labor Congress of Canada, and has received in its undertakings the practical support, besides, of many of the most influential of the international unions, in occupations as different as those of the shoe-workers, the carpenters and the miners. The rank and file of the local organizations, in city after city, have given the same hearty and unqualified approval to the League's pioneering work, in bringing the unorganized women and girls into the unions, and in carrying on a constant educative work among those already organized. As an instance of this openly expressed approval, take the cordial coöperation which the Chicago League has ever received from the Chicago Federation of Labor and its allied locals. But, owing to the complexity of women's lives, the varied and inconsistent demands that are made upon their energies, the organization of the League has to be somewhat different from that of any body which labor men would have formed for themselves.

Locally the relationship varies. In St. Louis the League has never been represented in the central body by its own delegates, but by members representing primarily their own organizations, such as Bindery Women and Boot and Shoe Workers. In Boston, New York and

Chicago each League is represented by its own delegates. In Kansas City, Missouri, again, not only are the delegates of the League seated in the central body, but every union of men in it pays a per capita tax into the funds of the Kansas City Women's Trade Union League.

The National League receives a certain amount of financial support from the American Federation of Labor, and from a number of the international unions, several of the latter being affiliated with the League. State federations, city central bodies, and local unions in different parts of the country give similar coöperation and money support.

As the labor movement is organized, it collects into suitable groups the different classes of wage-earners. But the average housekeeping, married woman, although both worker and producer, is not a wage-earner, although more and more, as the home industries become specialized is she becoming a wage-earner for at least part of her time. But, as our lives are arranged at present the largest proportion of married women and a considerable number of single women are ineligible for admission as members of any trade union. Are they therefore to be shut out from the labor movement, and from participation in its activities, no matter how closely their own interests are bound up with it, no matter how intensely they are in sympathy with its aims, no matter though as single girls they may have been members of a union?

We have noted already how much stronger the labor movement would be if the women and girls engaged in the trades were brought in through organization. Still further would organized men be advantaged if their movement were reinforced by this great body of home-keeping women, vast in numbers, and with their untouched reserves of energy and experience.

Again, it is only by making room for such women within the labor movement that women can be represented in sufficient numbers in the councils of labor. As long as there was no recognized way of admitting the home woman to even a tiny corner of the labor field, as long as entry was restricted solely to the wage-earning woman, there seemed no chance of women being ever in anything but a hopeless minority in either local or international union, and that minority, too, composed so largely of young and inexperienced girls. Is it any wonder, then, that the interests of the working-girls have suffered, and that, as a ready consequence, workingmen's interests have suffered, too.

The Women's Trade Union League is also bringing into touch with the labor movement other women's organizations, and especially winning their increased coöperation in the campaigns for legislation. It is largely through the ally [1] membership that the Women's Trade Union League has been able to reach the public ear as well as to attract assistance and coöperation, especially from the suffragists and the women's clubs. The suffragists have always been more or less in sympathy with labor organizations, while outside labor circles, the largest body to second the efforts of organized labor in the direction of humanity has been the women's clubs, whether expressing themselves through the General Federation, or through local activity in their home towns. An immense group of women thus early became com-

---

[1] An ally is a man or a woman of any class not a worker in any organized trade who believes in the organization of women and subscribes to the following League platform.
1. Organization of all workers into trade unions.
2. Equal pay for equal work.
3. Eight-hour day.
4. A living wage.
5. Full citizenship for women.

mitted to an active opposition to the employment of children either in factories, or under the even more dangerous and demoralizing conditions which await mere babies in the street or in tenement homes.

There is a similar movement going on within the National Young Women's Christian Association. The reason for this stand being taken by women's organizations was characteristic. The impelling force that urged those women on was something far deeper than mere philanthropy. It was the acceptance by a whole group of women of the old responsibilities of motherhood, in the new form that these must take on if new conditions are to be met. It was as if the motherhood of the country had said in so many words: "Social conditions are changing, but we are still the mothers of the new generation. Society is threatened with this calamity, that they will pass beyond our care before the needs and claims of childhood have been satisfied. As individuals we are now powerless. Let us see what coöperation will do to right conditions that are fast slipping beyond our control."

But how unconscious the vast number of women of this type were, either of the true nature of the force they were obeying or the point whither they were tending, was graphically illustrated at the Biennial Federation of Women's Clubs in St. Paul, in 1906, when a woman protested from the floor against the appointment of a committee to deal with industrial conditions. She added that she was all in favor of the Federation working against child labor, but they had no call to interfere in industrial questions.

This is an illustration of how the rank and file of the clubwomen became committed to industrial reform as part of their program, and incidentally, although there were those among their leaders who well knew whither the movement was tending. The Women's Trade Union League represents one of the forces that is leading on the most conservative among them to stand forth for industrial justice consciously and deliberately, while the League's special aims are brought the nearer to accomplishment by the support of this other group of women.

The Women's Trade Union League is, and as long as it fulfills its present function, will surely remain, a federation of trade unions with women members, but it finds a niche and provides an honorable and useful function for the wives of workingmen, for ex-trade-union women, and for others who endorse trade unionism and gladly give their support to a constructive work, aiming at strengthening the weakest wing of labor, the unorganized, down-driven, underpaid working-girls.

If the League is to be an organization open to, and aiming at including eventually the great majority of working-women, it must be so flexible as to admit the woman who works in the home without formal wages, as well as the woman who works for an employer for wages. Both are in many respects upon the same footing in relation to society. Both are earners and producers. Both require the help of organization. Both should be an integral part of the labor movement. Both therefore may be consistently received as dues-paying members into Women's Trade Union Leagues, even although we are still too confused and puzzled to permit of housewives forming their own unions, and therefore such members have to be received as allies.

In thus leaving open a door, however, through which all working-women may enter the League, the founders were mindful of the fact, and have it embodied in the constitution, that the main strength must lie in the increasing number of wage-earning girls and women who are socially developed up to the point of being themselves organized into trade unions. The League has so far grown, and can in the future grow normally, only so far as it is the highest organized expression of the ideals, the wishes and the needs of the wage-earning girl.

As for the woman of wealth, I should be the last to question her right to opportunities for self-development, or to deny her the joy of assisting her sorely driven sisters to rise out of the industrial mire, and stand erect in self-reliant independence. But if the League is to grow until it becomes the universal expression of the woman's part in organized labor, then the privilege of assisting with financial help the ordinary activities of the League can be hers only during the infancy of the body. No organization can draw its nurture permanently from sources outside of itself, although many a movement has been nursed through its early stages of uncertainty and struggle by the aid of the sympathetic and understanding outsider.

V

THE HUGE STRIKES

In September, 1909, the name of the Triangle Shirt Waist Company, which has since become a word of such ill omen, was known to few outside the trade. The factory had not then been wrapped in the flames and smoke of the Asch fire, that was to cut short the lives of one hundred and forty-three workers, and to blight the existence and mar the happiness of many more.

But by a not altogether inexplicable coincidence, it had been among the employés of this very firm that the smoldering flames of human discontent broke out, that were to grow into the "Strike of the Forty Thousand," a strike that proved to be but the first of a long series of revolts among the foreign garment-workers of the largest cities in the East and the Middle West.

It is true that in such an extensive trade as that of making ready-made clothes, with its low wages and its speeding-up, its sweating and its uncertainty of employment, there is always a strike on somewhere. At that very time, there were in progress two strikes of quite respectable size: one in Boston, under the Ladies' Tailors' and Dressmakers' Union, and the other in St. Louis, where the long-drawn-out Marx and Haas strike involving the makers of men's ready-made clothing, was in its first stage.

But outside of labor circles, these strikes were attracting no particular attention. The public were not even aware of what was happening, and would have been entirely indifferent if they had known.

The turning out of ladies' ready-made waists is an immense business in New York. The trade, like other branches of garment-making, is largely in the hands of Jewish employers. The workers are principally recently arrived foreigners, Russian and other Slavic Jews, Italians and other immigrants from eastern Europe. They are in an overwhelming majority women, or, to be more accurate, girls.

During all the earlier part of the year 1909 the Ladies' Waist Makers' Union No. 25 had been showing quite undue activity and unwelcome persistence in preaching unionism and its advantages among all and sundry of these foreign girls, and with quite unusual success. The managers of the Triangle Shirt Waist Company awoke one morning to a sense of what was happening. To quote from a writer in *The Outlook:*

One of the firm appeared before the girls and told them in kind phrases that the company was friendly to the union, and that they desired to encourage it, and that they might better give assistance, they would like to know what girls belonged to it. The girls, taken in by this speech, acknowledged their membership; only, instead of a few that the company had thought to discover and weed out, it developed that one hundred and fifty girls were members. That evening they were told, in the same kind way, that, because of a lull in the trade, due to an uncertainty as to fashions in sleeves, there was for the time being no more work. The girls took their discharge without suspicion; but the next morning they saw in the newspaper advertisements of the company asking for shirt-waist operators at once. Their eyes opened by this, the girls picketed the shop, and told the girls who answered the advertisement that the shop was on strike. The company retaliated by hiring thugs to intimidate the girls, and for several weeks the picketing girls

were being constantly attacked and beaten. These mêlées
were followed by wholesale arrests of strikers, from a dozen
to twenty girls being arrested daily.

Out of ninety-eight arrested all but nineteen were
fined in sums of from one to ten dollars.

With the aid of the police and a complaisant bench
the Triangle Company had been successful in its attempt
to empty the young union's treasury, and had likewise
intimidated the workers till their courage and spirit were
failing them. The manufacturers had accomplished their
object.

At this stage the New York Women's Trade Union
League took up the battle of the girls. Every morning
they stationed allies in front of the factory, to act as witnesses against illegal arrest, and to prevent interference
with lawful picketing. The wrath of the police was then
turned upon the League. First one and then another
ally was arrested, this performance culminating in the
unlawful arrest of Mary Dreier, president of the League.
The police were sadly fooled upon this occasion, and their
position was not in any degree strengthened, when they
angrily, and just as unreasonably freed their prisoner,
as soon as they discovered her identity. "Why didn't
you tell me you was a rich lady? I'd never have arrested you in the world."

This was good copy for the newspapers, and the whole
story of wrongful discharge, unlawful arrest and insult-
ing treatment of the strikers by the police began to filter
into the public mind through the columns of the daily
press. It was shown that what had happened in the case
of the Triangle employés had been repeated, with varia-
tions, in the case of many other shops. Respectable and
conservative citizens began to wonder if there might not
be two sides to the story. They learned, for instance,

of the unjust "bundle" system, under which the employer
gives out a bundle of work to a girl, and when she returns the completed work, gives her a ticket which she
can convert into cash on pay day. If the ticket, a tiny
scrap of paper, should be lost, the girl had no claim on
the firm for the work she had actually done. Again,
some employers had insisted that they paid good wages,
showing books revealing the astonishing fact that girls
were receiving thirty dollars, thirty-five dollars, and even
forty dollars per week. Small reason to strike here, said
the credulous reader, as he or she perused the morning
paper. But the protest of the libelled manufacturer lost
much of its force, when it was explained that these
large sums were not the wage of one individual girl, but
were group earnings, paid to one girl, and receipted for
by her, but having to be shared with two, three or four
others, who had worked with and under the girl whose
name appeared on the payroll.

Monday, November 22, was a memorable day. A mass
meeting had been called in Cooper Union to consider
the situation. Mr. Gompers was one of the speakers. At
the far end of the hall rose a little Jewish girl, and
asked to be heard. Once on the platform, she began
speaking in Yiddish, fast and earnestly. She concluded
by saying she was tired of talking, and so would put the
motion for a general strike of the whole trade. One who
was present, describing the tense dramatic moment that
followed, writes: "The audience unanimously endorsed
it. 'Do you mean faith?' said the chairman. 'Will you
take the old Jewish oath,' And up came 2,000 Jewish
hands with the prayer, 'If I turn traitor to the cause I
now pledge, may this hand wither and drop off at the
wrist from this arm I now raise.'" The girl was Clara
Lemlich, from the Leiserson factory. She did not com-
plain for herself, for she was a fairly well-paid worker,

making up to fifteen dollars in the rush season, but for her much poorer sisters.

The response within that hall typified the response next day outside. I quote the words of an onlooker:

From every waist-making factory in New York and Brooklyn, the girls poured forth, filling the narrow streets of the East Side, crowding the headquarters at Clinton Hall, and overflowing into twenty-four smaller halls in the vicinity. It was like a mighty army, rising in the night, and demanding to be heard. But it was an undisciplined army. Without previous knowledge of organization, without means of expression, these young workers, mostly under twenty, poured into the Union. For the first two weeks from 1,000 to 1,500 joined each day. The clerical work alone, involved in registering and placing recruits was almost overwhelming. Then halls had to be rented and managed, and speakers to be procured. And not for one nationality alone. Each hall, and there were twenty-four, had to have speakers in Yiddish, Italian and English. Every member of the League was pressed into service. Still small halls were not enough. Lipzin's Theatre was offered to the strikers, and mass meetings were held there five afternoons a week.

Meanwhile committees were appointed from each shop to settle upon a price list. As the quality of work differed in different shops, a uniform wage was impossible and had to be settled by each shop individually. When the hundreds of price lists were at last complete, meetings were arranged for each shop committee and their employers. Again the price list was discussed, and a compromise usually effected. In almost every shop, however, an increase of from 15 to 20 per cent. was granted.

Apart from wages, the contract insured significant improvements. Besides calling for recognition of the union it demanded full pay for legal holidays, limited night work during the rush season to eight P. M., abolished all Sunday work, did away with the inside contracting system, under which one girl took out work for several, and provided for a fair allotment of work in slack seasons.

After one hundred and ninety firms had signed up, and the majority of the strikers had returned to their shops, an attempt was made to settle with the still obdurate employers through arbitration, at the suggestion of the National Civic Federation.

Meanwhile picketing was going on; the pickets were being punished, not only with heavy fines, thus depleting the union's treasury, but with terms in the workhouse. Some of these criminals for principle were little girls in short skirts, and no attempt was made to separate them when in confinement from disorderly characters. But what was the result? The leaders saw to it that a photograph was taken of such a group, with "Workhouse Prisoners" pinned across the breast of each, and worn as a badge of honor, a diploma of achievement, and the newspapers were but too glad to print the picture. When that spirit of irrepressible energy and revolt once possesses men or women, punishment is converted into reward, disgrace transmuted into honor.

This it was, more even than the story of the wrongs endured, which had its effect on the public. In the rebound of feeling the illegality of the police behavior was admitted. The difficulties put in the way of the courageous little pickets led to the forming of parades, and the holding of meetings even in a class of society where no one had counted on receiving sympathy. The ladies of the rich and exclusive Colony Club learned from the girls themselves of the many disadvantages connected with waist-making. For instance that in the off season there was little regular work at all; and that all the time there were the fines and breakages. One girl told how she had been docked for a tucking foot, which, as she said, just wore out on her. "It wasn't really my fault," she concluded, "and I think the boss should look out for his own foots."

Said another: "When a girl comes five minutes late at my shop, she is compelled to go home. She may live outside of the city, it does not matter, she must go home and lose a day.

"We work eight days in the week. This may seem strange to you who know that there are only seven days in the week. But we work from seven in the morning till very late at night, when there's a rush, and sometimes we work a week and a half in one week."

The socialist women did yeoman service, protecting the pickets, attending the trials, speaking at meetings and taking a full share of the hard work. The organized suffragists and clubwomen were drawn into the thick of the fight. They spread the girls' story far and wide, raised money, helped to find bonds, and were rewarded by increased inspiration for their own propaganda.

The enormous extent of the strike, being, as it was, by far the largest uprising of women that has ever taken place upon this continent, while adding proportionately to the difficulties of conducting it to a successful issue, yet in the end deepened and intensified the lesson it conveyed.

In the end about three hundred shops signed up, but of these at least a hundred were lost during the first year. This was due, the workers say, partly to the terrible dullness in the trade following the strike, and partly to the fact that they were not entirely closed shops.

Since then, however, the organization has grown in strength. It was one of these coming under the protocol, covering the Ladies' Garment Workers, in so many branches, which was agreed to after the strikes in the needle trades of the winter of 1913. The name was changed from Ladies' Waist Makers, to Ladies' Waist and Dress Makers.

But the waist-makers' strike was not confined to New York. With the opening of their busy season, the New York manufacturers found themselves hard pressed to fill their orders, and they were making efforts to have the work done in other cities, not strike-bound. One of the cities in which they placed their orders was Philadelphia. It was with small success, however, for the spirit of unrest was spreading, and before many weeks were over, most of the Philadelphia waist-makers had followed the example of their New York sisters.

The girls were in many respects worse off in Philadelphia than in New York itself. Unions in the sewing trades were largely down and out there, and public opinion was opposed to organized labor.

When the disturbance did come, it was not so much the result of any clever policy deliberately thought out, as it was the sudden uprising and revolt of exasperated girls against a system of persistent cutting down extending over about four years. A cent would be taken off here, and a half-cent there, or two operations would be run into one, and the combined piece of work under one, and that a new, name would bring a lower rate of pay. The practice of paying for oil needles, cotton and silk had been introduced, a practice most irritating with its paltry deduction from a girl's weekly wage. Next there was a system of fines for what was called "mussing" work. Every one of these so-called improvements in discipline was deftly utilized as an excuse for taking so much off the girls' pay.

Patience became exhausted and the girls just walked out. Two-thirds of the waist-makers in the city walked out. Of these about eighty-five per cent., it is believed,

were Jewish girls, the rest made up of Italians with a
few Poles. The girls who did not go out were mostly
Americans. One observer estimated at the time that
about forty per cent. of those in the trade were under
twenty years of age, running down to children of twelve.

When the workers, with no sort of warning or explanation, or making any regular preliminary demands,
just quit, it upset matters considerably. A little girl
waist-maker may appear to be a very insignificant member of the community, but if you multiply her by four
thousand, her absence makes an appreciable gap in the
industrial machine, and its cogs fail to catch as accurately
as heretofore. So that even the decent manufacturers
felt pretty badly, not so much about the strike itself, as
its, to them, inexplicable suddenness. Such men were
suffering, of course, largely for the deeds of their more
unscrupulous fellow-employers.

One manufacturer, for instance, had gained quite a
reputation for his donations to certain orphanages. These
were to him a profitable investment, seeing that the institutions served to provide him with a supply of cheap
labor. He had in his shop many orphans, who for two
reasons could hardly leave his employ. They had no
friends to whom to go, and they were also supposed to be
under obligations of gratitude to their benefactor-em-
ployer. One of his girl employés, to whom he paid seven
dollars a week, turned out for that wage twelve dollars'
worth of work. This fact the employer admitted, justifying himself by saying that he was supporting her
brother in an orphanage.

It was a hard winter, and the first week of the strike
wore away without a sign of hope. Public opinion was
slow to rouse, and the newspapers were definitely adverse. The general view seemed to be that such a strike
was an intolerable nuisance, if not something worse. At

length the conservative *Ledger* came out with a two-column editorial, outlining the situation, and from then on news of the various happenings, as they occurred, could be found in all the papers. But the girls were unorganized. There was no money, and they faced the first days of the new year in a mood of utter discouragement. Organizers from the International of the Ladies' Garment Workers had, however, come on from New York to take charge. The strikers were supported by the Central Labor Union of Philadelphia, under the leadership of the capable John J. Murphy, and representatives of the National Women's Trade Union League, in the persons of Mrs. Raymond Robins and Miss Agnes Nestor, were already on the scene.

In the struggle itself, the New York experiences were repeated. The fight went on slowly and stubbornly. Arrests occurred daily and still more arrests. Money was the pressing need, not only for food and rent, but to pay fines and to arrange for the constantly needed bonds to bail out arrested pickets. At length a group of prominent Philadelphia women headed by Mrs. George Biddle, enlisted the help of some leading lawyers, and an advisory council was formed for the protection of legal rights, and even for directing a backfire on lawbreaking employers by filing suits for damages. With such interest and such help money, too, was obtained. The residents of the College Settlement, especially Miss Anna Davies, the head resident, and Miss Anne Young, the members of the Consumers' League, the suffragists and the clubwomen all gave their help.

These women were moved to action by stories such as those of the little girl, whom her late employer had been begging to return to his deserted factory. "The boss, he say to me, 'You can't live if you not work.' And I say to the boss, 'I live not much on forty-nine cents a day.'

As in New York, the police here overreached themselves in their zeal, and arrested a well-known society girl, whom they caught walking arm-in-arm with a striking waist-maker. Result, the utter discomfiture of the Director of Public Safety, and triumph for the fortunate reporters who got the good story.

An investigation into the price of food, made just then by one of the evening newspapers came in quite opportunely, forcing the public to wonder whether, after all, the girls were asking for any really higher wage, or whether they were not merely struggling to hold on to such a wage as would keep pace with the increasing prices of all sorts of food, fuel, lighting, the commonest clothing and the humblest shelter.

The strike had gone on for some weeks, when an effort was made to obtain an injunction forbidding the picketing of the Haber factory. This was finally to crush the strike and down the strikers. But in pressing for an injunction the manufacturers came up against a difficulty of their own making. The plea that had all along been urged upon the union had been the futility of trying to continue a strike that was not injuring the employers. "For," they had many times said, "we have plenty of workers, our factories are going full blast." Whereas the Haber witnesses in the injunction suit were bringing proof of how seriously the business was being injured through the success of the girl pickets in maintaining the strike, and, the money loss, they assured the court was to be reckoned up in thousands of dollars. This inconsistency impressed the judge, and the strikers had the chance of telling their story in open court. "Strikers' Day" was a public hearing of the whole story of the strike.

That night both sides got together, and began to discuss a working agreement. After twenty-five hours of conference between representatives of the Shirt Waist Makers' Union and of the Manufacturers' Association, an agreement was arrived at, giving the workers substantial gains; employment of all union workers in the shops without discrimination; a fifty-two-and-a-half-hour week and no work on Saturday afternoon; no charges for water, oil, needles or ordinary wear and tear on machinery; wages to be decided with the union for each particular shop, and all future grievances to be settled by a permanent Board of Arbitration; the agreement to run till May 1, 1911.

The workers' success was, unfortunately, not lasting. Owing to the want of efficient local leadership, the organization soon dropped to pieces. That gone, there was nothing left to stand between the toilers and the old relentless pressure of the competitive struggle, ever driving the employers to ask more, and ever compelling the wage-earners to yield more. The Philadelphia shirtwaist strike of 1910 furnishes a sad and convincing proof of how little is gained by the mere winning of a strike, however bravely fought, unless the strikers are able to keep a live organization together, the members coöperating patiently and steadily, so as to handle the fresh shop difficulties which every week brings, in the spirit of mutual help as well as self-help.

These first Eastern strikes in the garment trades, although local in their incidence, were national in their effects. There had been so much that was dramatic and unusual in the rebellion of the workers, and it had been so effectively played up in the press of the entire country that by the time spring arrived and the strikes were really ended, and ended in both cities with very tangible benefits for the workers, there was hardly anyone who had not heard something about the great strikes, and who had not had their most deeply rooted opinions modified.

It was an educational lesson on the grand scale. But the effects did not stop here. The impression upon the workers themselves everywhere was wholly unexpected. They had been encouraged and heartened to combine and thus help one another to obtain some measure of control over workshop and wages.

The echoes of the shirt-waist strikes had hardly died away, when there arose from another group of dissatisfied workers, the self-same cry for industrial justice.

There is no doubt that the Chicago strike which began among the makers of ready-made men's clothing in September, 1910, was the direct outcome of the strikes in New York and Philadelphia. While the Western uprising had many features in common with these, yet it presented difficulties all its own, and in its outcome won a unique success. Not only was the number of workers taking part greater than in the previous struggles, but, owing to the fact of a large number of the strikers being men, and a big proportion of these heads of families, the poverty and intense suffering resulting from months of unemployment extended over a far larger area. Also the variety of nationalities among the strikers added to the difficulties of conducting negotiations. Every bit of literature put out had to be printed in nine languages. And lastly, the want of harmony between certain of the national leaders of the union involved, and the deep distrust felt by some of the local workers and the strikers for a section of them, provided a situation which for complexity it would be hard to match. That the long-continued struggle ended with so large a measure of success for the workers was in part owing to the extraordinary skill and unwearied patience displayed in its handling, and in part to the close and intimate coöperation between the local strike leaders, both men and women, the Chicago Federation of Labor and the Chicago Women's Trade Union League. Much also had been learned from recent experience in the strikes immediately preceding.

The immediate cause of the first striker going out was a cut in the price of making pockets, of a quarter of a cent. That was on September 22 in Shop 21, in the Hart, Schaffner and Marx factories. Three weeks later the strike had assumed such proportions that the officers of the United Garment Workers' District Council No. 6 were asking the Women's Trade Union League for speakers. The League organized its own Strike Committee to collect money, assist the pickets and secure publicity. At the instance of the League also an independent Citizens' Committee was formed.

In time of sorest need was found efficient leadership. The garment-workers of Chicago, in their earlier struggles with the manufacturers, had had no such powerful combination to assist them as came to their aid now, when a Joint Strike Conference controlled the situation, with representatives upon it from the United Garment Workers of America International Executive Board, from the Chicago District Council of the same organization, from the Special Order Garment Workers, the Ready Made Garment Workers, the Chicago Federation of Labor and the Women's Trade Union League. The American Federation of Labor sent their organizer, Emmett Flood, the untiringly courageous and the ever hopeful.

The first step to be taken was to place before the public in clear and simple form the heterogeneous mass of grievances complained of. The Women's Trade Union League invited about a dozen of the girls to tell their story over a simple little breakfast. Within a week the story told to a handful was printed and distributed broadcast, prefaced, as it was, by an admirable introduction by the late Miss Katharine Coman, of Wellesley College, who happened to be in Chicago, and who was acting as chairman of the grievance committee. The Citizens' Committee, headed by Professor George Mead, followed with a statement, admitting the grievances and justifying the strike.

From then on the story lived on the front page of all the newspapers, and speakers to address unions, meetings of strikers, women's clubs and churches were in constant demand. Here again, the suffragist and the socialist women showed where their sympathies lay and of what mettle they were made. Visiting speakers, such as Miss Margaret Bondfield and Mrs. Philip Snowden, took their turn also. The socialist women of Chicago issued a special strike edition of the *Daily Socialist*. With the help of the striking girls as "newsies" they gathered in the city on one Saturday the handsome sum of $3,345. Another group of very poor Poles sent in regularly about two hundred dollars per week, sometimes the bulk of it in nickels and dimes. A sewing gathering composed of old ladies in one of the suburbs sewed industriously for weeks on quilts and coverings for the strikers. Some small children in a Wisconsin village were to have had a goose for their Christmas dinner, but hearing of little children who might have no dinner, sent the price of the bird, one dollar and sixty-five cents, into the strikers' treasury.

At first strike pay was handed out every Friday from out of the funds of the United Garment Workers. But on Friday, November 11, the number of applicants for strike pay was far beyond what it was possible to handle in the cramped office quarters. Through some misunderstanding, which has to this day never been explained, the crowd, many thousands of men, women and children, were denied admittance to the large wheat pit of the

Open Board of Trade, which, it was understood, had been reserved for their use. It was a heart-rending sight, as from early morning till late afternoon they waited in the halls and corridors and outside in the streets. At first in dumb patience and afterwards in bewilderment, but all along with unexampled gentleness and quietness.

At this point, Mr. John Fitzpatrick, president of the Chicago Federation of Labor, took hold of a situation already difficult, and which might soon have become dangerous. He explained to the crowd that everyone would be attended to in their various district halls, and that all vouchers already out would be redeemed. This relieved the tension, but the Joint Strike Committee were driven to take over at once the question of relief, so that none should be reduced to accept that hunger bargain, which, as Mrs. Robins put it, meant the surrender of civilization.

With such an immense number of strike-bound families to support, the utmost economy of resources was necessary, and it was resolved hereafter to give out as little cash as possible, but to follow the example of the United Mine Workers and others and open commissary stations. This plan was carried out, and more than any other one plan, saved the day. Benefits were handed over, in the form of groceries on a fixed ration scale. As far as we know, such a plan had never before been adapted to the needs of women and children, nor carried out by organized labor for the benefit of a large unorganized group. Of the economy of the system there is no question, seeing that a well-organized committee can always purchase supplies in quantities at wholesale price, sometimes at cost price, and frequently can, as was done in this instance, draw upon the good feeling of merchants and dealers, and receive large contributions of bread, flour, coal and other commodities. Commissary stations were established in different localities. Here is a sample ration as furnished at one of the stores, although, thanks to the kindness of friends, the allowance actually supplied was of a much more varied character:

Bread	18 loaves	Coffee	1 lb.
Sugar	5 lbs.	Beans	5 lbs.
Oatmeal	2 pkgs. (large)	Ham	10 lbs.

For Italians, oatmeal was replaced by spaghetti, and Kosher food for those of the orthodox Jewish faith was arranged for through orders upon local grocery stores and kosher butchers in the Jewish quarter. The tickets entitling to supplies were issued through the shop chairman at the local halls to those strikers known to be in greatest need.

The commissary plan, however, still left untouched such matters as rent, fuel, gas, and likewise the necessities of the single young men and girls. Also the little babies and the nursing mothers, who needed fresh milk, had to be thought of and provided for. There were certain strictly brought up, self-respecting little foreign girls who explained with tears that they could not take an order on a restaurant where there were strange people about, because "it would not be decent," a terrible criticism on so many of our public eating places. So a small separate fund was collected which gave two dollars a week per head, to tide over the time of trouble for some of these sorely pressed ones. There was a committee on milk for babies, and another on rent, and the League handled the question of coal.

With these necessities provided for, the strikers settled down to a test of slow endurance. Picketing went on as before, and although arrests were numerous, and fines followed in the train of arrests, the police and the court situation was at no time so acute as it had been in either New York or Philadelphia.

The heroism shown by many of the strikers and their families it would be hard to overestimate. Small inconveniences were made light of. Families on strike themselves, or the friends of strikers would crush into yet tighter quarters so that a couple of boys or two or three girls out of work might crowd into the vacated room, and so have a shelter over their heads "till the strike was over." A League member found her way one bitter afternoon in December to one home where lay an Italian woman in bed with a new-born baby and three other children, aged three, four and five years respectively, surrounding her. There was neither food nor fuel in the house. On the bed were three letters from the husband's employer, offering to raise his old pay from fifteen to thirty dollars per week, if he would go back to work and so help to break the strike. The wife spoke with pride of the husband's refusal to be a traitor. "It is not only bread we give the children. We live not by bread alone. We live by freedom, and I will fight for it though I die to give it to my children." And this woman's baby was one of 1,250 babies born into strikers' homes that winter.

To me those long months were like nothing so much as like living in a besieged city. There was the same planning for the obtaining of food, and making it last as long as possible, the same pinched, wan faces, the same hunger illnesses, the same laying of little ones into baby graves. And again, besides the home problems, there was the same difficulty of getting at the real news, knowing the meaning of what was going on, the same heart-wearing alternations of hope and dread.

Through it all, moreover, persisted the sense that this was something more than an industrial rising, although it was mainly so. It was likewise the uprising of a foreign people, oppressed and despised. It was the tragedy of the immigrant, his high hopes of liberty and prosperity in the new land blighted, finding himself in America, but not of America.

By the end of November the manufacturers were beginning to tire of watching their idle machinery, and the tale of unfilled orders grew monotonous. There began to be grumbles from the public against the disastrous effects upon business of the long-continued struggle. Alderman Merriam succeeded in having the City Council bring about a conference of the parties to the strike "to the end that a just and lasting settlement of the points in controversy may be made."

Messrs Hart, Schaffner and Marx, a firm employing in forty-eight shops between eight and nine thousand workers, agreed to meet with the committee and the labor leaders. After long hours of conferring a tentative agreement was at length arrived at, signed by the representatives of all parties, approved by the Chicago Federation of Labor, and, when referred to the army of strikers for their confirmation, was by them *rejected*. Indeed the great majority refused even to vote upon it at all. This was indeed a body blow to the hopes of peace. For the unfavorable attitude of the strikers there were, however, several reasons. The agreement, such as it was, did not affect quite a fourth of the whole number of workers who were out, and a regular stampede back to work of the rest with no guarantee at all, was greatly to be dreaded. Again, a clause discriminating against all who it should be decided had been guilty of violence during the strike, gave deep offense. It was felt to be adding insult to injury, to allude to violence during a struggle conducted so quietly and with such dignity and self-restraint. But a further explanation lay in the attitude of mind of the strikers themselves. The idea of compromise was new to them, and the acceptance of any compromise was a way out of the difficulty, that was not for one moment to be considered. Thus it came about that a settlement that many an old experienced organization would have accepted was ruled quite out of court by these new and ardent converts to trade unionism, who were prepared to go on, facing destitution, rather than yield a jot of what seemed to them an essential principle.

Organized labor, indeed, realized fully the seriousness of the situation. The leaders had used their utmost influence to have the agreement accepted, and their advice had been set aside.

What view, then, was taken of this development of these central bodies and by the affiliated trades of the city, who were all taxing themselves severely both in time and money for the support of the strike?

The democracy of labor was on this occasion indeed justified of its children, and the supreme right of the strikers to make the final decision on their own affairs and abide by the consequences was maintained. Plans were laid for continuing the commissary stores, and just at this stage there was received from the United Garment Workers the sum of $4,000 for the support of the stores. The strikers were also encouraged to hold out when on January 9 the firm of Sturm-Mayer signed up and took back about five hundred workers. Also, a committee of the state Senate began an inquiry into the strike, thus further educating the public into an understanding of the causes lying back of all the discontent, and accounting for much of the determination not to give in.

All the same, the prospects seemed very dark, and the strikers and their leaders had settled down to a steady, dogged resistance. It was like nothing in the world so much as holding a besieged city, and the outcome was as uncertain, and depended upon the possibility of obtaining for the beleaguered ones supplies of the primitive necessaries of life, food and fuel. And the fort was held until about the middle of January came the news that Hart, Schaffner and Marx had opened up negotiations, and presently an agreement was signed, and their thousands of employés were back at work.

They were back at work under an agreement, which, while it did not, strictly speaking, recognize the union, did not discriminate against members of the union. Nay, as the workers had to have representation and representatives, it was soon found that in practice it was only through their organization that the workers could express themselves at all.

This is not the place in which to enlarge upon the remarkable success which has attended the working out of this memorable agreement. It is enough to say that ever since all dealings between the firm and their employés have been conducted upon the principle of collective bargaining.

The agreement with Messrs. Hart, Schaffner and Marx was signed on January 14, 1911, and the Joint Conference Board then bent all its efforts towards some settlement with houses of the Wholesale Clothiers' Association and the National Tailors' Association for the twenty or thirty thousand strikers still out.

Suddenly, without any warning the strike was terminated. How and why it has never been explained, even to those most interested in its support. All that is known is that on February 3 the strike was called off at a meeting of the Strikers' Executive Committee, at which Mr. T. A. Rickert, president of the United Garment Workers of America, and his organizers, were present. This was done, without consulting the Joint Conference Board, which for fourteen weeks had had charge of the strike, and which was composed of representatives from the United Garment Workers of America, the Garment

Workers' local District Council, the strikers' own Executive Committee, the Chicago Federation of Labor, and the Women's Trade Union League.

This meant the close of the struggle. Three out of the four commissary stations were closed the following day, and the fourth a week later.

As regards the great mass of strikers then left, it was but a hunger bargain. They had to return to work without any guarantee for fair treatment, without any agency through which grievances could be dealt with, or even brought before the employers. And hundreds of the workers had not even the poor comfort that they could go back. Business was disorganized, work was slack, and the Association houses would not even try to make room for their rebellious employés. The refusal of work would be made more bitter by the manner of its refusal. Several were met with the gibe, "You're a good speaker, go down to your halls, they want you there." One employer actually invited a returned striker into his private office, shook hands with him as if in welcome, and then told him it was his last visit, he might go!

The beginning of the present stage of the industrial rebellion among working-women in the United States may be said to have been made with the immense garment-workers' strikes. All have been strikes of the unorganized, the common theory that strikes must have their origin in the mischief-breeding activities of the walking delegate finding no confirmation here. They were strikes of people who knew not what a union was, making protest in the only way known to them against intolerable conditions, and the strikers were mostly very young women. One most significant fact was that they had the support of a national body of trade-union women, banded together in a federation, working on the one hand with organized labor, and on the other bringing in as helpers large groups of outside women. Such measure of success as came to the strikers, and the indirect strengthening of the woman's cause, which has since borne such fruit, was in great part due to the splendid reinforcement of organized labor, through the efforts of this league of women's unions.

I need touch but lightly on the strikes in other branches of the sewing trades, where the history of the uprising was very similar.

In July, 1910, 70,000 cloak-makers of New York were out on strike for nine weeks asking shorter hours, increase of wages, and sanitary conditions in their workshops. All these and some minor demands were in the end granted by the Manufacturers' Association, who controlled the trade, but the settlement nearly went to pieces on the rock of union recognition. An arrangement was eventually arrived at, on the suggestion of Mr. Louis Brandeis, that the principle of preference to unionists, first enforced in Australia, should be embodied in the agreement. Under this plan, union standards as to hours of labor, rates of wages and working conditions prevail, and, when hiring help, union men of the necessary qualifications and degree of skill must have precedence over non-union men. With the signing of the agreement the strike ended.

January, 1913, saw another group of garment-workers on strike in New York. This time there were included men and women in the men's garment trades, also the white-goods-workers, the wrapper and kimono-makers, and the ladies' waist- and dress-makers. There is no means of knowing how many workers were out at any one time, but the number was estimated at over 100,000. The white-goods-workers embraced the very youngest girls, raw immigrants from Italy and Russia, whom the manufacturers set to work as soon as they were able to put plain seams through the machine, and this was all the skill they ever attained. These children from their extreme youth and inexperience were peculiarly exposed to danger from the approaches of cadets of the underworld, and an appeal went out for a large number of women to patrol the streets, and see that the girls at least had the protection of their presence.

The employers belonging to the Dress and Waist Manufacturers' Association made terms with their people, after a struggle, under an agreement very similar to that described above in connection with the cloakmakers.

One of the most satisfactory results of the strikes among the garment-workers has been the standardizing of the trade wherever an agreement has been procured and steadily adhered to. It is not only that hours are shorter and wages improved, and the health and safety of the worker guarded, and work spread more evenly over the entire year, but the harassing dread of the cut without notice, and of wholesale, uncalled-for dismissals is removed. Thus is an element of certainty and a sense of method and order introduced. Above all, homework is abolished.

In an unstandardized trade there can be no certainty as to wages and hours, while there is a constant tendency to level down under the pressure of unchecked competition from both above and below. There is too frequent breaking of factory laws and ignoring of the city's fire and health ordinances, because the unorganized workers dare not, on peril of losing their jobs, insist that laws and ordinances were made to be kept and not broken. Also, in any trade where a profit can be made by giving out work, as in the sewing trades, we find, unless this is prevented by organization or legislation, an enormous amount of home-work, ill-paid and injurious to all, cutting down the wages of the factory hands, and involving the wholesale exploitation of children.

Home-work the unions will have none of, and therefore, wherever the collective bargain has been struck and kept, there we find the giving out of work from the factory absolutely forbidden, the home guarded from the entrance of the contractor, motherhood respected, babyhood defended from the outrage of child labor, and a higher standard of living secured for the family by the higher and securer earnings of the normal breadwinners.

Everywhere on the continent the results of these strikes have been felt, women's strikes as they have been for the most part. The trade unionists of this generation have been encouraged in realizing how much fight there was in these young girls. All labor has been inspired. In trade after trade unorganized workers have learned the meaning of the words "the solidarity of labor," and it has become to them an article of faith. Whether it has been button-workers in Muscatine, or corset-workers in Kalamazoo, shoe-workers in St. Louis, or textile-workers in Lawrence, whether the struggle has been crowned with success or crushed into the dust of failure, the workers have been heartened to fight the more bravely because of the thrilling example set them by the garment-workers, and have thus brought the day of deliverance for all a little nearer hand.

Again, from the Atlantic to the Pacific, the public has been taught many lessons. The immense newspaper publicity, which could never have been obtained except for a struggle on a stupendous scale, has proved a campaign of education for young and old, for business man and farmer, for lawyer and politician, for housewife and for student. It has left the manufacturer less cocksure of the soundness of his individualist philosophy. More often is he found explaining and even apologizing for industrial conditions, which of yore he would have ignored as non-existent. He can no longer claim from the public his aforetime undisputed privilege of running his own business as he pleases, without concern for either the wishes or the welfare of employés and community.

The results are also seen in the fact that it is now so much easier to get the workers' story across the footlights in smaller local struggles, such as those of the porcelain-workers in Trenton and the waitresses in Chicago; in the increasing success in putting through legislation for the limitation of hours and the regulation of wages for the poorest paid in state after state. By state or by nation one body after another is set the task of doing something towards accounting for the unceasing industrial unrest, towards solving the general industrial problem. Even if to some of us the remedial plans outlined seem to fall far short of the mark, they still are a beginning and are a foretaste of better things ahead.

The conferences and discussions on unemployment are an admission, however belated, that a society which has, in the interests of the privileged classes, permitted the exploitation of the worker, must face the consequences, bear some of the burden, and do its share towards preventing the continuance of the evil. We do not cure smallpox by punishing the patient, nor do we thus prevent its recurrence among others. We handle the disease both by treating the sick person himself, and by finding the causes that lead to its spread, and arresting these. Industrial eruptive diseases have to be dealt with in like fashion, the cause sought for, and the social remedy applied fearlessly.

VI

THE IMMIGRANT WOMAN AND ORGANIZATION

The melting-pot of the races is also the melting-pot of nationalities. The drama that we are witnessing in America is a drama on a more tremendous scale than can ever have been staged in the world before. By the unawakened and so-called pure American the incoming Italian or Jew is regarded as an outsider, who may be graciously permitted to hew wood and draw water, to forge steel in a rolling-mill or to sew in a factory, to cut ice or make roads for the rest of us, and who may, on the other hand, be given the cold shoulder more or less politely, generally less, when it comes to acquaintanceship, to the simple democratic social intercourse which we share with those whom we admit as our equals. I, too, am an immigrant, although an English-speaking and Anglo-Saxon immigrant. Therefore I am accepted among Americans as one of themselves. But there comes to me often a bitter sense of separation from my fellow-immigrants, a separation by not one wall, but many. First, the wall we none of us can help, the wall raised by difference of language. Next, the wall raised by different manners and customs. This we might try to scale oftener than we do. Again, there are separating walls, harder than these either to surmount or to lay low, walls of provincial arrogance and crass self-satisfaction, and the racial pride that is mostly another name for primitive ignorance.

An ordinary city-dwelling American or an English-speaking foreigner earning a living in business or in one of the professions or even in some of the skilled trades might live a lifetime in the United States and never meet non-Americanized foreigners socially at all. In church or club or on the footing of private entertainment these first-comers and their friends keep themselves to themselves. And although among us such race-defined limits are less hard and fast than, say, the lines of class in old European countries, still there they are. The less enlightened do not even think about the immigrant within our shores at all. Those somewhat more advanced will talk glibly about the Americanization of the foreigner that is going on all the time. So is it. That is true, but the point here to be noted is that the desirable and inevitable process of the Americanization of the foreigner, and his assimilation by and into the American nation takes place outside the charmed circles wherein these good respectable folks dwell; takes place in spite of their indifference; takes place without their active assistance, without their coöperation, save and except so far as that coöperation is unconscious and unavoidable.

The Americanizing process takes place in the street, in the cars, in the stores, in the workshop, at the theater, and the nickel show, in the wheatfield and on the ice-field; best and quickest of all in the school, and nowhere so consciously as in the trade union, for all that section of foreigners whom organized labor has been able to reach and draw into its fold. Carried out for the most part in crude and haphazard fashion the process goes on, only in the vast majority of cases it is far slower than it need be.

Too many are but little touched, or touched only in painful ways by the Americanizing process, especially the married women who stay in their homes. Their lot is so often a tragedy. They have lost their own country and yet have not gained another. Even this is not the worst. The younger folks are in some fashion made over into American men and women. And here comes in the crucial question which concerns something more than universality of opportunity, quality of opportunity. These little Poles and Ruthenians and Bohemians are finally made over into Americans. Their life-contribution will be given to the generation now growing up, of which they will form a part. We want that contribution to be as fine as possible. They cannot give more than they themselves are. And what they are to be in very large part we are making them. Will they not be all the finer citizens-to-be if we come closer to them and to their parents in the warm friendly social relations of life?

The plane of social intercourse is the last to be transformed by democracy. Here is it that aristocratic and undemocratic limitations hamper us the longest. Here we are still far behind the fine, free and admirable planing out of differences, and rounding off of angles and making over of characters that is part of the democracy of the street and the marketplace. Here between strangers is the closest physical nearness. Here the common need to live and earn a living supplies a mutual education through the very acts of serving and being served, of buying and selling and using the common thoroughfares and means of transportation. And that basic democracy of the street and the marketplace is all between strangers.

It is the very fact that this blending of peoples, this rubbing off of racial angles, takes place in and through the commonplace surroundings of everyday life, that blinds most to the greatness and the wonder of the transformation and to the pressing importance of the right adjustments being made, and made early. But to the observer whose eyes are not holden, there comes a sense that he is every day witnessing a warfare of Titans, that in these prosaic American communities it is world powers that are in clash and in conflict while in preparation for the harmony to be.

Upon careful consideration it would appear that the immigrant problem is only a slightly varied expression of the general social and economic problem. It focuses public attention because the case of the immigrant is so extreme. For instance, whatever conditions, industrial or civic, press hardly upon the American worker, these conditions press with yet greater hardship upon the alien. The alien and his difficulties form therefore a first point of contact, the point where the social reformer begins with his suggestions for improvement. The very same thought unconsciously forms the basis of many of the proposed methods of dealing with the immigrant, however startlingly these may differ from one another in expression. On the one hand we have such suggestions as that of Mr. Paul Kellogg, which he called "A Labor Tariff, A Minimum Wage for the Immigrant." It does not take very acute reasoning to perceive that if such a proposal were ever to become law, it would not be very long before there would have to be a universal minimum wage for everyone.

On the other hand, Mr. Edward B. Whitney in his Memorandum appended to the Report of the Commission of the State of New York argues thus in discussing the claim made by the majority of the Commission that certain special help and protection is needed by the alien. He asks "whether, if a further extension of this kind of state charity is to be made, it would not be better to take up something for the benefit of our own citizens or for the benefit of citizen and alien alike." Mr. Whitney is entirely logical. Only progress rarely takes place for logical reasons, or on lines dictated by logic, but it does in almost all cases follow the line of least resistance, and the wise progressive accepts gratefully whatever he can get, without being too anxious as to whether it seems to be logically the next step or not.

The immigrant has hitherto been used as an excuse to permit the dehumanizing of our cities; he has been used industrially as an instrument to make life harder for the hardly pressed classes of workers whom he joined on his arrival here. That such has been his sorry function has been his misfortune as well as theirs. Would it not be equally natural and far more fair to utilize his presence among us to raise our civic and economic and industrial standards? It is no new story, this. Out of every social problem we can construct a stepping-stone to something better and higher than was before. The most that we know of health has been learned through a study of the misadjustments that bring about disease. What has been done educationally to assist the defective, the handicapped and the dependent has thrown a flood of light upon the training of the normal child. Through work undertaken in the first instance for the benefit of the exceptions, the minority, the whole community has benefited.

In this connection no one will deny that immigrants, both men and women, have their handicaps. In the great majority of instances they are handicapped by an upbringing among primitive conditions, by their unavoidable ignorance of our language and our customs, and by a quite natural mental confusion as to our standards of conduct, to them so curiously exacting in some respects as, for instance, where the schooling of their children is concerned, so incomprehensibly lax in others, say, in the unusual freedom accorded to those same children when grown but a little older.

We shall find that whatever we do for the immigrant

will be, in the end, so much accomplished for the good of all. Let us lessen this unfair pressure upon him, as far as we can, and we shall surely find that in helping him to help himself, we have, at the same time, benefited all workers.

It is easy to see that the great strikes in the sewing and textile trades of the last few years have proved a searchlight especially into women's industrial conditions, educating the whole public by informing them of the terrible price paid for our comfort by the makers of the commonest articles of household purchase and use, the sacrifice of youth, health, happiness, and life itself demanded by any industry which exacts of the employés cruelly long hours of work at an exhausting speed, and which for such overwork pays them wretchedly.

These uprisings have besides stimulated to an encouraging degree the forming of an intelligent public opinion upon the problem of the immigrant, and a wholesomely increased sense of responsibility towards the immigrant. And indeed it was time. Miss Grace Abbott, director of the Chicago League for the Protection of Immigrants, tells a story, illustrating how very unintelligent an educated professional man can be in relation to immigrant problems.

"Not long ago," she says, "I listened to a paper by a sanitary engineer, on the relation between the immigrant and public health. It was based on a study of typhoid fever in a certain city in the United States. He showed that most typhoid epidemics started among our foreign colonies, and spread to other sections. This, he explained, is because the foreigner has been accustomed to a pure water supply, and is therefore much more susceptible to typhoid than the American who has struggled since birth against the diseases which come from polluted water.

"Instead, then, of urging this as an additional reason for giving us all decent water, he drew the remarkable conclusion that in the interests of the public health, some new basis for the exclusion of immigrants must be adopted. In this way," Miss Abbott adds, "most discussions on the immigrant are diverted, and leave the fundamental problems quite untouched. For whether we adopt a literary and physique test, increase the head-tax, and do all the other things suggested by the restrictionists, thousands of immigrants will continue to come to us every year."

Apart from general considerations, these gigantic industrial upheavals have afforded to the public-spirited citizen an unsurpassed opportunity of understanding and appreciating the industrial problem as it affects and is affected by the immigrant girl and young woman. A few of us, here and there, from personal and trade experience knew the facts years ago as well as they are generally known today. But not all the Government reports, not an army of investigators could have imparted this knowledge to the public, and impressed upon them the sordid suffering of the working and living conditions of the foreign woman in the sewing trades in any great American city.

For in strikes of such magnitude, where whole groups of the participators themselves lived for months in a white heat of idealism and enthusiasm, life-stories are no longer dragged out of shy retiring girls, but are poured out in a burning flood by those very same girls, now quite transformed by the revolution through which they have passed, and by the new ideas of liberty and sisterhood with which they are possessed.

I speak of the woman worker here, because it is she who is my concern at present, and in all the now historic strikes she has played a very large part. Indeed in the first of these risings, in the shirtwaist strikes of 1909-1910 in New York and Philadelphia, very few men workers were involved, and in the huge Chicago strike, 1910-1911, among the makers of men's ready-made clothing, although there the girl strikers numbered only about one-fourth of the whole, even that fourth made up the very respectable total of, it is believed, somewhere around 10.000 individuals, the population of a small city. Indeed it would give most Americans pause to be told that in this same Chicago strike the whole of the workers, men and women together, numbered more than the troops that Washington was able to place in the field at any one time during the War of Independence.

Most of these strikes have been strikes of unorganized workers, who did not know even of the existence of a union till after they had gone out, and therefore with no idea of appealing to an organization for even moral support. In Chicago the strikers belonged to nine different nationalities, speaking as many different languages, so it is clear that the pressure must have been indeed irresistible that forced so many thousands with apparently no common meeting-ground or even common means of communication out of the shops into the street. When the organized strike, they know why. When the unorganized of one nationality and one tongue strike, they can tell one another why. Yet these people struck in spots all over the city almost simultaneously, although in most cases without any knowledge by one group that other groups were also resisting oppression and making a last stand against any further degradation of their poor standards of living. Amid every variety of shop grievance, and with the widest possible difference in race, language and customs, they shared two disadvantageous conditions: industrially they were oppressed, and socially they were subject races. Therefore they were one people, in spite of their nine nationalities. These two conditions acted and reacted upon one another complicating and intensifying the struggle. But because of this very intensity it has been easier for the onlooker to separate out the real questions at issue, easier for the sympathetic American to come into wholesome and human relationship with this large body of his brothers and sisters. To him they could be one group, for their interests were one, and they had been too long separated from him and from one another by the accidents of birth and speech.

So the searchlight turned on then on the sewing trades has since cast its enlightening beams on industrial conditions in other trades, in which, too, one race is perpetually played off against another with the unfailing result of cuts in wages and lowering of standards of living.

All tests of admission to secure some measure of selection among new arrivals are but experiments in an untried field. We have no tests but rough-and-ready ones, and even these are often inconsistent with one another. For instance, for a good many years now the immigration inspectors have taken such precautions as they could against the admission of the insane, but it is only recently that modified Binet tests have been used to check the entry of a socially far more injurious class, the congenitally feebleminded.

Those who have worked extensively among newly arrived foreign girls find that they arrive here with, as a rule, much less idea of what awaits them, what will be expected of them, and the difficulties and even dangers they may encounter, than the men. When the Chicago Women's Trade Union League began its immigration department a few years ago, it was found that three dollars was about the average sum which a girl had in her pocket when she reached the city of her destination. Ten dollars was felt to be a fortune, while I have since heard of young girls landing alone in a great city, and without a single cent with which to leave the depot. It is often said, why do their mothers let them go away (sixteen and eighteen are common ages) so young, so inexperienced? It must be remembered that many of the Polish and Lithuanian girls, for example, come from small villages. The mothers themselves have never seen a big city, and have not the remotest conception of any place of more than five hundred inhabitants, where the distances are short, and where everyone knows everyone else. They have no idea of the value of money, when it comes to earning and spending it in America. Three dollars a week is to mother, as to daughter, an ample sum for the young traveler.

It often happens that many of the young immigrants have had letters from those who had preceded them. But we know what human nature is. The person who succeeds proudly writes home the good news. The still more successful person is able to take a trip home and display the visible signs of his or her wealth. The unsuccessful, as a rule, either does not write at all, or writing, does not admit the humiliating truth.

In the ignorance and inexperience of the young foreign girl the white slaver finds his easiest prey, and the betrayer is too often the man speaking her own tongue. On this terrible subject the nation, like other nations, is beginning to wake up to its responsibilities in relation to the immigrant girl as in relation to other girls. This special danger to young womanhood is so linked with other social questions that I merely allude to it here, because of the certainty I entertain that much even of this danger would lessen if the trade-union movement among women were so strong and so extensive that any woman, young or old, could travel from place to place as a member of a truly world-wide organization. Then she would have a better chance of arriving well posted as to ways of earning her living, and of finding friends in every city and every town and village.

It may be urged that there exist already organizations world-wide in their scope, such as the religious associations, for the very purpose of safeguarding wandering girlhood. There are, and they accomplish a notable amount of good. But their appeal is not universal; they never have money or workers enough to cope adequately with a task like this, and they are not built upon the sound economic basis of the trade union.

The immigrant problem was not encountered by the first factory workers here, who were American-born. So we find the earliest leaders in the trade organization of women were wholly drawn from the daughters of the native settlers. They felt and spoke always as free-women, "the daughters of freemen." When this class of girls withdrew from the factories, they gave place to the Irish immigrant, in some respects a less advanced type than themselves. I have briefly traced some of the economic reasons which affected the rise, growth and eventual passing away of the various phases of trade unionism among women in this country. The progress of these was radically modified by the influx into the trades of workers from one nation after another; by the passing from a trade or a group of trades of body after body of the old workers, starved out or giving way before the recent arrivals, whose pitiful power to seize the jobs of the others and earn some sort of a living, has lain in their very weakness and helplessness.

So the first Irish girls who came into the factory life of New England were peasants, with no knowledge of city life, but quick and ready to learn. They went into the new occupations, and picked up the new ways of doing things. And by the time they had grasped the meaning of this strange industrial world in which they found themselves, they were in the relentless grasp of machine-controlled industry. Under untold handicaps they had to begin at the very beginning, and start rebellions on their own account. From the sixties on we can detect the preponderance of Irish names in the annals of early trade unionism. When they had adapted themselves to their conditions, for they quickly became Americanized, they showed in the trade unions which they organized the remarkable qualities for political leadership · which the Irish and Irish-Americans have ever since displayed in this country. The important rôle which Irish and Irish-American men have played in the councils of American trade unionism is well known, and their power today remains very great. So as regards the women, by glancing over the past we can readily trace the influence of the Irish girl, in the efforts after organization, unsuccessful as these often were. It was Maggie McNamara who led the Brooklyn Female Burnishers' Association in 1868. It was during the sixties that Kate Mullaney was leading her splendid body of Troy laundresses, and twenty years later we find Leonora Barry, another Irish girl, as the leading spirit among the women of the Knights of Labor.

Except in isolated instances, no other race has come to the front among working-women until recently. We read of German women and Bohemian women as faithful unionists. But Germans, Bohemians and Scandinavians advanced or lost ground along with the others. By this time, moreover, the nation had become more habituated to absorbing immigrants from various nations, and the distinction between races was less accentuated after a few years' residence. On the part of the Germans and Scandinavians, amalgamation has been so speedy, and in the end so complete, that most of those who have been here some time, and invariably the children of the first-comers, are Americans through and through.

With the foreign peoples that we have with us today, the situation is somewhat different. Certain general principles are common to the course of all these migrations. They originate, on the one hand, in economic pressure, complicated not unfrequently with religious wars or persecutions, and on the other, in the expectation of better times in a new country. They meet the demands of a new country, asking for labor, and are further subject to the inducements of agents. Under our haphazard social arrangements, the newly arrived often meet wretched conditions, and have no means of knowing how they are being used to lower yet further wages for themselves and others.

Always, whatever their own descent and history, the older inhabitants feel resentment, knowing no more than their unfortunate rivals what is the underlying reason of the trouble. Milder forms of antagonism consist in sending the immigrant workers "to Coventry," using contemptuous language of or to them, as we hear every day in "dago" or "sheeny," and in objections by the elders to the young people associating together, while the shameful use that is continually made of the immigrants as strike-breakers may rouse such mutual indignation that there are riots and pitched battles as a consequence.

The first indignant efforts to exclude the intruders are vain. More and more do experienced trade unionists admit this, and plead for the acceptance of the inevitable, and turn all their energies towards the organization of the unwelcome rivals. Scabs they must be, if left alone. Better take them in where they can be influenced and controlled, and can therefore do less damage. Here is where the help of the foreign organizer is so essential to overcome the indifference and quell the misgivings of the strangers in a situation where the influence of the employer is almost always adverse.

At length the immigrant gains a footing; he is left in possession, either wholly or partly, and amalgamation to a great degree takes place. A generation grows up that knew not the sad rivalry of their fathers, for fresh industrial rivalries on different grounds have replaced the old, as sharply cut, but not on race lines.

Every one of these stages can be seen today in all the industrial centers and in many rural ones, with one people or another.

While the tendency of the organized labor movement, both in the United States and in Canada, is towards restriction, whether exercised directly through immigration laws, or indirectly through laws against the importation of contract labor, there exist wide differences of opinion among trade unionists, and in the younger groups are many who recognize that there are limits beyond which no legislation can affect the issue, and that even more important than the conditions of admission to this new world is the treatment which the worker receives after he passes the entrance gate. If it is necessary in the interests of those already in this country to guard the portals carefully, it is equally necessary for the welfare of all, that the community through their legislators, both state and national, should accept the responsibility of preventing the ruthless exploitation of immigrants in the interest of private profit. Exploited and injured themselves, these become the unconscious instruments of hardly less ruthless exploitation and injury to their fellows in the competitive struggle for a bare subsistence.

Such exploitation could be in some degree checked

through the authorities assuming control, and especially by furnishing to the new arrivals abundant information and advice, acquainting them with the state of the labor market in different localities and at different times. It is for the authorities also to see that the transportation of newly arrived foreigners from place to place is rendered secure; to encourage their early instruction in the language and laws of the country and the ordinances of the city, along with enlightenment as to the resources in time of trouble, which lie open to the poorest, if they but know where to turn.

In the first number of the *Immigrants in America Review,* the editor, Frances A. Kellor, points out what an unusual opportunity has been granted to America to formulate a definite program with reference to alien residents. Now is the time, she insists, to perfect laws, establish systems and improve conditions, when, owing to the European War, but few immigrants are arriving, and therefore, when no great rush of people demand expedients. "Now is the time to build, to repair, to initiate, so we may obviate the necessity for expedients."

The writer shows that efforts ought to be directed along seven lines, and the work on these seven lines should be closely coördinated.

1. *Transportation.* The safe transportation of admitted aliens to their destination.

2. *Employment.* Security of employment, and adequate, coördinated, regulated labor-market organization.

3. *Standards of living.* Making it possible for the immigrant to adopt and maintain better standards of living, by removal of discriminations in localities, housing and sanitation, and by preventing overcrowding.

4. *Savings.* Information regarding savings banks, loan funds, agricultural colonies, and legislation regarding the same.

5. *Education.* Reduction of illiteracy, the teaching of civics, and extension of opportunity of education and industrial training.

6. *Citizenship.* Higher and simpler naturalization requirements, and processes, and placing the legal status of the alien upon a just and consistent foundation.

7. *Public Charges.* National and state coöperation in the care of any who may become public charges.

No one can suppose that every Greek boy desires to become a shoeblack, or that every Scandinavian girl is fitted for domestic service and for nothing else; that every Slavic Jewess should become a garment-worker; that every Italian man should work on the roads; that the Lithuanian and Hungarian, no matter what their training or their ability, should be compelled to go into the steel-rolling mills. All this because they land speaking no English, and not knowing how to place themselves in occupations better adapted to their inclinations and qualifications. No one knows how many educated and trained men and women are thus turned into hewers of wood and drawers of water, to the ruin of their own lives and the loss of the community.

The unregulated private employment office, the padrone and the sweat-shop are the agencies who direct the newcomers to jobs, whether it be in the city or out in the country camp.

Many of the new arrivals would gladly take up agriculture, if they knew where to go, and were safeguarded against imposition—having a fee taken, for instance, and then landed several hundred miles away, penniless, to find all the jobs gone.

The immigrant on landing is very much like the child leaving school to go to work, and requires vocational guidance just as sorely.

The needs of the alien are closely related to the

general question of unemployment. He suffers in an acute degree from the want of system in the regularization of industry, and the fact that we have failed to recognize unemployment, and all irregularity of employment as a condition to be met and provided against by industry and the community.

Americans take credit to themselves that so many immigrants do well, succeed, become prosperous citizens and members of society, but wish to shoulder none of the blame when the alien falls down by the way, or lives under such home conditions that his babies die, and his older children fall out of their grades, drift into the street trades or find their way into the juvenile court. Americans forget how many of all these evil results are due to the want of social machinery to enable the alien to fit into his new surroundings, or the neglect to set such social machinery agoing where it already exists. In the small towns it is not unusual for health ordinances to be strictly enforced in the English-speaking localities, and allowed to remain a dead letter in the immigrant districts. In Chicago it was in the stockyards district that garbage was dumped for many years; garbage, the product of other wards, that the residents of those other wards insisted be removed from their back-doors. How much of the high infant death-rate among stockyards families has been due to the garbage exposed and decaying, so carefully brought there, from the fine residential districts?

Legally the alien suffers under a burden of disabilities of which he is usually wholly unaware, until he has broken some law or regulation devised, it would appear, often for his discomfiture, rather than for anyone's else benefit. These laws and regulations, in themselves sometimes just and sometimes unjust, make up a mass of the most inconsistent legislation. State laws, varying from state to state, and city ordinances equally individual limit the employment of aliens on public work. Peddlers' and fishers' licenses come under similar restrictions; so with the owning of property, the right to leave property by will, say, to a wife and children in Europe, and the right even to protection of life, in violation of treaty rights. "The state courts have never punished a single outrage of this kind" [violence at the hands of a mob]. The federal government, Miss Kellor states, makes a payment to a victim's heirs out of a secret service fund "if the ambassador is persistent, and threatens to withdraw from Washington if the murder of his country-men is not to be punished."

These are all most serious handicaps, and certainly the need for investigation of all laws, the codifying of many, and the abolition of some is urgent.

If some of these handicaps were lifted from the im-migrant, complaint against under-cutting competition of cheap foreign labor would largely cease, and the task of organizers among the foreign workers would be much simplified, even while we are waiting for the day when it will be possible for all to obtain work without turning others out of their jobs, which can only come about when we produce intelligently for the use of all, instead of for the profit of the exceptional few.

Here and there work on the lines sketched out is be-ginning, even though much of it is as yet unrelated to the rest. The community is making headway, in the acknowledgment by various states, headed by New York, of the just claim of the immigrant, once he is admitted within our borders, to the protection of the government. For long after the Federal authorities took over the control of immigration, their concern was limited to some degree of restriction over the entry of foreigners, and the enforcement of deportation, when such was considered necessary. Quite a fresh departure, however, was made in the year 1910, when the state of New York, following the recommendations of its State Commission on Immigration (1909), established its Bureau of Industries and Immigration, which really grew out of the activities of a private society. Other communities are also realizing their responsibility. California established a permanent Commission on Immigration and Housing in 1913, and the Investigating Commissions of Massachusetts and New Jersey recommended similar agencies in their reports to the legislatures in 1914.

New York has already accomplished excellent results, and more important still, has shown the direction, in which other states may both follow and coöperate. A few years more may see us with interstate legislation insuring the better care and protection of immigrants all over the country, interstate legislation being the curiously indirect method which the United States has hit upon to overcome the imperfections and deficiencies of its national instrument of government. One of these days may even find the Federal House at Washington taking over, in other lines besides that of foreign workers, the functions outlined for it in the first instance by the daughter states.

The United States Government has recently entered a new field in the passage of a law, authorizing the protection of immigrants in transit to their destination, and providing for the establishment of a station in Chicago, where the immigrants will go on their arrival, and will thus be protected from the gross frauds from which they have so long suffered. The present administration also promises an experiment in the development of the Bureau of Information in the Immigration Department.

It is not so easy for any of us to give the same

dispassionate consideration to the problem that is with us as to that which has long been settled, and has passed away into the calm atmosphere of history. And truly, there are complications in the present situation which our fathers had not to face. And first, the much greater dissimilarity in training, mental outlook, social customs, and in the case of the men and women from eastern Europe, not to speak of Asia, the utter unlikeness in language, makes mutual knowledge and understanding much more difficult, and the growth of mutual confidence, therefore, much slower.

No one has yet analyzed the effects upon the nervous system of the migrating worker, of the unsettlement of habits, and the change of surroundings and social environment, working in connection with the changed climatic conditions, and the often total change in food. This is one phase of the immigrant problem which deserves the most careful study. And when, as too often in the case of the Russian Jew, this complete alteration of life is piled on top of the persecutions so many of them have endured, and the shocks so many have sustained before leaving their native land, the normal, usual effects of the transition are emphasized and exaggerated, and it may take a generation or longer before complete Americanization and amalgamation is brought about.

The longer such a change is in being consummated, the more is the new generation likely to retain some of their most characteristic qualities permanently; to retain and therefore to impress these upon the dominant race, in this case upon the American nation, through association, and finally, through marriage. Especially is this a probable result where we find such vitality and such intensely prepotent power as among the Jews.

In reference to trade-union organization among women, while each nationality presents its own inherent problem, there is equally no doubt but that each will in the future make its own special contribution towards the progress and increased scope of the movement among the women workers.

As matters are developing today, the fulfillment of this promise of the future has already begun most markedly among the Slavic Jewesses, especially those from Russia. These young women have already brought, and are every day bringing into the dreary sweatshop and the speeded-up factory a spirit of fearlessness and independence both in thought and action, which is having an amazing effect upon the conditions of factory industry in the trades where they work. So also, supporting and supported by the men of their own race, these Russian Jewish girls, many of them extremely young, are inspiring their fellow-workers and interpenetrating the somewhat matter-of-fact atmosphere of American trade unionism with their own militant determination and enthusiasm. With most, the strike has been their initiation into trade unionism, often the general strike in their own trade, the strike on a scale hitherto unparalleled in trades where either the whole or a very considerable proportion of the workers are women. Some again, especially among the leaders, approach unionism through the ever open door of socialism. If I speak here of the women of the Slavic Jewish race, it is not that I wish to ignore the men. I have to leave them on one side, that is all.

These girls add to courage and enthusiasm, such remarkable gifts of intellect and powers of expression as to make them a power wherever they have become awakened to the new problems that face them here and now, and to their own responsibilities in relation thereto. They are essentially individualists. They do not readily or naturally either lean upon others or cooperate with others, nor yet confide in others. They come here with a history generations long of ill-treatment and persecution. Many thousands of them have witnessed their dearest tortured, outraged and killed with the narrowest possible escape from some similar fate themselves. To most any return to their native country is completely barred, and they do not therefore nurse the hope, so inveterately cherished by the Italians, for instance, that they may some day be able to go back.

When the Russian Jewish girl first hears of a trade union, she has usually been some years in one of our cities, working in a factory or a sweatshop, let us say as a garment-worker. The religious and social liberty which she has here learnt to consider her due has stimulated her desire for further freedom, while the tremendous industrial pressure under which she earns her daily bread stirs the keenest resentment. One day patience, Jewish girlish patience, reaches its limit. A cut in wages, exhausting overtime, or the insults of an overbearing foreman, and an unpremeditated strike results. It may be small, poorly managed, and unsuccessful. The next time things may go better, and the girls come in touch with a union, and take their first lessons in the meaning of collective bargaining. (What is passing in the minds of the rank and file at this stage I am not certain. The obscurities of their psychology are more difficult to fathom.) But I am sure that to the leaders of the young protestants it is not so much in the light of a tower of refuge that the trade union presents itself, but rather as an instrument by means of which they believe that they can control a situation which has become unbearable. As happens to many endowed with the gift of leadership, they travel much farther than they had any idea of when they set out. As time goes on, if they are real leaders, they learn to understand human nature in its varied aspects, the human nature of bosses, as well as the human nature of their fellow-wage-earners. After a year or two as presidents or secretaries of their local, you will hear these fiery-tongued little orators preaching endurance, in order to gain an end not obtainable today, aye, even advising compromise, they to whom the very word compromise had erstwhile been impossible. This implies no loss of principle, no paltering with loyalty, but merely putting in practice the wisdom of the experienced statesman. Nearly all, sooner or later, embrace the socialist philosophy, and many are party members. In that philosophy they find a religious sanction in their most determined struggles after victory, and unfailing support and consolation in the hour of defeat.

As for the rank and file, with them, too, something of the same mental processes probably goes on in a minor degree; but they are much longer in learning their lesson, and meanwhile are often exceedingly hard to direct. They are impulsive beyond belief. It used once to be remarked that Jewish girls were the easiest of all to organize during a strike, and the hardest of all to hold in the union afterwards. This is fortunately not so true today, now that there are a few trained leaders of their own race, whom they trust, and who understand their moods, and know, better than most Americans, how to handle them.

The alien is forever being resented as an obstacle, even if an unconscious one, in the way of organization. Yet as far as women are concerned, it is to this group of aliens in particular that is due the recent tremendous impulse towards organization among the most poorly paid women. In the sewing trades, and in some other trades, such as candy-making, it is the American girls who have accepted conditions, and allowed matters to drift from bad to worse. It is the foreign girl, and especially the Slavic Jewess who has been making the fight for higher wages, shorter hours, better shop management, and above all, for the right to organize; and she has kept it up, year after year, and in city after city, in spite of all expectations to the contrary.

One of the indirect benefits of the colossal strikes in the sewing trades in which these Jewish girls have played so conspicuous a part has been the increasing degree in which those of differing nationalities have come to understand one another, as men and women having common difficulties and common rights, as all alike members of the great working people.   Through sore trial many have learnt the meaning of "class consciousness," who never heard of the word.

The new spirit is beginning to touch the Italian girl, and as time goes on, she, too, will be brought into the fold of unionism.   To meet with large success, we need as leaders and organizers, Italians, both men and women, of the type of Arthur Carotti, as capable and devoted. The Italian girl is guarded in her home as is the girl of no other race, and this works both for good and for evil.   The freedom of the streets, accorded so unquestioningly to their girls by the parents of other nationalities, is conscientiously denied to the Italian girl. No respectable family would permit their daughters to go to any sort of an evening gathering, to attend church or dance or union meeting, unless accompanied by father, mother or brother.   While no one can help deeply respecting the principles of family affection and responsibility which dictate this code of manners, there is equally no blinking the fact that it raises a most serious barrier in the way of organizing girls of Italian parentage. Nor on the other hand is it of the least avail to protect the girl against the evils of the industrial system of which the whole family form a part.   In especial it does not serve to shield her from the injurious effects of cruel overwork. In no class of our city population do we find more of this atrocious evil, misnamed home-work than among Italian families, and whether it is sew-ing, artificial-flower- or feather-making or nut-picking, neither grown daughters nor little children are spared here. Along with the mother and under her eye, the whole group work day after day, and often far into the night at occupations in themselves harmless enough under proper conditions, but ruinous to health and happiness when permitted to intrude under the family roof. For the wrong of home-work is not to be measured even by the injury suffered by the workers themselves. All parasitic trades, such as these, lower wages in the open market. The manufacturer is continually impelled to cut down wages in his shops to keep pace with the com-petition of the ill-remunerated home-worker.

As I have said above, I believe that every race that has settled down here in this America has some special contribution to bestow, which will work for good to the whole labor movement. I have instanced the case of the Slavic Jewess as one who has certainly arrived. From the others the gift has still to come. From the Italian girl it will come in good time, for they are beginning to enter the unions now, and from the lips of their own fellow-countrywomen even Italian mothers will learn to accept for their daughters the gospel they will not listen to from foreigners like ourselves. The most severely handicapped of all the nationalities so far, to my thinking, is the Polish. They are what is called pure Slavs, that is, with no Jewish blood. They are peasant girls and cannot be better described than they are in a pamphlet on "The Girl Employed in Hotels and Restaurants," published by the Juvenile Protective League of Chicago.

In these places Polish girls are chosen for the following reasons:

1. Because they come of strong peasant stock, and accomplish a large amount of work.

2. They are very thorough in what they do.

3. They are willing to take low wages.

4. They are very submissive, that is, they never protest.

5. They are ignorant of the laws of this country, and are easily imposed upon.

6. They never betray their superiors, no matter what they see.

What a scathing indictment of the American people is set forth in this brief summing up!

The trades that swallow up these strong, patient, long-enduring creatures are work in the meat-canning plants, and dish-washing and scrubbing in restaurants and hotels. These really valuable qualities of physical strength and teachableness, unbalanced by any sense of what is due to themselves, let alone their fellow-workers, prove their industrial ruin.

It is only when they are fortunate enough to get into a better class of work, and when they chance upon some well-organized establishment and are drawn into the union as a matter of course that we find Polish girls in unions at all. Intellectually they are not in the running with the Russian Jewess and the peasant surroundings of their childhood have offered them few advantages. One evening, for instance, there were initiated into a glove-workers' local seventeen new Polish members. Of these two only were able to read and write English, and of the remainder not more than half were able to read and write Polish. As to what is to be the later standing and the ultimate contribution of the Polish girl, I cannot hazard a guess. I only know that she possesses fine qualities which we are not utilizing and which we may be obliterating by the cruel treatment so many thousands of Polish girls are receiving at our hands.

I cannot see any prospect of organizing them in any reasonable numbers at present. The one thing we can do to alleviate their hard lot is to secure legislation—legislation for shorter hours and for the minimum wage.

Their suspiciousness is perhaps the chief barrier in the way of social elevation of the Poles. That Poles can be organized is shown by the remarkable success of the Polish National Alliance and kindred societies. Their capacity for coöperation is seen in their establishment of their own coöperative stores.

VII

THE WOMAN ORGANIZER

The problems that face the woman organizer are many and complex. They are the harder to handle, inasmuch as there is very little assistance to be had from any body of tradition on the subject among women workers. The movement for organization among women is still so inchoate. The woman organizer turns to the more experienced men leaders, and finds that often, even with the best will in the world, they cannot help her. The difficulties she meets with are, in detail, so different from theirs that she has to work out her own solutions for herself.

It is indeed a blind alley in which she has so often to move. The workers are young and ignorant, therefore, by all odds, they require the protection of both legislation and organization. Again, the workers are young and ignorant, and therefore they have not learnt the necessity for such protection. Their wages are in most cases low, too low for decent self-support. But just because their wages are so inadequate for bare needs it is in many cases all the more difficult to induce them to deduct from such scanty pay the fifty cents a month which is the smallest sum upon which any organization can pay its way and produce tangible benefits for its members.

Left to her own devices, the solution of her financial difficulties which the average girl finds is always to lessen her expenses so as to manage on the lessening wage that is inevitable in all trades if not resisted. To find a cheaper room, to take one more girl into her room, to spend a few cents a day less for food—these are the near-hand economies that first present themselves to the girlish mind. This is on the economizing side. When it comes to trying to earn more, to work longer hours is surely the self-evident way of increasing the contents of the weekly pay envelope. The younger and inexperienced the worker, the more readily is she fooled into believing that the more work she turns out, under a piece-work system, the more money will she earn, not only in that week but in the succeeding weeks.

To this child-like and simple code of worldly wisdom and of ethics, the policy advised by the organizer is indeed entirely foreign. To some very good girls, indeed, it seems ethically wrong not to work your hardest, or, as they say, do your best, especially when you are urged to. To more, it seems a silly, not to say impossible plan, not to try and earn as big a wage as possible. But the organizer comes in and she approaches the question from the other end. She does not talk about a standard of living, but she preaches it all the time. It is her business and her vocation to bring the girls to see that the first step towards getting more wages is to want more wages, to ask for more wages, and then, seeing that the single girl has no power of bringing about this result by herself, to show them that they must band together with the determination to make their wage square with their ideas of living, and not think that they must forever square their mode of living with their wage.

In the acceptance into the mind of this idea is involved a complete revolution.

It is in making of this ideal theory a living force, by helping girls to put it into practice in everyday shop life that the girl organizer has her special work cut out

for her. And here she necessarily contrasts favorably
with the average man organizer when he tries to deal
with girls, because she understands the girl's work and
the girl's problems better, and the girl knows that she
does.

I have taken wages as the prime subject of the organizer's activities only because wages form the crux of
the whole question. There, without any deceiving veils
falling between, we come close up to the real point at
issue between the employer and the employed, between
the employé and the community, the standard of living
that is possible, as measured by the employé's share of the
product of labor. But in practice, money wages form
only one element of the standard of living problem, although the one around which least confusion gathers.

Whatever form the demands of labor organizations
may take, the essence of the demand is the same : better
terms for the worker always, however temporary circumstances or technical details may obscure the issue.

That this holds of reductions in hours of work has
become a truism among trade unionists, who recognize
that any reduction of hours of work eventually, though
not perhaps immediately, results in a readjustment of
wages, whether week-workers or piece-workers or both
be involved, till the original money wage at any rate is
reached, supposing, of course, that no other influence
enters in as an element to lessen rates of pay.

The question of equal pay for equal work involves
indeed much more complicated issues, as regards both
the individual worker and the whole body of women
workers in the trade or branch of the trade affected.
But even here, the underlying purpose is the same, the
assuring, to the total number of workers whose labor
has gone into the production, of a certain amount of
finished marketable work, of an increased, or at the least,

not a lessened share of the product of their toil. It is not to be questioned that if women are permitted to work at the same operations as men for a lesser remuneration, the man's wage must go down. In addition, he may, even at the lowered rate, lose his job, as the employer may cherish the not altogether groundless hope that he may cut down the women's wage yet further and employ yet more women and yet fewer men.

In the same way the provision of better sanitary conditions, the fencing off of dangerous machinery, the prohibition usually of dangerous processes or of the use of dangerous materials, such as lead or white phosphorus, all involve an addition small or large, to the cost of manufacture. If, however, there be in all these instances an increase in the cost of manufacture there are also results to the well-being of the workers, which, if they could be measured in money, would be out of all proportion to the money cost to the employer or to the purchasing community. But again, it is the maintenance of the workers' ideal standard of living which causes the trade union to demand that their share of the product of their toil shall not be lessened by needless or avoidable risks to life or limb or health.

I have taken these demands in the order, in which, generally speaking, the organizer can induce the young girl worker to consider them in her own case. Better pay makes by far the easiest appeal, whether it be to the very young girl with her eager desire for a good time or to her older sister upon whom, quite surely, years have laid some of life's increasing burdens.

Next in order of attractiveness came shorter hours, especially if the wage-earners can be assured that wages will stay where they are.

But nothing short of both years and trade experience, apparently, will impress upon the worker all that is implied in those words that we write so easily and pronounce so glibly—sanitary conditions.

The young girls have all the blessed, happy-go-lucky care-free-ness of children, the children they are in years. They start out on their wage-earning career with the abounding high spirits and the stores of vitality of extreme youth. They are proud of their new capacity to earn, to begin to keep themselves and to help the mother and the others, and at first it does not seem to them as if anything could break them down or kill them. They do not at first associate bad air with headaches or sore throats, nor long standing with backaches, nor following the many needles of a power sewing-machine with eye trouble. The dangerous knife-edge on the revolving wheel, or the belting that may catch hair or clothing is to them only an item in the shop-furnishings, that they hope may not catch them napping.

All along the progress of labor organization has been exceedingly slow among women as compared with men, and has been far indeed from keeping pace with the rate at which increasing numbers of women have poured into the industrial field. So that it was not strange that well-meaning labor men, judging from personal experiences or arguing from analogy, came to the conclusion, paralyzing indeed to their own strivings after an all-inclusive, nation-wide organization of the workers, that women could not be organized. Or if such a labor man did not like to put it quite so bluntly, even to himself, he would shake his head, and regretfully remark that women did not make good trade unionists. If someone less experienced or more hopeful came along with plans for including or for helping women, the veteran trade unionist had too often a number of facts to bring forward, the bald accuracy of which was not to be disputed, of how in his own trade the women were scabbing on the men by working for a lower wage, or that they were so indifferent about the meetings, or worse still, how that women's local did so fine during the strike, and then just went to pieces, and now there wasn't any local at all.

"Facts are not to be explained away," he would conclude. No, they are not to be explained away, but some facts may be explained, and not unfrequently the explanation is based upon some other fact, which has been overlooked. With the present question, the one important fact which explains a good deal is the youth of so many women workers. This by no means disposes of each particular situation with its special difficulties, but it does help to explain the general tendency among the women to be neglectful of meetings and to let their local go to pieces, which so distracts our friend.

This new competitor with men, whom we think of and speak of as a woman, is in many cases not a woman at all, but only a girl, very often only a child. From this one fact arises a whole class of conditions, with resulting problems and difficulties totally different from any the man trade unionist has to deal with among men.

The first and most palpable difficulty is that the majority of workers are yet at the play age. They are still at the stage when play is one of the rightful conditions under which they carry on their main business of growing up. Many of them are not ready to be in the factory at all. Certainly not for eight, ten or twelve hours a day. And so those young things, after an unthankful and exhausting day's toil, are not going to attend meetings unless these can be made attractive to them. And the meeting that may appear entirely right and even attractive to the man of thirty or forty will be tiresome and boring past endurance to the girl of sixteen or eighteen.

Then there are other huge difficulties to encounter.

The very first principles of coöperative action and mutual responsibility are unknown to the great majority of the young workers. Too rarely does it happen, that in her own home the girl has learnt anything about trade unionism, at least trade unionism for women. The greater number of girls are not the daughters of factory mothers. The mother, whether American or foreign-born, grew up herself in simpler conditions, and does not begin to comprehend the utterly changed environment in which her little daughter has to work when she enters a modern factory. If American, she may have married just out of her father's home, and if foreign-born she may have been tending silkworms or picking grapes in Italy, or at field-work in Poland or Hungary. Very different occupations these from turning raw silk into ribbon or velvet in an Eastern mill, or labelling fruit-jars in an Illinois cannery.

Again, neither in the public nor in the parochial school are the workers-to-be taught anything concerning the labor movement or the meaning of collective bargaining. Even if they should have attained the eighth grade with its dizzy heights of learning, the little teaching they have received in civics has not touched upon either of the most vital problems of our day, the labor movement or the woman movement.

The mere youth, however, of the girl workers is not in itself the chief or the most insuperable difficulty. If these girls were boys we might look forward to their growing up in the trade, gaining experience and becoming ever more valuable elements in the union membership. But after a few years the larger percentage of the girls marry and are lost to the union and to unionism for good. Nay, a girl is often such a temporary hand that she does not even remain out her term of working years in one trade, but drifts into and out of half-a-dozen unskilled or semi-skilled occupations, and works for twenty different employers in the course of a few years. The head of a public-school social center made it her business to inquire of fifty girls, all over sixteen, and probably none over eighteen how long each had held her present job. Two only had been over a year at the one place. The rest accounted for such short periods as four months, six weeks, two weeks, at paper-box-making, candy-packing or book-binding with, of course, dull seasons and periods of unemployment between.

In the organized trades conditions are not quite so exasperating, but even in these the short working term of the girl employé means an utter lack of continuity in the membership of the trade and therefore of the union. The element of permanence in men's organizations is in great measure the result of the fact that men, whether they remain in one particular trade or shift to another, are at least in industry for life as wage-earners, unless indeed they pass on into the employing or wage-paying class.

But instead of seeing in the temporary employment of so many girls only another reason why they need the protection and the educational advantages of organization, we have been too contented to let ill alone, and all alike, the girl, the workingman, and the community are suffering for this inertia.

In this connection the first and most important matter to take up is that of women organizers, for women workers will never be enrolled in the labor movement of America in adequate numbers except through women organizers. And where are these today?

A most emphatic presentation of the practical reasons why the man organizer can rarely handle effectively young women workers, and why therefore women are absolutely necessary if the organization on any large scale is to be successful, was made before the Convention of the American Federation of Labor in Toronto in 1909. The speaker was Mr. Thomas Rumsey of Toledo. He described his own helplessness before the problem. He told, how, to begin with, it was not possible for a man to have that readiness of access to the girl workers when in their own homes and in their leisure hours which the woman organizer readily obtained.

"If a girl is living at home," he said, "it is not quite so awkward, but if she is in lodgings I can't possibly ask to see her in her own room. If I talk to her at all it will be out on the street, which is not pleasant, especially if it is snowing or freezing or blowing a gale. It is not under these conditions that a girl is likely to see the use of an organization or be attracted by its happier and more social side." Then he went on to say that he himself often did not know what best to say to his girl when he had caught her. He was ignorant, perhaps almost as ignorant as an outsider, of the conditions under which she did her work. He might know or be able to find out her wages and hours; he might guess that there was fining and speeding up, but he would know nothing of the details, and on any sanitary question or any moral question he would be utterly at sea. He could neither put the questions nor get the answers, nor in any way win the girl's confidence. Therefore, Mr. Rumsey concluded, if the American Federation of Labor is going to acknowledge its responsibilities in the great field of labor propaganda among women it must seriously take up the question of organizing women by women.

On a similar basis of reasoning it is easy to see that in the great majority of cases the successful organization of the women in any particular trade can be best carried out by one of themselves, a woman from their own trade. Not only do the girls believe that she understands their difficulties better than anyone else, but in most instances she does indeed bring to her work that exact knowledge of details and processes which gives the girls confidence that she can fairly state their case, that she will not, through technical ignorance, ask for impossibilities, nor on the other hand permit herself to be browbeaten by a foreman or superintendent because she does not know anything about the quality of material used, the peculiarities of a machine or the local or seasonal needs of the trade. Employers and managers also quickly recognize when organizers know whereof they talk. They, like the employés, realize that with such competent and efficient organizers or business agents they, too, are on firmer ground, even though they may not always acknowledge it.

To these sound general rules there are exceptions. There are cases where a man organizer can be invaluable, especially in some great, even if temporary, crisis. Also, there are in the American labor movement a few women who possess a genius for organizing on the very broadest lines. So profound is their sympathy with all their sisters, so thorough their grasp of general principles, so quick their perception of details, so intimate their knowledge of human nature and so sound and cool their judgment that they can be sent far afield into trades quite foreign to those of which they have had personal experience, and make a success of it. But such as these are rare and, when found, to be prized and cherished. The ordinary everyday way of drawing the women workers into the union and into the labor movement would be to have in every trade women from that trade at work all the time organizing their fellow-workers and holding them in the organization.

When the preliminary difficulties of organization have been met and overcome, when the new union has been set on its feet or the old one strengthened, there remains for the girl leader to keep her forces together.

The commonest complaint of all is that women members of a trade union do not attend their meetings. It is indeed a very serious difficulty to cope with, and the reasons for this poor attendance and want of interest in union affairs have to be fairly faced.

At first glance it seems curious that the meetings of a mixed local composed of both men and girls, should have for the girls even less attraction than meetings of their own sex only. But so it is. A business meeting of a local affords none of the lively social intercourse of a gathering for pleasure or even of a class for instruction. The men, mostly the older men, run the meeting and often are the meeting. Their influence may be out of all proportion to their numbers. It is they who decide the place where the local shall meet and the hour at which members shall assemble. The place is therefore often over a saloon, to which many girls naturally and rightly object. Sometimes it is even in a disreputable district. The girls may prefer that the meeting should begin shortly after closing time so that they do not need to go home and return, or have to loiter about for two or three hours. They like meetings to be over early. The men mostly name eight o'clock as the time of beginning, but business very often will not start much before nine. Then, too, the men feel that they have come together to talk, and talk they do while they allow the real business to drag. Of course, the girls are not interested in long discussions on matters they do not understand and in which they have no part and naturally they stay away, and so make matters worse, for the men feel they are doing their best for the interests of the union, resent the women's indifference, and are more sure than ever that women do not make good unionists.

Among the remedies proposed for this unsatisfactory state of affairs is compulsory attendance at a certain number of meetings per year under penalty of a fine or even losing of the card. (A very drastic measure this last and risky, unless the trade has the closed shop.)

Where the conditions of the trade permit it by far the best plan is to have the women organized in separate locals. The meetings of women and girls only draw better attendances, give far more opportunity for all the members to take part in the business, and beyond all question form the finest training ground for the women leaders who in considerable numbers are needed so badly in the woman's side of the trade-union movement today.

Those trade-union women who advocate mixed locals for every trade which embraces both men and women are of two types. Some are mature, perhaps elderly women, who have been trade unionists all their lives, who have grown up in the same locals with men, who have in the long years passed through and left behind their period of probation and training, and to whose presence and active coöperation the men have become accustomed. These women are able to express their views in public, can put or discuss a motion or take the chair as readily as their brothers. The other type is represented by those individual women or girls in whom exceptional ability takes the place of experience, and who appreciate the educational advantages of working along with experienced trade-union leaders. I have in my mind at this moment one girl over whose face comes all the rapture of the keen student as she explains how much she has learnt from working with men in their meetings. She ardently advocates mixed locals for all. For the born captain the plea is sound. Always she is quick enough to profit by the men's experience, by their ways of managing conferences and balancing advantages and losses in presenting a wage-scale or accepting an agreement. At the same time she is not so overwhelmed by their superiority, born of long practice in handling such situations, but that she retains her own independence of judgment and clearness of vision, and at the fitting moment will rise and place the woman's point of view before her male co-workers. Oh yes, for herself she is right, and for the coming woman she is right, too. But the risk is rather that she and such as she pressing on in their individual advancement will outstep the rank and file of their sisters at the present stage while trade unionism among women is still so young a movement, and one which under the most hopeful circumstances will have to fulfill for many years the task of receiving, teaching and assimilating vast numbers of young and quite untrained, in many cases non-English-speaking girls.

The mixed local for all mixed trades is, I believe, the ultimate goal which women trade unionists ought to keep in mind. But with the average girl today the plan does not work. The mixed local does not, as a general rule, offer the best training-class for new girl recruits, in which they may obtain their training in collective bargaining or coöperative effort. To begin with, they are often so absurdly young that they stand in the position of children put into a class at school two or three grades ahead of their capacity and expected to do work for which they have had no preparation through the earlier grades. Many of the discussions that go on are quite above the girls' heads. And even when a young girl has something to say and wishes to say it, want of practice and timidity often keep her silent. It is to be regretted, too, that some trade-union men are far from realizing either the girls' needs in their daily work or their difficulties in meetings, and lecture, reprove or bully, where they ought to listen and persuade.

The girls, as a rule, are not only happier in their own women's local, but they have the interest of running the meetings themselves. They choose their own hall and fix their own time of meeting. Their officers are of their own selecting and taken from among themselves. The rank and file, too, get the splendid training that is conferred when persons actually and not merely nominally work together for a common end. Their introduction to the great problems of labor is through their practical understanding and handling of those problems as they encounter them in the everyday difficulties of the shop and the factory and as dealt with when they come up before the union meeting or have to be settled in bargaining with an employer.

But there are other and broader reasons still why it is women who should in the main be the leaders and teachers of women in the trade union, that newest and best school for the working-women. Women have always been the teachers of the race. It was in the far-back ages with motherhood as their normal school that primitive women learnt their profession and handed on to their daughters their slowly acquired skill. Whenever woman has been left to self-development on her own lines her achievements have always been in the constructive direction. Always she has been busy helping to make some young thing grow, whether the object of her solicitous attention were a wild grass, a baby, or an art. What does education mean but the drawing forth of latent qualities? Is not the best teacher the one who calls these forth? Are not women teachers, trained, wise, and patient, urgently needed in the labor movement of our day? Just now, when the number of young girls in industry is so great, the girls need them, we know. Possibly the men also would be the gainers through their influence. The labor movement is a constant fight, it is true, but it is also a school of development. In the near future we hope it will mean to all workers even more than a discipline, a storehouse of culture, a provider of joy and of pleasure, of care in sickness, of support in adversity, and best of all, a preparation for and a hastener on of that coöperative commonwealth for which more and more of us ever watch and pray.

The need for the woman organizer admitted, the demand for women organizers becomes pressing. And where are they to be found? The reply is that they are not to be found, not yet. If the organizers were to be obtained such requests would be increased fourfold. But the material is ready to hand. The born organizer, with initiative, resource, courage and patience exists in every trade, in every city, and she comes of every race. But on the one hand she is untrained, and on the other cannot stop to receive training unless for a little while she is relieved from the pressing necessity of earning her living.

The problem of how to provide women organizers in response to the demand for such workers, with its solution, was admirably put by Mrs. Raymond Robins, in her presidential address before the Fourth Biennial Convention of the National Women's Trade Union League in St. Louis, in June, 1913, when she said:

The best organizers without question are the trade-union girls. Many a girl capable of leadership and service is held within the ranks because neither she as an individual nor her organization has money enough to set her free for service. Will it be possible for the National Women's Trade Union League to establish a training-school for women organizers, even though in the beginning it may be only a training-class, offering every trade-union girl a scholarship for a year?

The course finally outlined included a knowledge of the principles of trade unionism, and their practical application in field-work, a knowledge of labor legislation, of parliamentary law, and practice in writing and speaking.

In the following year, 1914, the League was able to give several months of training to three trade-union girls. Cordial coöperation was received from both the University of Chicago and Northwestern University. For the present no further students have been received, because of the need of larger financial resources to maintain classes in session regularly.

The need for a training-school is attested by the constant demands for women organizers received at the headquarters of the League from central labor bodies and men's unions, and by the example of the thorough training given to young women taking up work in other fields somewhat analogous. Such a school for women might very well prove in this country the nucleus of university extension work in the labor movement for both men and women, similar to that which has been so successfully inaugurated in Great Britain, and which is making headway in Canada and in Australia.

At the Seattle Convention of the American Federation of Labor held in November, 1914, a resolution was passed levying an assessment of one cent upon the entire membership to organize women. Efforts were mainly concentrated upon workers in the textile industry, to which special organizers, both men and women, were assigned. There is no trade which has worse conditions, and consequently wages and regularity of employment are immediately affected adversely by any industrial depression.

Women in the labor movement will have to make their own mistakes and earn their own experience. I have dwelt elsewhere upon the many advantages that accrue to women and girls from belonging to an organization so vital and so bound up with some of our most fundamental needs, as the trade union. On the very surface it is evident that in such a body working-women learn to be more business-like, to work together in harmony, to share loyally the results of their united action, whether these spell defeat or success. If they err, they promptly learn of their mistakes from their fellow-workers, men or women, from employers, and from their families.

Here, however, is perhaps the place to call attention to one markedly feminine tendency, which should be discouraged in these early days lest in process of time it might even gain the standing of a virtue, and that is the inclination among the leaders to indulge in unlimited overwork in all their labor activities. Labor men overwork too, but not, as a rule, to the same degree, nor nearly so frequently as women.

Do not mistake. Women do not fall into this error because they are trade unionists, or because they are inspired by the labor movement or by the splendid ideals or by the aspiration after a free womanhood.

No! Trade-union and socialist and suffrage women overwork because they are women, because through long ages the altruistic side has been overdeveloped. They have brought along with them into their public work the habit of self-sacrifice, and that overconscientiousness in detail which their foremothers acquired during the countless generations when obedience, self-immolation and self-obliteration were considered women's chief duties. Personally these good sisters are blameless. But that does not in the least alter the hard fact that such overdevotion is an uneconomical expenditure of nervous energy.

When a wiser onlooker, wise with the onlooker's

wisdom, urges moderation even in overwork, there is put forward the pathetic plea, variously worded:

"So much to do, so little time to do it."

I have never heard that hard-to-be-met argument so well answered as by a woman physician, who gave these reasons to her patient, one of the overdevoted ilk.

"Agreed," she said, "there is so much to do that you cannot possibly do it all, nor the half, nor the tenth, nor the fiftieth part of it. Furthermore, the struggle is going on for a long, long time, and there are occasions ahead when your aid will be needed as badly or more badly than today. And when that hour comes, if you do not take care of yourself now, you will not be there to furnish the help others require. Not that I think you are dangerously ill, but I'm reminding you that, at the rate you are going, your working years, the years during which your energy and your initiative will last, are going to be few, so pull up and go slow!

"You are a leader, and you are so, partly at least, because you are a highly trained person. It has taken many years to train you up to this pitch of efficiency. You can handle agreements, at a pinch you can draft a bill. You are a favorite and influential speaker. You are invaluable in a strike, and you have often prevented strikes. We all want you to go on doing all these things. Now, tell me, which is the most valuable to the whole labor movement, a few years of your activity, or many years?"

That puts the matter in a nutshell.

I do not wish to overlook the fact that there are exceptional occasions when overwork to the extent of breakdown or even death is justified, or to have it supposed that I think mere life our most valuable possession, or that there may not be many a time when truly to save your life is to lose it. But I repeat that habitual, everyday overwork, is uneconomical, injurious to the cause we serve, and likely to lessen rather than heighten the efficiency of the indispensable leaders when the supreme test comes.

VIII

THE TRADE UNION IN OTHER FIELDS

When we begin to survey the vast field of industry covered by different occupations we get the same sense of confusion that comes to us when we look at an ant-heap. The workers are going hither and thither, with apparently no ordered plan, with no unity or community of purpose that we can discover. But those who have given time and patience to the task have been able to read order even in the chaos of the ant-hill. And so may we, with our far more complex human ant-hill, if we will set to work. The material for such a study lies ready to our hand in bewildering abundance; but to make any practical studies which shall aid the workers and the thinking public to follow the line of least resistance in raising standards of wages and of status as well will be the work of many years and of many minds. Even today there are some general indications of how the workers are going to settle their own problems.

Some foreign critics and some critics at home are very severe upon the backwardness of the labor movement in the United States, and in these criticisms there is a large element of truth. Yet there is one difficulty under which we labor on this continent, which these critics do not take into consideration. That is the primal one of the immense size of the country, along with all the secondary difficulties involved in this first one. There has never been any other country even attempting a task so stupendous as ours—to organize, to make one, to obtain good conditions for today, to insure as good and better conditions for tomorrow, for the wage-earning ones out of a population of over ninety millions spread over three million square miles. And with these millions of human beings of so many different races, with no common history and often no common language, this particular task has fallen to the lot of no other nation on the face of this earth. Efforts at organization of the people and by the people, are perpetually being undermined. Capitalism is nationally fairly well organized, so that there has been all the time more and more agreement among the great lords of finance, not to trespass on one another's preserves. But it is not so with the workers. Even in trades where there exists a formal national organization, there will be towns and states where it will either be non-existent or extremely weak, so that workers, especially the unskilled, as they drift from town to town in search of work, tend to pass out of, rather than into, the union of their trade. And thus members of every trade organization live in dread of the inroad into their city or their state of crowds of unorganized competitors for their particular kind of employment. Why, if it were Great Britain or Germany, by the time we had organized one state, we should have organized a whole country.

But the big country is ours, and the big task must be shouldered.

It is only natural that trade-union organization should have progressed furthest in those occupations which, as industries, are the most highly developed. The handicrafts of old, the weaving and the carving and the pottery, have through a thousand inventions become specialized, and the work of the single operative has been divided up into a hundred processes. These are the conditions, and this the environment under which the workers most frequently organize. The operations have become more or less defined and standardized, and the operatives are more readily grouped and classified. Also, even amid all the noise and clatter of the factory, they have opportunity for becoming acquainted, sometimes while working together, or at the noon hour, or when going to or coming from work. There are still few enough women engaged in factory work who have come into trade unions, but the path has at least been cleared, both by the numbers of men who have shown the way, and by the increasing independence of women themselves. Similar reasoning applies to the workers in the culinary trades. These also are the modern, specialized forms of the old domestic arts of cooking and otherwise preparing and serving food. The workers, the cooks and the waitresses, have their separate, allotted tasks; they also have opportunities of even closer association than the factory operatives. These opportunities, which may be used among the young folks to exchange views on the latest nickel show, to compare the last boss with the present one, may also, among the older ones, mean talking over better wages and hours and how to get them, and here may spring up the beginnings of organization.

The number of women organized into trade unions is still insignificant, compared with those unreached by even a glimmering of knowledge as to what trade unionism means. The movement will not only have to become stronger numerically in the trades it already includes. It must extend in other directions, taking in the huge army of the unskilled and the semi-skilled, outside of those trades, so as to cover the fruit-pickers in the fields and the packers in the canneries, the paper-box-makers, the sorters of nuts and the knotters of feathers, those who pick the cotton from the plant, as well as those who make the cotten into cloth. Another group yet to be enrolled are the hundreds of thousands of girls in stores, engaged in selling what the girls in factories have made, and still other large groups of girls in mercantile offices who are indirectly helping on the same business of exchange of goods for cash, and cash for goods, and who are just as truly part of the industrial world and of commercial life. But the pity is that the girl serving at the counter and the girl operating the typewriter do not know this.

Take two other great classes of women, who have to be considered and reckoned with in any wide view of the wage-earning woman. These are nurses and teachers. The product of their toil is nothing that can be seen or handled, nothing that can be readily estimated in dollars and cents. But it must none the less be counted to their credit in any estimate of the national wealth, for it is to be read in terms of sound bodies and alert minds.

Large numbers of women and girls are musicians, actresses and other theatrical employés. The labor movement needs them all, and, although few of them realize it, they need the labor movement. These are professions with great prizes, but the average worker makes no big wage, has no assurance of steadiness of employment, of sick pay when out of work, or of such freedom while working as shall bring out the very best that is in her.

In almost all of these occupations are to be found the beginnings of organization on trade-union lines. The American Federation of Musicians is a large and powerful body, of such standing in the profession that the entire membership of the Symphony Orchestras in all the large cities of the United States and Canada (with the single exception of the Boston Symphony Orchestra) belongs to it. Women, so far, although admitted to the Federation, have had no prominent part in its activities.

Nurses and attendants in several of the state institutions of Illinois have during the last two years formed unions. Already they have had hours shortened from the old irregular schedule of twelve, fourteen and even sixteen hours a day to an eight-hour workday for all, as far as practicable. The State Board is also entirely favorable to concede higher wages, one day off in seven, and an annual vacation of two weeks on pay, but cannot carry these recommendations out without an increased appropriation from the legislature.

There are now eight small associations of stenographers and bookkeepers and other office employés, one as far west as San Francisco, while there is at least one court reporters' union.

The various federations of school-teachers have worked to raise school and teaching standards as well as their own financial position. They have besides, owing to the preponderance of women in the teaching profession, made a strong point of the justice of equal pay for equal work. Women teachers are perhaps in a better position to make this fight for all their sex than any other women.

The fact that so many bodies of teachers have one after another affiliated with the labor movement has had a secondary result in bringing home to teachers the needs of the children, the disadvantages under which so many of them grow up, and still more the handicap under which most children enter industry. So it has come about that the teaching body in several cities has been roused to plead the cause of the workers' children, and therefore of the workers, and has brought much practical knowledge and first-hand information before health departments, educational authorities, and legislators.

Yet another angle from which the organization of teachers has to be considered is that they are actually, if not always technically, public employes. Every objection that can be raised against the organization of public employés, if valid at all, is valid here. Every reason that can be urged why public employés should be able to give collective expression to their ideas and their wishes has force here.

The domestic servant, as we know her, is but a survival in culture from an earlier time, and more primitive environment. As a personal attendant, with no limitation of hours, without defined and standardized duties, and taking out part of her wages in the form of board and lodging, also at no standardized valuation, she will have to be improved out of existence altogether.

On the other hand as a skilled worker, she fills an important function in the community, satisfying permanent human needs, preparing food to support our bodies, and making clean and beautiful the homes wherein we dwell. Surely humanity is not so stupid that arrangements cannot be planned by which domestic workers can have their own homes, like other people, hours of leisure, like other workers, and organizations through which they may express themselves. The main difficulty in the immediate future is that the very reason why organization is so urgently needed by domestic workers is the reason why it is so difficult to form organizations, the individual isolation in which the girls live and work. The desire for common action assuredly is there; one little group after another are meeting and talking over their difficulties, and planning how they can overcome them. The obstacles in the way of forming unions of domestic workers are tremendous. What such groups need, above all, is a union headquarters, with comfortable and convenient rooms, in which girls could meet their friends during their times off, or in which they could just rest, if they wanted to, for many have no friend's house to go to during their precious free days. Such a headquarters should conduct an employment agency. Other activities would probably grow out of such a center, and the workers coöperating would help towards the solving of that domestic problem which is their concern even more intimately than it is that of those whom, as things are, they so unwillingly serve. That the finest type of women are already awake, and nearing the stage when they themselves recognize the need of organization, is evident from the fact that in Chicago, Buffalo and Seattle, there lately sprang up almost simultaneously, small associations of household workers formed to secure regular hours and better living conditions.

There is no class of women or girls more urgently in need of a radical change in their economic condition than department-store clerks. To this need even the public has of late become somewhat awakened, thanks mainly to a troop of investigators and to the writers in the magazines, who on the one hand have roused nation-wide horror by means of revelations regarding the white-slave traffic, and on the other have brought to that same national audience painful enlightenment as to the chronic starvation of both soul and body endured by so many brave and patient young creatures, who on four, five or six dollars a week just manage to exist, but who in so doing, are cheated of all that makes life worth living in the present, and are disinherited of any prospect of home, health and happiness in the future.

This story has been told again and again. Yet the public has not yet learned to relate it to any effectual remedy. Undoubtedly organization has done a great deal for this class in other countries, notably in England and in Germany, and in this country also, in the few cities where it has been brought about. But meanwhile their numbers are increasing, and it hardly seems human for us to wait while all these young lives are being ruined in the hope that a few years hence the department-store clerks succeeding them may be able to save themselves through organization, when there is another remedy at hand. That remedy is legislation to cover thoroughly hours, wages and conditions of work. No one suggests depending exclusively on laws. One reason, probably, why the freeing of the negro slave has been so often merely a nominal freeing is because he was able to play so small a part himself in the gaining of his freedom. It was a gift, truly, from the master race. But no one, surely, would use that argument in reference to children, and an immense proportion of the department-store employés are but children, children between fourteen and eighteen, and in some states much younger. One hears of occasional instances in which even children have banded together and gone on strike. School-children have done it. The little button-sewers of Muscatine, Iowa, formed a juvenile union during the long strike of 1911. But these are such exceptional instances that they can hardly count in normal times. And that such a large body of children and very young girls are included among department-store employés adds immensely to the difficulty of gaining over the grown-up women to organization.

Perhaps at some future time children may mature mentally earlier. If along with this, education is more efficient, and the civic duty of a common responsibility for the good of all is taught universally in our schools, even the child at fourteen may become class-conscious, and willing to fight and struggle for a common aim. But if that day ever comes, it will be in the far future, and let us hope that then childish energies may be free to find other channels of expression and childish coöperation

A Bindery

Hand folders on platform. Machine folder and hand gatherers below

Interior of one of the Largest and Best Equipped Waist and
Cloak Factories in New York City

be exerted for happier aims. The child of today is often temporarily willful and disobedient, but on the whole he (and more often she) is pathetically patient and long-suffering under all sorts of hardships and injustices, and has no idea of anything like an industrial rebellion. Indeed overwork and ill-usage have upon children the markedly demoralizing effect of cowing them permanently, so that in oppressing a child you do more than deprive him of his childhood, you weaken what ought to be the backbone of his maturity. But improve conditions, whether by law or otherwise, and you will have a more independent "spunky" child, a better prospect of having him, when grown up, a more wholesomely natural rebel. Indeed more or less, this applies to human beings of any age.

As regards the minimum wage, the objection raised by certain among the conservative labor leaders has been that it will retard organization and check independence of spirit. This reasoning seems quite academic, in view of the fact that it is the most oppressed workers who are usually the least able and willing to assert themselves. Give them shorter hours or better wages, and they will soon be pleading for still shorter hours and yet higher wages. Wherever the regulation of wages, through that most democratic method, that of wages boards composed of representatives of workers and employers, has been attempted, organization has been encouraged, and this plan of legalized collective bargaining has been applied to trade after trade. In Victoria, Australia, the birthplace of the system, and the state where it has been longest in force, and more fully developed than anywhere else, the number of trades covered has grown in less than twenty years from the four experimental trades of shoemaking, baking, various departments of the clothing trades and furniture-making to 141 occupations, including such varied employments as engravers, plumbers, miners and clerical workers.

It is hardly necessary to say that minimum wages boards in Australia control the wages of men as well as of women. This question, however, does not enter into practical labor statesmanship in the United States today, but the minimum wage for women is a very live issue, and its introduction in state after state is supported by the working-women, both speaking as individuals and through their organizations.

The objections of employers to any regulation of wages is partly economic, as they fear injury to trade, a fear not sustained by Australian experience, or by the experience of employers in trades in this country, in which wages have been raised and are largely controlled by strong labor organizations. In especial, employers object to an unequal burden imposed upon the state or states first experimenting with wages boards. This has no more validity than a similar objection raised against any and all interference between employer and employé, whether it be limitation of hours, workmen's compensation acts or any other industrial legislation. It is only that another adjustment has to be made, one of the many that any trade and any employer has always to be making to suit slightly changing circumstances. And often the adjustment is much less, and the advantage to the employer arising from having more efficient and contented employés greater than anticipated. Competition is then not for the cheapest worker, but for the most efficient.

Public responsibility for social and economic justice is likely to be quickened and maintained by the very existence of these permanent boards created not so much to remedy acute evils as to establish in the industry conditions more nearly equitable.

It has ever been found that in regard to ordinary factory legislation, organized employés were the best inspectors to see that the law was enforced. This principle holds good in even a more marked degree, where the representatives of the workers have themselves a say in the decision, as is the case during the long sessions of a wages board, where all who take part in the discussions and in the final agreement are experts in the trade, and intimately acquainted with the practical details of the industry.

The very same misgivings as are felt and expressed by employers and by the public regarding the effect of legislation for the regulation of wages have been heard on every occasion when any legal check has been proposed upon the downward pressure upon the worker, inevitable under our system of competition for trade and markets. What a cry went up from the manufacturers of Great Britain when a bill to check the ruthless exploitation of babies in the cotton mills was introduced into the House of Commons. The very same arguments of interference with trade, despotic control over the right of the employé to bargain as an individual, are urged today, no matter how often their futility and irrelevance have been exposed.

The question of organization and the white alien has been dealt with in another chapter, but organization cannot afford to stop even here. It will never accomplish all that trade unionists desire and what the workers need until those of every color, the Negro, the Indian, the Chinese, the Japanese, the Hindoo are included. The southern states are very imperfectly organized, and trade unionism on any broad scale will never be achieved there until the colored workers are included. In this the white workers, neither in the North nor in the South, have yet recognized their plain duty. It is not the American Federation itself which is directly responsible, but the national and local unions in the various trades, who place difficulties in the way of admitting colored members. "Ordinarily," writes Dr. F. E. Wolfe in his "Admission to Labor Unions," published by the Johns Hopkins University Press, "the unimpeded admission of Negroes can be had only where the local white unionists are favorable. Consequently, racial antipathy and economic motive may, in any particular trade, nullify the policies of the national union." This applies even in those cases where the national union itself would raise no barrier. I think it may be safely added that there are practically no colored women trade unionists, the occasional exception but serving to emphasize our utter neglect, as regards organization, of the colored woman.

Yet another world waiting to be conquered is the Dominion of Canada, Canada with its vast area and its still small population, yet with its cities, from Montreal to Vancouver, facing the very same industrial problems as American cities, from New York to San Francisco. The organization of women is, so far, hardly touched in any of the provinces.

One encouraging circumstance, and significant of the intimate connection between the two halves of North America, is the fact that the international union of each trade includes those dwelling both in the United States and in Canada; these internationals are in their turn, for the most part affiliated with both the American Federation of Labor and the Trades and Labor Congress of Canada.

Whenever, then, the women of Canada seriously begin to unionize, advance will be made through these existing international organizations. As mentioned elsewhere, the Canadian Trades and Labor Congress of Canada has endorsed the work of the National Women's Trade

Union League of America, and seats a fraternal delegate from the League at its conventions.

It can only be a question of time, and of increasing industrial pressure, when an active trade-union movement will spring up among Canadian women. Among those who advocate and are prepared to lead in such a movement are the President of the Trades and Labor Congress, Mr. J. C. Watters, Mr. James Simpson of the Toronto *Industrial Banner,* Mrs. Rose Henderson of Montreal, Mr. J. W. Wilkinson, President of the Vancouver Trades and Labor Council, and Miss Helena Gutteridge, also of Vancouver.

The President of the National Women's Trade Union League, in her opening address before the New York convention in June, 1915, summed up the situation as to the sweated trades tellingly:

For tens of thousands of girl and women workers the average wage in sweated industries still is five, eight and ten cents an hour, and these earnings represent, on the average, forty weeks' work out of a fifty-two week year. Further, in the report of the New York State Factory Investigation Commission we find that out of a total of 104,000 men and women 13,000 receive less than $5.00 a week, 34,000 less than $7.00 a week, 68,000 less than $10.00 a week and only 17,000 receive $15.00 a week or more. These low wages are not only paid to apprentices either in factories or stores but to large numbers of women who have been continuously in industry for years. Again, the New York State Factory Investigating Commission tells us that half of those who have five years' experience in stores are receiving less than $8.00 a week, and only half of those with ten years' experience receive $10.00 a week. Dr. Howard Woolston of the Commission has pointed out: "Even for identical work in the same locality, striking differences in pay are found. In one wholesale candy factory in Manhattan no male laborer and no female hand-dipper is paid as much as $8 a week, nor does any female packer receive as much as $5.50. In another establishment of the same class in the same borough every male laborer gets $8 or over, and more than half the female dippers and packers exceed the rates given in the former plant. Again, one large department store in Manhattan pays 86 per cent. of its saleswomen $10 or over, another pays 86 per cent of them less. When a representative paper-box manufacturer learned that cutters in neighboring factories receive as little as $10 a week, he expressed surprise, because he always pays $15 or more. This indicates that there is no well-established standard at wages in certain trades. The amounts are fixed by individual bargain, and labor is 'worth' as much as the employer agrees to pay."

It has been estimated by the Commission that to raise the wages of two thousand girls in the candy factories from $5.75 to $8.00 a week, the confectioners in order to cover the cost will have to charge eighteen cents more per hundred pounds of candy. It is also estimated that if work shirts cost $3.00 a dozen, and the workers receive sixty cents for sewing them we can raise the wages ten per cent and make the labor cost sixty-six cents. The price of those dozen shirts has been raised to $3.06. The cost of labor in the sweated industries is a small fraction of the manufacturing cost.

In the face of such evidence is there anyone who can still question that individual bargaining is a menace against the social order and that education and equipment in organization and citizenship become a social necessity?

Women unionists, like men in the labor movement, are continually asked to support investigations into industrial conditions, investigations and yet more investigations. They are asked to give evidence before boards and commissions, they are asked to furnish journalists and writers of books with information. They have done so willingly, but there is a sense coming over many of us that we have had investigations a-plenty; and that the hour struck some time ago for at least beginning to put an end to the conditions of needless poverty and inexcusable oppression, which time after time have been unearthed.

No one who heard Mrs. Florence Kelley at the Charities and Corrections Conference in St. Louis in 1910 can forget the powerful plea she made to social workers that they should not be satisfied with investigation. Not an investigation has ever been made but has told the same story, monotonous in its lesson, only varying in details; workers, and especially women workers, are inadequately paid. Further she considers that investigations would be even more thorough and drastic if the investigators, the workers and the public knew that something would come out of the inquiry beyond words, words, words.

Investigation alone never remedied any evil, never righted any injustice. Yet as far as the community are concerned, average men and women seem quite content when the investigation has been made, and stop there. What is wrong? Will no real improvement take place till the workers are strong enough individually and collectively to manage their own affairs, and through organization, coöperation, and political action, or its equivalent insure adequate remuneration, and prevent overwork, speeding up, and dangerous and insanitary conditions?

In a degree investigation has prepared the way for legislation. Legislation will undoubtedly play even a bigger part than it has done in the protection of the workers. Almost all laws for which organized labor generally works affect women as well as men, whether they are anti-injunction statutes, or workmen's compensation acts, or factory laws. But there is another class of laws, specially favoring women, about which women have naturally more decided opinions than men. These are laws as to hours, and more recently as to wages, which are or are to be applicable to women alone. A just and common-sense argument extends special legislative protection to women, because of their generally exploited and handicapped position; but the one strong plea used in their behalf has been health and safety, the health and safety of the future mothers of society. At this point we pause. In all probability such protection will be found so beneficial to women that it will be eventually extended to men.

One group of laws in which labor is vitally interested is laws touching the right of the workers to organize. Many of the most important judicial decisions in labor cases have turned upon this point. In this are involved the right to fold arms, and peacefully to suggest to others to do the same; the right to band together not to buy non-union goods, and peacefully to persuade others not to buy.

One angle from which labor views all law-making is that of administration. A law may be beneficial. It is in danger on two sides. The first the risk of being declared unconstitutional, a common fate for the most advanced legislation in this country; or, safe on that side, it may be so carelessly or inefficiently administered as to be almost useless. In both cases, strong unions have a great influence in deciding the fate and the practical usefulness of laws.

Whether in the making, the confirming, or the administering of laws, the trade unions form the most important channel through which the wishes of the workers can be expressed. Organized labor does not speak only for trade unionists; it necessarily, in almost every case, speaks for the unorganized as well, partly because the needs of both are usually the same, and partly because there is no possible method by which the wishes of the working people can be ascertained, save through the accepted representatives of the organized portion of the workers.

An excellent illustration of how business can and does adjust itself to meet changing legal demands is seen in what happened when the Ten-Hour Law came in force in the state of Illinois in July, 1909.

The women clerks on the elevated railroads of Chicago, who had been in the habit of working twelve hours a day for seven days a week at $1.75 a day, were threatened with dismissal, and replacement by men. But what happened? At first they had to accept as a compromise a temporary arrangement under which they received eleven hours' pay for ten hours' work. Their places were not, however, filled by men, and now, they are receiving for their ten-hour day $1.90 or 15 cents more than they had previously been paid for a twelve-hour day, and in addition they now are given every third Sunday off duty. This showed the good results of the law, particularly when there was a strong organization behind the workers. Mercantile establishments came in under the amended Ten-hour Law two years later.

The new law was, on the whole, wonderfully well observed in Chicago, and as far as I have been able to learn, in the smaller towns as well. There were some violations discovered, and plenty more, doubtless, remained undiscovered. But the defaulting employers must have been very few compared with the great majority of those who met its requirement faithfully and intelligently. The proprietors and managers of the large Chicago department stores, for instance, worked out beforehand a plan of shifts by which they were able to handle the Christmas trade, satisfy their customers, and at the same time, dismiss each set of girls at the end of their ten-hour period. To meet the necessities of the case a staff of extra hands was engaged by each of the large department stores. This was a common arrangement. The regular girls worked from half-past eight till seven o'clock, with time off for lunch. The extra hands came on in the forenoon at eleven o'clock and worked till ten in the evening, with supper-time off. Certain of the stores varied the plan somewhat, by giving two hours for lunch. These long recesses are not without their disadvantages. They mean still a very long day on the stretch, and besides, where is a girl to spend the two hours? She cannot go home, and it is against the law for her to be in the store, for in the eye of the law, if she remains on the premises, she is presumably at work, and if at work, therefore being kept longer than the legal ten hours.

That a law which had been so vigorously opposed should on the whole have been observed so faithfully in the second largest city in the United States, that it should in that city have stood the test, at its very initiation, of the rush season, is a fact full of hope and encouragement for all who are endeavoring to have our laws keep pace with ideals of common justice.

Some time afterwards the constitutionality of the law was tested in the courts. Since then, complaints have died away. There is no record of trading establishments having been compelled to remove to another state, and we no longer even hear of its being a ruinous handicap to resident manufacturers. Even reactionary employers are now chiefly concerned in putting off the impending evil, as they regard it, of an eight-hour day, which they know cannot be very far off, as it has already arrived on the Pacific Coast.

If the acquiescence of Illinois employers was satisfactory, the effect upon the girls was remarkable and exceeded expectations. During that Christmas week, the clerks were tired, of course, but they were not in the state of exhaustion, collapse, and physical and nervous depletion, which they had experienced in previous years. This bodily salvation had been expected. It was what organized women had pleaded for and bargained for, what the defending lawyers, Mr. Louis D. Brandeis and Mr. William J. Calhoun had urged upon the judges, when the Supreme Court of Illinois had been earlier called upon to pass upon the validity of the original ten-hour law, although department-store employés had not been included within the scope of its protection.

But the girls were more than not merely worn-out to the point of exhaustion. Most of them were more alive than they had ever been since first they started clerking. They were happy, and surprised beyond measure at their own good fortune. Those juniors who could just remember how different last Christmas had been, those seniors whose memories held such searing recollections of many preceding Christmases, were one in their rejoicing and wonderment. They caught a dim vision of a common interest. Here was something which all could share. That one was benefited did not mean another's loss.

From girl after girl I heard the same story. I would ask them how they were getting on through the hard time this year. "Oh," a girl would answer, "it wasn't so bad at all. You see we've got the ten-hour law, and we can't work after the time is up. It's just wonderful. Why, I'm going to enjoy Christmas this year. I'm tired, but nothing like I've always been before. Last Christmas Day I couldn't get out of bed, I ached so, and I couldn't eat, either."

And yet, while the girls, thanks to the new law, were having something like decent, though by no means ideal hours of work, the young elevator boys, in the same store were working fourteen hours and a half, day in, day out.

So imperfect yet are the results of much that is accomplished!

There are now two states, Mississippi and Oregon, which have ten-hour laws, applying to both men and women, and including the larger proportion of the workers. There are also federal statutes, state laws and municipal ordinances limiting the hours and granting the eight-hour day to whole groups of workers, either in public or semi-public employ, or affecting special occupations such as mining. Thus it is clear, that for both sexes there is now abundant legal precedent for any shortening of hours, which has its place in a more advanced social and industrial development.

IX

WOMEN AND THE VOCATIONS

The profound impression that has been left upon contemporary thought by the teaching of Lester Ward and those who have followed him, that woman is the race, has been felt far and wide outside the sphere of those branches of science, whose students he first startled with the thought. His idea is indeed revolutionary as far as our immediate past and our present social arrangements and sex relations are concerned, but is natural, harmonious and self-explanatory if we regard life, the life of our own day, not as standing still, but as in a state of incessant flux and development, and if we are at all concerned to discover the direction whither these changes are driving us. It indeed may well have been that the formal enunciation of the primary importance of woman in the social organism has played its own part in accelerating her rise into her destined lofty position, though in the main, any philosophy can be merely the explanation and the record of an evolution wherein we are little but passive factors.

This much is certain, that the insistent driving home by this school of thinkers of woman, woman, woman, as the center and nucleus whence is developed the child and the home, and all that civilization stands for, and whose rights as an independent human being are therefore to be held of supreme importance in the normal evolution of the race, has served as an incessant reminder to practical workers and reformers in the sphere of education as well as to leaders of the woman movement. Especially has this been true when tackling the problems more immediately affecting women, because these are the truly difficult problems. Whatever touches man's side of life alone is comparatively simple and easily understood, and therefore easier of solution. So in the rough and ready, often cruel, solutions which nature and humanity have worked out for social problems, it has always been the man whose livelihood, whose education and whose training have been first considered, and whose claims have been first satisfied. For this there are several reasons. Man's possession of material wealth, and his consequent monopoly of social and political power have naturally resulted in his attending to his own interests first. The argument, too, that man was the breadwinner and the protector of the home against all outside antagonistic influences, which in the past he has generally been, furnished another reason why, when any class attained to fresh social privileges, it was the boy and the man of that class, rather than the woman and the girl, who benefited by them first. The woman and the girl would come in a poor second, if indeed they were in at the dividing of the spoils at all.

There is, however, another reason, and one of profound significance, which I believe has hardly been touched upon at all, why woman has been thus constantly relegated to the inferior position. Her problems are, as I said above, far more difficult of settlement. Because of her double function as a member of her own generation and as the potential mother of the next generation, it is impossible to regard her life as something simple and single, and think out plans for its arrangement, as we do with man's. So in large measure we have only been following the line of least resistance, in taking up men's difficulties first. We have done so quite naturally, because they are not so overwhelmingly hard to deal with, and have attacked woman's problems, and striven to satisfy her needs, only when we could find time to get round to them. This is most strikingly exemplified in the realm of education. Take the United States alone. It was ever to the boy that increasing educational advantages were first offered.

In the year 1639 the authorities of the town of Dorchester, Massachusetts, hesitated as to whether girls should be admitted to the apparently just established school. The decision was left "to the discretion of the elders and seven men." The girls lost. In "Child Life in Colonial Days" Mrs. Annie Grant is quoted. She spent her girlhood in Albany, N. Y., sometime during the first half of the eighteenth century. She says it was very difficult at that time to procure the means of instruction in those districts. The girls learned needlework from their mothers and aunts; they learnt to read the Bible and religious tracts in Dutch; few were taught writing. Similar accounts come from Virginia.

Was it university education that was in question, how many university-trained men had not American colleges turned out before Lucy Stone was able to obtain admission to Oberlin?

Harvard was opened in 1636. Two hundred years elapsed before there was any institution offering corresponding advantages to girls. Oberlin granted its first degree to a woman in 1838. Mount Holyoke was founded in 1837, Elmira in 1855 and Vassar in 1865.

That a perfectly honest element of confusion and puzzle did enter into the thought of parents and the views of the community, it would be vain to deny. These young women were incomprehensible. Why were they not content with the education their mothers had had, and with the lives their mothers had led before them?

Why did they want to leave comfortable homes, and face the unknown, the hard, perhaps the dangerous? How inexplicable, how undutiful! Ah! It was the young people who were seeing furthest into the future; it was the fathers and mothers who were not recognizing the change that was coming over the world of their day.

If then, for the combination of reasons outlined, women have always lagged in the rear as increasing educational advantages of a literary or professional character have been provided or procured for boys, it is not strange, when, in reading over the records of work on the new lines of industrial education, trade-training and apprenticeship we detect the very same influences at work, sigh before the same difficulties, and recognize the old weary, threadbare arguments, too, which one would surely think had been sufficiently disproved before to be at least distrusted in this connection. This, however, must surely be the very last stand of the non-progressivists in education as regards the worker. The ideals of today aim at education on lines that will enable every child, boy and girl alike, born in or brought into any civilized country, to develop all faculties, and that will simultaneously enable the community to benefit from this complete, all-round development of every one of its members.

There is one consideration to which I must call attention, because, when recognized, it cannot but serve as the utmost stimulus to our efforts to arrange for vocational education for girls on the broadest lines. It is this. Whatever general, national or state plans prove the most complete and satisfactory for girls, will, speaking generally, at the same time be found to have solved the problem for the boy as well. The double aim, of equipping the girl to be a mother as well as human being, is so all-inclusive and is therefore so much more difficult of accomplishment, that the simpler training necessary for a boy's career will be automatically provided for at the same time. Therefore the boy is not likely to be at a disadvantage under such a coeducational system as is here implied. For it is to nothing short of coeducation that the organized women of the United States are looking forward, coeducation on lines adapted to present-day wants. What further contributions the far-off future may hold for us in the never wholly to be explored realm of human education in its largest acceptance, we know not. Until we have learned the lesson of today, and have set about putting it in practice, such glimpses of the future are not vouchsafed to us.

In such an age of transition as ours, any plan of vocational training intended to include girls must be a compromise with warring facts, and will therefore have to face objections from both sides, from those forward-looking ones who feel that the domestic side of woman's activities is overemphasized, and from those who still hark back, who would fain refuse to believe that the majority of women have to be wage-earners for at least part of their lives. These latter argue that by affording to girls all the advantages of industrial training granted or which may be granted to boys, we are "taking them out of the home." As if they were not out of the home already!

This assumption will appear to most readers paradoxical, if indeed it does not read as a contradiction in terms. A little thought, however, will show that it is just because we are all along assuming the economic primacy of the boy, that the girl has been so disastrously neglected. It is true that the boy is also a potential father, and that his training for that lofty function is usually ignored and will have to be borne in mind, though no one would insist that training for fatherhood need occupy a parallel po-

sition with training for motherhood. But popular reasoning is not content with accepting this admission; it
goes on to draw the wholly unwarranted conclusion that
while the boy ought to be thoroughly taught on the wage-
earning side, and while such teaching should cover all the
more important occupations, to which he is likely to be
called, the girl's corresponding training shall as a matter
of course be quite a secondary matter, fitting her only for
a limited set of pursuits, many of these ranking low in
skill and opportunities of advancement, and necessarily
among the most poorly paid; these being all occupations
which we choose to assume girls will enter, such as sewing or box-making. Only recently have girls been prepared for the textile trades, though they have always
worked in these, first in the home and since then in the
factories. Still less is any preparation thought of for the
numberless occupations that necessity and a perpetually
changing world are all the while driving girls to take
up. There were in 1910, 8,075,772 women listed as
wage-earners in the United States. Would it not be as
well, if a girl is to be a wage-earner, that she should have
at least as much opportunity of learning her trade properly, as is granted to a boy?

Setting aside for the moment the fact that girls are already engaged in so many callings, it is poor policy and
worse economy to argue that because a girl may be but
a few years a wage-earner, it is therefore not worth
while to make of her an efficient, capable wage-earner.
That is fair to no one, neither to the girl herself nor to
the community. The girl deserves to be taken more seriously. Do this, and it will then be clear that a vocational
system wide enough and flexible enough to fit the girl to
be at once a capable mother-housekeeper, and a competent wage-earner, will be a system adequate to the vocational training of the boy for life-work in any of the

industrial pursuits. It is self-evident that the converse would not hold.

And first, to those readers of advanced views who will think that I am conceding even too much in thus consenting apparently to sink the human activities of the woman in those of the mother during the greater part of maturity. Touching the question of personal human development, I concede nothing, as I assert nothing, but I accept present-day facts, and desire to make such compromise with them as shall clear the way for whatever forms of home and industrial life shall evolve from them most naturally and simply. We may observe with satisfaction and hopefulness that the primitive collection of unrelated industries which have so long lingered in the home to the detriment of both and which have confused our thoughts as to which were the essential and permanent, and which the merely accidental and temporary functions of the home, are gradually coming within the range of the specialized trades, and as such are freeing the home from so much clutter and confusion, and freeing the woman from so many fettering bonds. But the process is a slow one, and again, it may not even go on indefinitely. There may be a limit in the process of specializing home industries. So far as it has gone, different classes of women are very unequally affected by it. In the United States, where these changes have gone on faster and further than anywhere else, the two classes whose occupations have been most radically modified have been, first and chiefly, the young girl from fourteen to twenty-four, of every class, and next the grown-up woman, who has taken up one of the professions now for the first time open to women, and this almost irrespective of whether she is married or single.

As to the young girl, the transformation of the home plus industries to the home, pure and simple, a place

to live in and rest in, to love in and be happy in, has
so far already been effected, that in the home of the
artisan and the tradesman there is not now usually sufficient genuine, profitable occupation for more than one
growing or grown girl as assistant to her mother. For
two reasons the other daughters will look out of doors
for employment. The first reason is that under re-
arranged conditions of industry, there is nothing left for
them to do at home. The second is not less typical of
these altered conditions. The father cannot, even if he
would, afford to keep them at home as non-producers.
If the processes of making garments and preparing food
are no longer performed by the members of the family
for one another, the outsiders who do perform them
must be remunerated, and that not in kind, as, for example, with board and lodging and clothing, but in money
wages, in coin. And their share of the money to enable
this complicated system of exchange of services to be
carried out, must be earned by the unmarried daughters of the house through their working in turn at some
wage-earning occupation, also outside.

The young woman who has entered medicine, or law,
or dentistry, who paints pictures or writes books, is on
very much the same economic basis as the young working-girl. She, too, is accepted as part of the already established order of things, and the present generation has
grown up in happy ignorance of the difficulties experienced by the pioneers in all these professions in establishing their right to independent careers. The professional
woman who has married finds herself so far on a less
secure foundation. Every professional woman who has
children has to work out for herself the problem of the
mutual adjustment of the claims of her profession and
her family, but so many have solved the difficulties and
have made the adjustment that it seems only a question

of time when every professional woman may accept the happiness of wifehood and motherhood when it is offered to her without feeling that she has to choose once for all between a happy marriage and a successful professional career.

Not a few professional women, writers, and speakers, have gone on to infer that a similar solution was at hand for the working-girl on her marriage. Not yet is any such adjustment or rather readjustment of domestic and industrial activities in sight for her. Whatever changes may take place in the environment of the coming American woman, the present generation of working-girls as they marry are going to find their hands abundantly filled with duties within the walls of their own little homes. We know today how the health and the moral welfare of children fare when young mothers are prematurely forced back into the hard and exhausting occupations from which marriage has withdrawn them.

Again, the factory conditions of modern industry have been brought to their present stage with one end in view—economy of time and material with the aim of cheapening the product. The life and the smooth running of the human machine, when considered at all, has been thought of last, and in this respect America is even one of the most backward of the civilized nations. Hence factory life is hard and disagreeable to the worker. Especially to the young girl is it often unendurable. A girl who has been some years in a factory rarely wants her young sister to come into it, too. She herself is apt to shift from one shop to another, from trade to trade, always in the hope that some other work may prove less exhausting and monotonous than that with which she is familiar by trying experience. Two forces tend to drive girls early out of industrial life: on the one hand, the perfectly normal instinct of self-protection in escaping from unnatural and health-ruining conditions and on the other the no less normal impulse leading to marriage. But oftener than we like to think, the first is the overmastering motive.

Let us now take up the objections of those far more numerous to whom the provision of trade-training for girls seems superfluous, when not harmful, and who especially shrink from the suggestion of coeducation. To satisfy them, let us marshal a few facts and figures.

Of every kind of education that has been proposed for girls, whether coeducational or not, we have always heard the same fears expressed. Such education would make the girl unwomanly, it would unfit her for her true functions, a man could not wish to marry her, and so on. The first women teachers and doctors had indeed a hard time. After being admitted to the profession only at the point of the sword, so to speak, they had to make good, and in face of all prejudice, prove their ability to teach or to cure, so as to keep the path open for those who were to follow after them. No similar demand should be logically made of the working-girl today when she demands coeducation on industrial lines. For she is already in the trades from which you propose so futilely to exclude her, by denying her access to the technical training preparatory to them, and for fitting her to practice them.

Take some other occupations which employ women in great numbers: textile mill operatives, saleswomen, tobacco-workers, cigar-workers, boot- and shoe-workers, printers, lithographers, and pressmen, and book-binders. You can hardly say that these are exceptions, for here are the figures, from the occupational statistics of the census of 1910.[1]

---

[1] The statement that appeared in the report on "Occupations" in the census returns of 1910, that there were but nine occupa-

Textile mill operatives	330,766
Saleswomen	250,438
Tobacco-workers and cigar-makers	71,334
Boot- and shoe-makers and repairers............	61,084
Printers, lithographers and pressmen	27,845
Book-binders	22,012

Just here we can see a rock ahead. In the very prospects that we rejoice over, of the early introduction of public industrial training, we can detect an added risk for the girl. If such technical instruction is established in one state after another, but planned primarily to suit the needs of boys only, and the only teaching afforded to girls is in the domestic arts, and in the use of the needle and the pastebrush for wage-earning, where will our girls be when a few years hence the skilled trades are full of her only too well-trained industrial rivals? In a greater degree than even today, the girl will find herself everywhere at a disadvantage for lack of the early training the state has denied to her, while bestowing it upon her brother, and the few industrial occupations for which instruction is provided will be overcrowded with applicants.

---

tions in which women were not employed, has been widely commented upon.

An explanation appearing in the corresponding volume of the census report for 1910 shows the great difficulties that enumerators and statisticians experience in getting at exact facts, wherever the situation is both complex and confused. The census officials admit their inability to do so in the present instance, although they have revised the figures with extreme care. With all possible allowance for error, women still appear in all but a minority of employments. The classification of occupations is on a different basis, and the number of divisions much larger; yet even now out of four hundred and twenty-nine separately listed, women are returned as engaged in all but forty-two. On the other hand there is only one trade which does not embrace men, that of the (untrained) midwife.

That women should take such an inferior position in the trades they are in today is regrettable enough. But far more important is it to make sure that they obtain their fair share of whatever improved facilities are provided for "the generation knocking at the door" of life. Working-women or women intimately acquainted with working-women's needs, should have seats on all commissions, boards and committees, so that when schemes of state industrial training are being planned, when schools are built, courses outlined, the interests of girls may be remembered, and especially so that they be borne in mind, when budgets are made up and appropriations asked for.

If not, it will only be one other instance of an added advantage to the man proving a positive disadvantage to the woman. You cannot benefit one class and leave another just as it was. Every boon given to the bettered class increases the disproportion and actually helps to push yet further down the one left out.

Among the many influences that make or mar the total content of life for any class, be that class a nation, a race, an industrial or economic group, there is one, the importance of which has been all too little realized. That influence we may call expectance. It is impossible for anyone to say how far a low standard of industrial or professional attainment held out before the girl at her most impressionable age, a standard that to some degree, therefore, develops within her, as it exists without her, ends in producing the very inefficiency it begins by assuming. But psychology has shown us that suggestion or expectance forms one element in the developing of faculty, and this whether it be manual dexterity, quickness of memory or exercise of judgment and initiative.

In all probability, too, this element of expectance has indirect as well as direct effects, and the indirect are not the least fruitful in results. To illustrate: it is certain that if we start out by assuming that girls are poor at accounts, that they cannot understand machinery, that they are so generally inefficient as to be worth less wages than boys, any such widespread assumption will go a long way to produce the ignorant and incompetent and inefficient creatures it presupposes girls to be. But it will do more than this. Such poor standards alike of performance and of wages will not end with the unfortunate girls themselves. They will react upon parents, teachers, and the community which so largely consists of the parents and which employs the teachers. Those preëssentials and antecedents of the competent worker, training, trainers, and the means and instruments of training, will not be forthcoming. What is the use of providing at great expense industrial training for girls, when the same money, spent upon boys, would produce more efficient workers? What is the use of giving girls such training, when they are presumably by nature unfitted to benefit by it?

X

WOMEN AND VOCATIONAL TRAINING

The United States started its national existence with an out-of-doors people. Until comparatively recent years, the cities were small, and the great bulk of the inhabitants lived from the natural resources of the country, that is to say, from the raw products of the mines and the forests, and the crops grown upon the plains by a most primitive and wasteful system of agriculture. But the days have forever gone when a living can be snatched, so to speak, from the land in any of these ways. The easily gotten stores of the mines and forests are exhausted; the soil over many millions of acres has been robbed of its fertility. The nation is now engaged in reckoning up what is left in the treasury of its natural resources, estimating how best to conserve and make profitable use of what is left.

The nation might have done this sooner, but there was in the West always fresh land to open up and in the East, after a time, a new source of income in the factory industries, that were more and more profitably absorbing capital and labor. So that although pioneer conditions gradually passed away, and it became less easy to wrest a living from plain or mountain or mine, the idea of finding out what was wrong, improving methods of agriculture, conserving the forest wealth by continual replanting or working the less rich mines at a profit through new processes, or the utilization of by-products, did not at first suggest itself.

When, on the other hand, we turn to the manufacturing occupations, we find that they have followed an analogous, though not precisely similar, course of evolution. Certainly from the first the manufacturers showed themselves far ahead of their fellows in the economical management of the raw material, in the adoption of every kind of labor and time-saving device and in the disposal of refuse. But in their way they have been just as short-sighted. They carried with them into the new occupations the very same careless habits of national extravagance. They, too, went ahead in a similar hustling fashion. This time the resources that were used up so recklessly were human resources, the strength and vitality of the mature man, the flesh and blood of little children, their stores of energy and youthful joy and hope. By overwork or accident, the father was cut off in his strong manhood, the boy was early worn out, and the young girl's prospects of happy motherhood were forever quenched.

There are now signs of a blessed reaction setting in here, too, and it is largely owing to the efforts of organized labor. The principles of conservation and of a wise economy, which are re-creating the plains of the West and which will once more clothe with forests the slopes of the mountains, are at work in the realm of industry. Not a year passes but that some state or another does not limit anew the hours during which children may work, or insist upon shorter hours for women, or the better protection from dangerous machinery, or the safeguarding of the worker in unhealthy occupations. Organized labor, ever running ahead of legislation in its standards of hours and sanitary conditions, provides a school of education and experiment for the whole community, by procuring for trade unionists working conditions which afterwards serve as the model for enlightened employers, and as a standard that the community in the end must exact for the whole body of workers.

But more must be done than merely keeping our people alive, by insisting they shall not be killed in the earning of their bread. Leaders of thought and many captains of industry have at last grasped the fact that the worker, uneducated and not trained in any true sense, is at once a poor tool and a most costly one. Other countries add their quota of experience, to back up public opinion and legislative action. Hence the demand heard from one end of the land to the other for industrial training. The public everywhere after a century of modern factory industry are at length beginning to have some definite ideas regarding industrial training for boys who are to supply the human element in the factory scheme. (Regarding girls, they still grope in outer darkness.)

For many years economists were accustomed to express nothing but satisfaction over the ever-advancing specialization of industry. They saw only the cheapening of the product, the vast increase in the total amount produced, and the piling up of profits, and they beheld in all three results nothing but social advantage. Verily both manufacturer and consumer were benefited. When the more thoughtful turned their attention to the actual makers through whose labors the cloth and the shoes and the pins of specialized industry were produced, they satisfied themselves that the worker must also be a sharer in the benefits of the new system; for, said they, everyone who is a worker is also a consumer. Even though the worker who is making shoes has to turn out twenty times as much work for the same wages, still as a consumer he shares in the all-round cheapening of manufactured articles, and is able to buy clothes and shoes and pins so much the cheaper. That the cost of living on the whole might be greater, that the wage of the worker might be too low to permit of his purchasing the very articles into the making of which his own labor had gone, did not occur to these *à priori* reasoners. It has taken a whole century of incredibly swift mechanical advance, associated at the same time with the most blind, cruel, and brutal waste of child life and adult life, to arrive at the beginning of an adjustment between the demands of machine-driven industry and the needs and the just claims of the human workers. We have only just recovered from the dazed sense of wonderment and pride of achievement into which modern discoveries and inventions, with the resultant enormous increase of commerce and material wealth, plunged the whole civilized world. We are but beginning to realize, what we had well-nigh totally overlooked, that even machine-driven industry with all that it connotes, enormously increased production of manufactured goods, and the spread of physical comfort to a degree unknown before among great numbers, is not the whole of national well-being; that by itself, unbalanced by justice to the workers, it is not even an unmixed boon.

I have tried to follow up the evolution of our present industrial society on several parallel lines: how industry itself has developed, how immigration affects the labor problem as regards the woman worker, and the relation of women to the vocations in the modern world. Let us now glance at our educational systems and see how they fit in to the needs of the workers, especially of the working-women. For our present purpose I will not touch on education as we find it in our most backward states, but rather as it is in the most advanced, since it is from improvement in these that we may expect to produce the best results for the whole nation.

Free and compulsory public education was established to supply literary and cultural training at a time when children still enjoyed opportunities of learning in the home, and later in small shops something of the trades they were to practice when grown-up. I know of a master plumber, who twenty years ago, as a child of eleven, made friends with the blacksmith and the tinsmith in the little village where he lived, and taught himself the elements of his trade at the blacksmith's anvil and with the tinsmith's tools. At fourteen that boy knew practically a great deal about the properties of metals, could handle simple tools deftly, and was well prepared to learn his trade readily when the time came.

As the most intelligent city parents cannot as individuals furnish their children with similar chances today, we must look to the public schools, which all citizens alike support, to take up the matter, and supply methodically and deliberately, that training of the eye and hand, and later that instruction in wage-earning occupations which in former days, as in the case quoted, the child obtained incidentally, as it were, in the mere course of growing up.

On the literary side, it is true, schools are improving all the time. History is now taught by lantern slides, showing the people's lives, instead of by a list of dates in a catechism. Geography is illustrated in the garden plot of the school playground. But in responding to the new claims which a new age and a changed world are making upon them, schools and teachers are only beginning to wake up. The manual training gradually being introduced is a hopeful beginning, but nothing more. The most valuable and important work of this kind is reserved for the upper grades of the grammar schools and for certain high schools, and the children who are able to make use of it are for the most part the offspring of comfortably off parents, enjoying all sorts of educational privileges already. Education, publicly provided, free and compulsory, therefore presumably universal, was established primarily for the benefit of the workers' children, yet of all children it is they who are at this moment receiving the least benefit from it. Many circumstances combine to produce this unfortunate result. The chief direct cause is poverty in the home. So many families have to live on such poor wages—five and six hundred dollars a year—that the children have neither the health to profit by the schooling nor the books nor the chance to read books at home when the home is one or perhaps two rooms. The curse of homework in cities ties the children down to willowing feathers or picking nuts or sewing on buttons, or carrying parcels to and from the shop that gives out the work, deprives them of both sleep and play, makes their attendance at school irregular, and dulls their brains during the hours they are with the teacher. In the country the frequently short period of school attendance during the year and the daily out-of-school work forced from young children by poverty-harassed parents has similar disastrous results.

Even in those states which have compulsory attendance up to fourteen, many children who are quite normal are yet very backward at that age. The child of a foreign-speaking parent, for instance, who never hears English spoken at home, needs a longer time to reach the eighth grade than the child of English-speaking parents.

Chicago is fairly typical of a large industrial city, and there the City Club found after investigation that forty-three per cent. of the pupils who enter the first grade do not reach the eighth grade; forty-nine per cent. do not go through the eighth grade; eleven per cent. do not reach the sixth grade, and sixteen per cent. more do not go through the sixth grade.

A child who goes through the eighth grade has some sort of an equipment (on the literary side at least) with which to set out in life. He has learned how to read a book or a newspaper intelligently, and how to express himself in writing. If he is an average child he has acquired a good deal of useful information. He will remember much of what he has learned, and can turn what knowledge he has to some account. But the child who leaves school in the fifth or sixth grade, or, perhaps, even earlier, is apt to have no hold on what he has been taught, and it all too soon passes from his memory, especially if he has in his home surroundings no stimulus to mental activity. Poor little thing! What a mockery to call this education, so little as it has fitted him to understand life and its problems! What he has learned out of school, meanwhile, as often as not, is harmful rather than beneficial.

The school door closes and the factory gate stands open wide. The children get their working papers, and slip out of the one, and through the other. At once, as we arrange matters, begins the fatal effect of handing over children, body and soul, into the control of industry. After a few days or weeks of wrapping candy, or carrying bundles or drawing out bastings, the work, whatever it is, becomes but a mere mechanical repetition. A few of the muscles only, and none of the higher faculties of observation, inquiry and judgment come into play at all, until, at the end of two years the brightest school-children have perceptibly lost ground in all these directions.

Two of the most precious years of life are gone. The little workers are not promoted from performing one process to another more difficult. They are as far as ever from any prospect of learning a trade in any intelligent fashion. The slack season comes on. The little fingers, the quick feet are not required any longer. Once more there is a scurrying round to look for a job, less cheerfully this time, the same haphazard applying at another factory for some other job, that like the first needs no training, like the first, leads nowhere, but also like the first, brings in three or four dollars a week, perhaps less. A teacher at a public-school social center inquired of a group of fifty girls, cracker-packers, garment-workers and bindery girls, how long each had been in her present situation. Only one had held hers eighteen months. No other had reached a year in the same place. The average appeared to be about three or four months.

Worse still is another class of blind-alley occupation. These are the street trades. The newsboy, the messenger and the telegraph boy often make good money to begin with. Girls, too, are being employed by some of the messenger companies. These are all trades, that apart from the many dangers inseparable from their pursuit, spell dismissal after two or three years at most, or as soon as the boy reaches the awkward age. The experience gained is of no use in any other employment, and the unusual freedom makes the messenger who has outgrown his calling averse to the discipline of more regular occupations.

What a normal vocational education can be, and a normal development of occupation, is seen in the professions, such as law and medicine. The lawyer and the doctor are, it is true, confining themselves more and more to particular branches of their respective callings, and more and more are they becoming experts in the branch of law or medicine selected. The lawyer specializes in criminal cases or in damage suits, in commercial or constitutional law; he is a pleader or a consultant. The doctor may decide to be a surgeon, or an oculist, an anesthetist or a laboratory worker. And the public reap the benefit in more expert advice and treatment. But the likeness between such professional specialization and the dehumanizing and brain-deadening industrial special- ization, which is the outgrowth of the factory system, is one in name only as was admirably put by Samuel Gom- pers, when presiding over the Convention of the Ameri- can Federation of Labor at Toronto in 1909.

"It must be recognized that specialists in industry are vastly different from specialists in the professions. In the professions, specialists develop from all the elements of the science of the profession. Specialists in industry are those who know but one part of a trade, and abso- lutely nothing of any other part of it. In the professions specialists are possessed of all the learning of their art; in industry they are denied the opportunity of learning the commonest elementary rudiments of industry other than the same infinitesimal part performed by them per- haps thousands of times over each day."

When the speaker emphasized these points of unlike- ness, he was at the same time, and in the same breath, pointing out the direction in which industry must be transformed. Training in the whole occupation must precede the exercise of the specialty. Furthermore, as all professional training has its cultural side, as well as its strictly professional side, so the cultural training of the worker must ever keep step with his vocational training.

The motto of the school should be, "We are for all," for it is what teachers and the community are forever forgetting. Think of the innumerable foundations in the countries of the old world, intended for poor boys, which have been gradually appropriated by the rich. Of others again, supposed to be for both boys and girls, from which the girls have long been excluded. The splendid techni- cal schools of this country, nominally open to all boys, at least, are by their very terms closed to the poor boy, however gifted. To give to him that hath is the tendency against which we must ever guard in planning and administering systems of public education. With many, perhaps most, educational institutions, as they grow older, more and more do they incline to improve the standards of their work, technically speaking, but to bestow their benefits upon comparatively fewer and fewer recipients.

I would not be understood to deprecate original research, or the training of expert professional workers in any field, still less as undervaluing thoroughness in any department of teaching. But I plead for a sense of proportion, that as long as the world is either so poor or its wealth and opportunities so unequally distributed, a certain minimum of vocational training shall be insured to all.

We recognize the need for thorough training in the case of the coming original investigator, and the expert professional, and they form the minority. We do not recognize the at least equally pressing need for the thorough training of the whole working population, and these make up the vast majority. In so far as the prevocational work in primary schools, the manual work and technical training in high schools, the short courses, the extension lectures and the correspondence instruction of universities are meeting this urgent popular need, just so far are they raising all work to a professional standard, just so far are they bringing down to the whole nation the gifts of culture and expert training that have hitherto been the privilege of the few.

I have often noticed college professors, in turning over the leaves of a university calendar or syllabus of lectures, pass lightly over the pages recounting the provision made for short courses, summer schools, extension or correspondence work, and linger lovingly over the fuller

and more satisfactory program outlined for the teacher
or the professional worker. The latter is only apparently
the more interesting. Take Wisconsin's College of Agriculture, for example. It sends forth yearly teachers and
original investigators, but quite as great and important
a product are the hundreds of farmers and farmers' sons
who come fresh from field and dairy to take their six
weeks' training in the management of cattle or of crops,
and to field and dairy return, carrying away with them
the garnered experience of others, as well as increased
intelligence and self-reliance in handling the problems of
their daily toil.

Anna Garlin Spencer, in her "Woman and Social Culture," points out how our much-lauded schools of domestic economy fail to benefit the schoolgirl, through this
very overthoroughness and expensiveness how they are
narrowed down to the turning out of teachers of domestic economy and dietitians and other institutional
workers. Domestic economy as a wage-earning vocation
cannot be taught too thoroughly, but what every girl is
entitled to have from the public school during her school
years is a "short course" in the simple elements of domestic economy, with opportunity for practice. It is
nothing so very elaborate that girls need, but that little
they need so badly. Such a course has in view the girl
as a homemaker, and is quite apart from her training as
a wage-earner.

When again we turn to that side, matters are not any
more promising. If the boy of the working classes is
badly off for industrial training, his sister is in far worse
case. Some provision is already made for the boy, and
more is coming his way presently, but of training for the
girl, which shall be adequate to fit her for self-support, we
hear hardly anything. We have noted that women are
already in most of the trades followed by men, and that

the number of this army, of working, wage-earning women is legion; that they are not trained at all, and are so badly paid that as underbidders they perpetually cut the wages of men. Nay, the young working-girl is even "her own worst competitor—the competitor against her own future home, and as wife and mother she may have to live on the wage she herself has cheapened."

And to face a situation like this are we making any adequate preparation? With how little we are satisfied, let me illustrate. In the address of Mrs. Raymond Robins as president of the National Women's Trade Union League of America before their Fourth Biennial Convention in St. Louis, in June, 1913, she told how "in a curriculum of industrial education we find that under the heading 'Science' boys study elementary physics, mechanics and electricity, and girls the action of alkalies, and the removal of stains. While under 'Drawing' we read, 'For boys the drawing will consist of the practical application of mechanical and free-hand work to parts of machinery, house plans, and so forth. Emphasis will be placed upon the reading of drawings, making sketches of machine parts quickly and accurately. For the girls the drawing will attempt to apply the simple principles of design and color to the work. The girls will design and stencil curtains for the dining- and sewing-rooms and will make designs for doilies for the table. They will plan attractive spacing for tucks, ruffles and embroidery for underwear.' Women have entered nearly three hundred different occupations and trades in America within the past quarter of a century, three hundred trades and occupations, and they are to qualify for these by learning to space tucks attractively."

In the very valuable Twenty-fifth Annual Report of the Commissioner of Labor, published in 1910, which is devoted to industrial education, there is but one chapter dealing with girls' industrial schools, in itself a commentary upon the backwardness of the movement for industrial education where girls are affected. It is true that the schools included under this heading do not account for all the school trade-training given to girls in this country, for the classification of industrial schools, where there is no general system, is very difficult, and under no plan of tabulation can there be an all-inclusive heading for any one type. For instance a school for colored girls might be classified either as a school for Negroes or as a school for girls, as a public school, a philanthropic school, or an evening school, and a school giving trade-training to boys might also include girls. The writer of this most exhaustive report, however, states definitely that "trade schools for girls are rare, and even schools offering them industrial courses as a part of their work are not common."

It is impossible to consider vocational training without bearing in mind the example of Germany. Germany has been the pioneer in this work and has laid down for the rest of us certain broad principles, even if there are in the German systems some elements which are unsuitable to this country. These general principles are most clearly exemplified in the schools of the city of Munich. Indeed, when people talk of the German plan, they nearly always mean the Munich plan. What it aims at is:

1. To deal in a more satisfactory way with the eighty or ninety per cent. of children who leave school for work at fourteen, and to bridge over with profit alike to the child, the employer and the community the gap between fourteen and sixteen which is the unsolved riddle of educators everywhere today.

2. To retain the best elements of the old apprenticeship system, though in form so unlike it. The boy (for it mainly touches boys) is learning his trade and he is

also working at his trade, and he has cultural as well as industrial training, and this teaching he receives during his working hours and in his employer's time.

3. To provide teachers who combine ability to teach, with technical skill.

4. To insure, through joint boards on which both employers and workmen are represented, even if these boards are generally advisory, only an interlocking of the technical class and the factory, without which any system of vocational instruction must fall down.[1]

5. To maintain a system which shall reach that vast bulk of the population, who, because they need technical training most urgently, are usually the last to receive it.

Many of the most advanced educators in this country join issue with the usual German practice on some most important points. These consider that it is not sufficient that there be a close interlocking of the technical school and class and the factory. It is equally essential that vocational education, supported by public funds, shall be an integral part of the public-school system, of which it is indeed but a normal development, and therefore that we must have a unit and not a dual system. Only thus can we insure that vocational education will remain education at all and not just provide a training-school for docile labor as an annex and a convenient

---

[1] As to how far this is the case, there is a difference of opinion among authorities. Professor F. W. Roman, who has made so exhaustive a comparative study of vocational training in the United States and Germany, writes: "In Germany, there is very little local control of schools, or anything else. The authority in all lines is highly centralized." (The Industrial and Commercial Schools of the United States and Germany, 1915, p. 324.) Dr. Kerchensteiner is quoted by the Commercial Club of Chicago as saying, in a letter to Mr. Edwin G. Cooley, that the separate administrative school-boards of Munich form an essential part of the city's school-system.

entrance hall to the factory system. Only thus can we insure democracy in the control of this new branch of public activity. Only thus can the primary schools be kept in touch with the advanced classes, so that the teacher, from the very kindergarten up, may feel that she is a part of a complete whole. Then indeed will all teachers begin to echo the cry of one whom I heard say: "You ask us to fit the children for the industries. Let us see if the industries are fit for the children."

Another point in which we must somewhat modify any European model is in the limited training provided for girls. A country which is frankly coeducational in its public schools, state universities and professional colleges, must continue to be so when installing a new educational department to meet the changed and changing conditions of our time.

The parliament of organized labor in the United States has taken a liberal view and laid down an advanced program on the subject of vocational training. In 1908 the American Federation of Labor appointed a committee on industrial education consisting of nineteen members, of whom two were women, Agnes Nestor, International Secretary of the Glove Workers' Union, and Mrs. Raymond Robins, President of the National Women's Trade Union League of America. Its very first report, made in 1909, recommended that the Federation should request the United States Department of Commerce and Labor to investigate the subject of industrial education in this country and abroad.

The report of the American Federation of Labor itself, includes a digest of the United States Bureau of Labor's report, and was published as Senate Document No. 936. It is called "The Report of the Committee on Industrial Education of the American Federation of Labor, compiled and edited by Charles H. Winslow."

Whatever narrowness and inconsistency individual trade unionists may be charged with regarding industrial education, the leaders of the labor movement give it their endorsement in the clearest terms. For instance, this very report commends those international unions which have already established supplemental trade courses, such as the Typographical Union, the Printing Pressmen's Union, and the Photo Engravers' Union, and other local efforts, such as the School for Carpenters and Bricklayers in Chicago and the School for Carriage, Wagon, and Automobile Workers of New York City. All trade unions which have not adopted a scheme of technical education are advised to take the matter up.

On the question of public-school training, the American Federation of Labor is no less explicit and emphatic, favoring the establishment of schools in connection with the public-school system in which pupils between fourteen and sixteen may be taught the principles of the trades, with local advisory boards, on which both employers and organized labor should have seats. But by far the most fundamental proposal is the following. After outlining the general instruction on accepted lines, they proceed as follows:

"The shop instruction for particular trades, and for each trade represented, the drawing, mathematics, mechanics, physical and biological science applicable to the trade, the history of that trade, and a sound system of economics, including and emphasizing the philosophy of collective bargaining."

The general introduction of such a plan of training would mean that the young worker would start out on his wage-earning career with an intelligent understanding of the modern world, and of his relations to his employer and to his fellow-laborers, instead of, as at present, setting forth with no knowledge of the world he is entering, and moreover, with his mind clogged with a number of utterly out-of-date ideas, as to his individual power of control over wages and working conditions.[1]

If we wish to know the special demands of working-women there is no way so certain as to consult the organized women. They alone are at liberty to express their views, while the education they have had in their unions in handling questions vital to their interests as wage-earners, and as leaders of other women gives clearness and definiteness to the expression of those views.

If organized women can best represent the wage-earners of their sex, we can gain the best collective statement of their wishes through them. At the last convention of the National Women's Trade Union League in June, 1913, the subject of industrial education received very close attention. The importance of continuation schools after wage-earning days have commenced was not overlooked. An abstract of the discussion and the

---

[1] History, as it is usually taught, is not considered from the industrial viewpoint, nor in the giving of a history lesson are there inferences drawn from it that would throw light upon the practical problems that are with us today, or that are fast advancing to meet us. When a teacher gives a lesson on the history of the United States, there is great stress laid upon the part played by individual effort. All through personal achievements are emphasized. The instructor ends here, on the high note that personal exertion is the supreme factor of success in life, failing unfortunately to point out how circumstances have changed, and that even personal effort may have to take other directions. Of the boys and girls in the schools of the United States today between nine and fourteen years of age, over eight millions in 1910, how many will leave school knowing the important facts that land is no longer free, and that the tools of industry are no more, as they once were, at the disposal of the most willing worker? And that therefore (Oh, most important therefore!) the workers must work in coöperation if they are to retain the rights of the human being, and the status signified by that proud name, an American citizen.

chief resolutions can be found in the issue of *Life and Labor* for August, 1913.

After endorsing the position taken up by the American Federation of Labor, the women went on to urge educational authorities to arm the children, while yet at school, with a knowledge of the state and federal laws enacted for their protection, and asked also "that such a course shall be of a nature to equip the boy and girl with a full sense of his or her responsibility for seeing that the laws are enforced," the reason being that the yearly influx of young boys and girls into the industrial world in entire ignorance of their own state laws is one of the most menacing facts we have to face, as their ignorance and inexperience make exploitation easy, and weaken the force of such protective legislation as we have.

Yet another suggestion was that "no working certificates be issued to a boy or girl unless he or she has passed a satisfactory examination in the laws which have been enacted by the state for their protection."

In making these claims, organized working-women are keeping themselves well in line with the splendid statement of principles enunciated by that great educator, John Dewey:

The ethical responsibility of the school on the social side must be interpreted in the broadest and freest spirit; it is equivalent to that training of the child which will give him such possession of himself that he may take charge of himself; may not only adapt himself to the changes that are going on, but have power to shape and direct them.

When we ask for coeducation on vocational lines, the question is sure to come up: For how long is a girl likely to use her training in a wage-earning occupation? It is continually asserted and assumed she will on the average remain in industry but a few years. The mature woman as a wage-earner, say the woman over twenty-five, we have been pleased to term and to treat as an exception which may be ignored in great general plans. Especially has this been so in laying out schemes for vocational training, and we find the girl being ignored, not only on the usual ground that she is a girl, but for the additional, and not-to-be-questioned reason that it will not pay to give her instruction in any variety of skilled trades, because she will be but a short time in any occupation of the sort. Hence this serves to increase the already undue emphasis placed upon domestic training as all that a girl needs, and all that her parents or the community ought to expect her to have. This is only one of the many cases when we try to solve our new problems by reasoning based upon conditions that have passed or that are passing away.

In this connection some startling facts have been brought forward by Dr. Leonard P. Ayres in the investigations conducted by him for the Russell Sage Foundation. He tried to find the ages of all the women who are following seven selected occupations in cities of the United States of over 50,000 population. The occupations chosen were those in which the number of women workers exceeds one for every thousand of the population. The number of women covered was 857,743, and is just half of all the women engaged in gainful employment in those cities. The seven occupations listed are housekeeper, nursemaid, laundress, saleswoman, teacher, dressmaker and servant. No less than forty-four per cent. of the housekeepers are between twenty-five and forty-four. Of dressmakers there are fifty-one per cent. between these two ages; of teachers fifty-eight per cent.; of laundresses forty-nine per cent., while the one occupation of which a little more than half are under twenty-five years is that of saleswoman, and even here there are barely sixty-one per cent., leaving the still considerable proportion of thirty-nine per cent. of saleswomen over the age of twenty-five. It is pretty certain that these mature women have given more than the favorite seven years to their trade. It is to be regretted that the investigation was not made on lines which would have included some of the factory occupations. It is difficult to see why it did not. Under any broad classification there must be more garment-workers, for instance, in New York or Chicago, than there are teachers. However, we have reason to be grateful for the fine piece of work which Dr. Ayres has done here.

The *Survey,* in an editorial, also quotes in refutation of the seven-year theory, the findings of the commission which inquired into the pay of teachers in New York. The commissioners found that forty-four per cent. of the women teachers in the public schools had been in the service for ten years or more, and that only twenty-five per cent. of the men teachers had served as long a term.

It can hardly be doubted that the tendency is towards the lengthening of the wage-earning life of the working-woman. A number of factors affect the situation, about most of which we have as yet little definite information. There is first, the gradual passing of the household industries out of the home. Those women, for whom the opportunity to be thus employed no longer is open, tend to take up or to remain longer in wage-earning occupations.

The changing status of the married woman, her increasing economic independence and its bearing upon her economic responsibility, are all facts having an influence upon woman as a wage-earning member of the community, but how, and in what degree, they affect her length of service, is still quite uncertain. It is probable too, that they affect the employment or non-employment of women very differently in different occupations, but how, and in what degree they do so is mere guess-work at present.

Much pains has been expended in arguing that any system of vocational training should locally be co-related with the industries of the district. Vain effort! For it appears that the workers of all ages are on the move all the time. Out of 22,027 thirteen-year-old boys in the public schools of seventy-eight American cities, only 12,699, or a little more than half, were living in the places of their birth. And considering the *wanderlust* of the young in any case, is anything more probable than that the very first thing a big proportion of this advancing body of "vocationally trained" young men and women will want to do will be to try out their training in some other city? And why should they not?

If there has ever been voiced a tenderer plea for a universal education that shall pass by no child, boy or girl, than that of Stitt Wilson, former Socialist Mayor of Berkeley, I do not know it. If there has ever been outlined a finer ideal of an education fitting the child, every child, to take his place and fill his place in the new world opening before him, I have not heard of it. He asks that we should submit ourselves to the leadership of the child —his needs, his capacities, his ideal hungers—and in so doing we shall answer many of the most disturbing and difficult problems that perplex our twentieth-century civilization. Even in those states which make the best attempt at educating their children, from three-fourths to nine-tenths, according to the locality, leave the schools at the age of thirteen or fourteen, and the present quality of the education given from the age of twelve to sixteen is neither an enrichment in culture, nor a training for life and livelihood. It is too brief for culture, and is not intended for vocation.

Mr. Wilson makes no compromise with existing conditions; concedes not one point to the second-rate standards that we supinely accept; faces the question of cost, that basic difficulty which most theoretical educators waive aside, and which the public never dreams of trying to meet and overcome. Here are some of his proposals.

The New Education [he writes] will include training and experience in domestic science, cookery and home-making; agriculture and horticulture; pure and applied science, and mechanical and commercial activities with actual production, distribution and exchange of commodities. Such training for three to six millions of both sexes from the age of twelve to twenty-one years will require land, tools, buildings of various types, machinery, factory sites by rail and water, timber, water and power sources.

As all civilization is built upon the back of labor, and as all culture and leisure rests upon labor, and is not possible otherwise, so all cultural and liberal education, as generally understood, shall be sequent to the productive and vocational. The higher intellectual education should grow out of and be earned by productive vocational training.

Hence our schools should be surrounded by lands of the best quality obtainable, plots of 10, 50, 100 and more acres. These lands should be the scene of labor that would be actually productive and not mere play. * * * * In such a school the moral elements of labor should be primary, viz.: joy to the producer, through industry and art; perfect honesty in quality of material and character of workmanship; social coöperation, mutualism, and fellowship among the workers or students; and last, but not least, justice—that is, the full product of labor being secured to the producer.

He plans to make the schools largely self-supporting, partly through land endowments easier to obtain under the system of taxation of land values that is possibly near at hand in the Golden State, for which primarily the writer is planning. The other source of income would be from the well-directed labor of the students themselves, particularly the older ones. He quotes Professor Frank Lawrence Glynn, of the Vocational School at Albany, New York, as having found that the average youth can, not by working outside of school hours, but in the actual process of getting his own education, earn two dollars a week and upward. Elsewhere, Mr. Wilson shows that the beginnings of such schools are to be found in operation today, in some of the best reform institutions of the country.

For all who desire university training, this would open the door. They would literally "work their way" through college. One university president argues for some such means of helping students: "We need not so much an increase of beneficiary funds as an increase of the opportunities for students to earn their living." This is partly to enable them to pay for their courses and thereby acquire an education, but chiefly because through supporting themselves they gain self-confidence and therefore the power of initiative.[1]

[1] "The social and educational need for vocational training is equally urgent. Widespread vocational training will democratize the education of the country: (1) by recognizing different tastes and abilities, and by giving an equal opportunity to all to prepare for their lifework; (2) by extending education through part-time and evening instruction to those who are at work in the shop or on the farm." Report of the Commission on National Aid to Vocational Instruction, 1914, page 12.

XI

THE WORKING WOMAN AND MARRIAGE

It is a lamentable fact that the wholesome and normal tendency towards organization which is now increasingly noticeable among working-women has so far remained unrelated to that equally normal and far more deeply rooted and universal tendency towards marriage.

As long as the control of trade unionism among women remained with men, no link between the two was likely to be forged; the problem is so entirely apart from any that men unionists ever have to face themselves. It is true that with a man the question of adhering to a union alike in times of prosperity or times of stress may be complicated by a wife having a "say-so," through her en-thusiasm or her indifference when it means keeping up dues or attending meetings; yet more, when belonging to a union may mean being thrown out of work or ordered on strike, just when there has been a long spell of sickness or a death with all the attendant expenses, or when perhaps a new baby is expected or when the hard winter months are at hand and the children are lacking shoes and clothes. Still, roughly speaking, a man worker is a unionist or a non-unionist just the same, be he single or married.

But how different it is with a girl! The counter influence exerted by marriage upon organization is not confined to those girls who leave the trade, and of course the union, if they have belonged to one, after they have married. The possibility of marriage and espe-

cially the exaggerated expectations girls entertain as to
the improvement in their lot which marriage will bring
them is one of the chief adverse influences that any
organization composed of women or containing many
women members has to reckon with, an influence acting
all the time on the side of those employers who oppose
organization among their girls.

It has been the wont of many men unionists in the
past and is the custom of not a few today, to accept at
its face value the girl's own argument: "What's the
use of our joining the union? We'll be getting married
presently." It is much the same feeling, although un-
spoken, that underlies the ordinary workingman's un-
willingness to see women enter his trade and his indifference to their status in the trade once they have entered it. The man realizes that this rival of his is but
a temporary worker, and he often, too often, excuses
himself tacitly, if not in words, from making any effort to
aid her in improving her position or from using his influence and longer experience to secure for her any sort
of justice, forgetting that the argument, "She'll soon get
married" is a poor one at best, seeing that as soon as one
girl does marry her place will immediately be filled by
another, as young, as inexperienced as she had been, and
as utterly in need of the protection that experienced and
permanent co-workers could give her. The girl, although
she guesses it not, is only too frequently made the instrument of a terrible retribution; for the poor wage,
which was all that she in her individual helplessness was
able to obtain for herself, is used to lower the pay of
the very man, who, had he stood by her, might have
helped her to a higher wage standard and at the same
time preserved his own.

Again, the probability of the girl marrying increases on
all sides the difficulties encountered in raising standards

alike of work and of wages. Bound up with direct payment are those indirect elements of remuneration or deduction from remuneration covered by length of working-hours and by sanitary conditions, since whatever saps the girl's energy or undermines her health, whether overwork, foul air, or unsafe or too heavy or overspeeded machinery, forms an actual deduction from her true wages, besides being a serious deduction from the wealth-store, the stock of well-being, of the community.

Up till comparatively recent times the particular difficulties I have been enumerating did not exist, since, under the system of home industries universal before the introduction of steam-power, there was not the same economic competition between men and women, nor was there this unnatural gap between the occupation of the woman during her girlhood and afterwards in her married life. In the majority of cases, indeed, she only continued to carry on under her husband's roof the very trades which she had learned and practiced in the home of her parents. And this applied equally to the group of trades which we still think of as part of the woman's natural home life, baking and cooking and cleaning and sewing, and to that other group which have become specialized and therefore are now pursued outside the home, such as spinning and weaving. It was true also in large part of the intrinsically out-of-door employments, such as field-work.

In writing about a change while the process is still going on, it is extremely difficult to write so as not to be misunderstood. For there are remote corners, even of the United States, where the primitive conditions still subsist, and where woman still bears her old-time relation to industry, where the industrial life of the girl flows on with no gap or wrench into the occupational life of the married woman. Through wifehood and motherhood she indeed adds to her burdens, and complicates her responsibilities, but otherwise she spends her days in much the same fashion as before, with some deduction, often, alas, inadequate, to allow for the bearing and rearing of her too frequent babies. Also in the claims that industry makes upon her in her relation to the productive life of the community, under such primitive conditions, her life rests upon the same basis as before.

As a telling illustration of that primitive woman's occupations, as she carries them on among us today, the following will serve. Quite recently a friend, traveling in the mountainous regions of Kentucky, at the head of Licking Creek, had occasion to call at a little mountain cabin, newly built out of logs, the chinks stopped up with clay, evidently the pride and the comfort of the dwellers. It consisted of one long room. At one end were three beds. In the center was the family dining-table, and set out in order on one side a number of bark-seated hickory chairs made by the forest carpenters. On the other a long bench, probably intended for the younger members of the family. Facing the door, as the visitor entered, was a huge open fireplace, with a bar across, whence hung three skillets or kettles for the cooking of the food. The only occupant of the cabin at that hour in the afternoon was an old woman. She was engaged in combing into smoothness with two curry-combs a great pile of knotted wool, washed, but otherwise as it came off the sheep's back. The wool was destined to be made into blankets for the household. The simple apparatus for the carrying-out of the whole process was there at hand, for the spinning-wheel stood back in a corner of the room, while the big, heavy loom had, for convenience' sake, been set up on the porch. That old woman's life may be bare and narrow enough in many ways, but at least she is rich and fortunate in having the opportunity for the exercise of a skilled trade, and in it an outlet for self-expression, and even for artistic taste in the choice of patterns and colors. Far different the lot of the factory worker with her monotonous and mindless repetition of lifeless movements at the bidding of the machine she tends. The Kentucky mountain woman was here practicing in old age the art she had acquired in her girlhood. Those early lessons which had formed her industrial education, were of life-long value, both in enriching her own life, and by adding to her economic and therefore social value, alike as a member of her own household, and as a contributor to the wealth of the little community.

We once had, universally, and there still can be found in such isolated regions, an industrial arrangement, soundly based upon community and family needs, and even more normally related to the woman's own development, better expressing many sides of her nature than do the confused and conflicting claims of the modern family and modern industry render possible for vast numbers today. And this, although wide opportunity for personal and individual development was so sadly lacking, and the self-abnegation expected from women was so excessive, that the intellectual and emotional life must often have been a silent tragedy of repression.

Among our modern working-women in urban localities, we find today no such settled plan for thus directing the activities of women to meet modern needs and conditions. Neither home nor school furnishes our girls with a training fitting them for a rich and varied occupational life. The pursuits into which most of them drift or are driven, do indeed result in the production of a vast amount of manufactured goods, food, clothing, house and personal furnishings of all sorts, and of machinery with which may be manufactured yet more goods. Much of this product is both useful and beneficial to us all, but there are likewise mountains of articles fashioned, neither useful nor beneficial, nor resulting in any sort of use, comfort or happiness to anyone: adulterated foods, shoddy clothes, and toys that go to pieces in an hour.

Certainly the girl worker of this twentieth century produces per head, and with all allowances made for the cost of the capital invested in factory and machinery, and for superintendence, far and away more in amount and in money value than did her girl ancestor of a hundred years ago, or than her contemporary girl ancestor of to-day in the Kentucky and Tennessee mountains, or than her other sister, the farmer's daughter in agricultural regions, who still retains hold of and practices some of the less primitive industries.

But the impulse to congratulate ourselves upon this vastly increased product of labor is checked when we take up the typically modern girl's life at a later stage. We have observed already that her life during her first fourteen years is utterly unrelated to the next period, which she spends in store or factory. The training of her childhood has been no preparation for the employments of her girlhood. She is but an unskilled hand, the last cog in a machine, and if these prove but seven lean years for her, it is only what we might expect. When they are ended, and married life entered upon, we are again struck by the absence of any relation between either of these two life-periods and the stage preceding, and by the fact that at no time is any intelligent preparation made either for a wage-earning or a domestic career. This means an utter dislocation between the successive stages of woman's life, a dislocation, the unfortunate results of which, end not with the sex directly affected, but bring about a thousand other evils, the lowering of the general wage standard, the deterioration of home life, and serious loss to the children of the coming generation. As far as we know, such a dislocation in the normal development of women's lives never took place before on any large scale. I am speaking of it here solely in relation to the sum of the well-being of the whole community. As it affects the individual girl and woman herself it has been dealt with under other heads.

The cure which the average man has to propose is pithily summed up in the phrase: "Girls ought to stay at home." The home as woman's sole sphere is even regarded as the ultimate solution of the whole difficulty by many men, who know well that it is utterly impracticable today. A truer note was struck by John Work, when addressing himself specially to socialist men:

It would be fatal to our prospects of reaching the women with the message of socialism if we were to give the millions of wage-earning women to understand that we did not intend to let them continue earning their own living, but proposed to compel them to become dependent upon men. They prize what little independence they have, and they want more of it.

It would be equally fatal to our prospects of reaching the women with the message of socialism if we were to give the married women to understand that they must remain dependent upon men. It is one of the most hopeful signs of the times that they are chafing under the galling chains of dependence.

* * * * * *

Far from shutting women out of the industries, socialism will do just the opposite.

It will open up to every woman a full and free opportunity to earn her own living and receive her full earnings.

This means the total cessation of marrying for a home.

The degree of irritation that so many men show when expressing themselves on the subject of women in the trades is the measure of their own sense of incompetence to handle it. The mingled apathy and impatience with which numbers of union men listen to any proposal to organize the girls with whom they work arises from the same mental attitude. "These girls have come into our shop. We can't help it. We didn't ask them. They should be at home. Let them take care of themselves."

The inconsistency of such a view is seen when we consider that in the cities at least an American father (let alone a foreign-born father) is rarely found nowadays objecting to his own girls going out to work for wages. He expects it, unless one or more are needed by their mother at home to help with little ones or to assist in a small family store or home business. He takes it as a matter of course that his girls go to work as soon as they leave school, just as his boys do. And yet the workman in a printing office, we will say, whose own daughter is earning her living as a stenographer or teacher, will resent the competition of women type-setters, and will both resent and despise those daughters of poorer fathers, who have found their way into the press or binding-rooms. Unionists or non-unionists, such men ignore the fact that all these girls have just as much right to earn an honest living at setting type, or folding or tipping and in so doing to receive the support and protection of any organization there is, as their own daughters have to take wages for the hours they spend in schoolroom or in office. The single men but echo the views of the older ones when such unfortunately is the shop tone, and may be even more indifferent to the girls' welfare and to the bad economic results to all workers of our happy-go-lucky system or no-system.

I do not wish to be understood as accepting either the girl's present economic position or the absorption in purely domestic occupations of the workingman's wife as a finality. It is a transitional stage that we are considering. I look forward to a time, I believe it to be rapidly approaching, when the home of the workingman, like everyone's else home, will be truly the home, the happy resting-place, the sheltering nest of father, mother and children, and when through the rearrangement of labor, the workingman's wife will be relieved from her monotonous existence of unrelieved domestic drudgery and overwork, disguised under the name of wifely and maternal duties, when the cooking and the washing, for instance, will be no more part of the home life in the humblest home than in the wealthiest. The workingman's wife will then share in the general freedom to occupy part of her time in whatever occupation she is best fitted for, and, along with every other member of the community she will share in the benefits arising from the better organization of domestic work.

However, this blessed change has not yet come to pass, and of all city-dwellers, the wife of the workingman seems to be furthest away from the benefits of the transformation. Therefore, in considering the connection between the girl's factory life and her probable occupational future in married life, I have purposely avoided dwelling upon what is bound to arrive some time in the future, and have tried to face facts as they exist today, dealing as far as possible with the difficulties of the generation of girls now in the factories, those about to enter, and those passing out, remembering only, with a patience-breeding sense of relief, that the conditions of today may not necessarily be the conditions of tomorrow.

I therefore accept in its full meaning domesticity, as practiced by the most domestic woman, and as preached by the domestic woman's most ardent advocate among men. Nor am I expressing resentment at the fact that when a girl leaves the machine-speeded work of the factory, it is only to take up the heavy burden of the workingman's wife, as we know it. She must be wife and mother, and manager of the family income, and cook and laundress and housemaid and seamstress. The improvement of her position and the amelioration of her lot can only come slowly, through social changes, as expressed in the woman movement, and through the widening scope of the principle of specialization.

Even today, without any such radical changes as are foreshadowed above, the gap between schooldays and working years, between working years and married life, can to some extent be bridged over if we plan to do so from the beginning. As has been shown, organized women are already advocating some such orderly plan for the girl's school training, as should blend book-learning with manual instruction and simple domestic accomplishments. But also, in order to deal justly and fairly by the girl, any reasonable scheme of things would also presuppose such strict control of the conditions of industry, that hours would be reasonably short, that in the building and running of machinery there should be borne in mind always the safety and health of the workers, instead of, as today, expecting almost all the adaptation to be on the part of the worker, through pitting the flexible, delicate, and easily injured human organism against the inflexible and tireless machine. Other essential conditions would be the raising of the standard of living, and therefore of remuneration, for all, down to the weakest and least skilled, and the insistence upon equal pay for equal work, tending to lessen the antagonism between men and women on the industrial field. Thus doubly prepared and adequately protected the girl would pass from her wage-earning girlhood into home and married life a fresher, less exhausted creature than she usually is now. Further, she would be more likely to bring to the bearing and rearing of her children a constitution unenfeebled by premature overwork and energies unsapped by its monotonous grind. Again, her understanding of industrial problems would make her a more intelligent as well as a more sympathetic helpmate. Hand in hand, husband and wife would more hopefully tackle fresh industrial difficulties as these arose, and they would do so with some slight sense of the familiarity that is the best armor in life's battle.

Besides there is the other possibility, all too often realized, that lies in the background of every such married woman's consciousness. She may be an ideally domestic woman, spending her time and strength on her home and for the welfare of her husband and children, yet through no fault of hers, her home may be lost to her, or if not lost, at least kept together only by her own unremitting efforts as a wage-earner. It often happens that marriage in course of time proves to be anything but an assurance of support. Early widowed, the young mother herself may have to earn her children's bread. Or the husband may become crippled, or an invalid, or he may turn out a drunkard and a spendthrift. In any of these circumstances, the responsibility and the burden of supporting the entire family usually falls upon the wife. Is it strange that the group so often drift into undeserved pauperism, sickness and misery, perhaps later on, even into those depths of social maladjustment that bring about crime?

The poorly paid employment of office-cleaning is sadly popular among widows and deserted wives, because, being followed during the evening, and sometimes night hours, it leaves a mother free during the day to attend to her cooking and housework and sewing, and be on the spot to give the children their meals. Free! The irony of it! Free, that is, to work sixteen hours or longer per day, and free to leave her little ones in a locked-up room, while she earns enough to pay the rent and buy the food. Ask any such widowed mother what she is thinking of, as she plies mop and scrubbing-brush after the offices are closed and the office force gone home, and she will tell you how she worries for fear something may have happened to the baby while she is away. She wonders whether she left the matches out of the reach of four-year-old Sammy; and Bessie, who isn't very strong, is always so frightened when the man on the floor above comes home late and quarrels with his wife.

The theory on which the poor woman was paid her wages when as a single girl she used to draw her weekly pay-envelope, that a fair living wage for a woman is what is barely sufficient to support herself, rather falls down when a whole household has to be kept out of a girl's miserable pay.

All these difficulties would be eased for such over-burdened ones, if their early training had been such as to leave them equipped to meet the vicissitudes of fortune on fairer terms, and if the conditions of industrial life, allotting equal pay to workers of both sexes, had also included reasonable opportunities for advancement to higher grades of work with proportionately increased pay.

Meanwhile, married women, less handicapped than these, are experimenting on their own account, and are helping to place the work of wives as wage-earners on a more settled basis. The wife of the workingman who has no children, and who lives in a city finds she has not enough to do in the little flat which is their home. The stove in winter needs little attention; there is not enough cooking and cleaning to fill up her time, and as for sewing she can buy most of their clothing cheaper than she can make it. But any little money she can earn will come in useful; so she tries for some kind of work, part-time work, if she can find it. In every big city there are hundreds of young married women who take half-time jobs in our department stores or who help to staff the lunch-rooms or wash up or carry trays, or act as cashiers in our innumerable restaurants. As half-day girls such waitresses earn their three or four dollars a week, besides getting their lunch. Very frequently they do not admit to their fellow-workers that they are married, for the single girl with her own hard struggle on her hands is apt to resent such competition. A worker who is in a position to accept voluntarily a half-time job of this sort is one who must have some other means of meeting part of her living expenses. A home in the background is such an aid. The increasingly large number of part-time workers, lessen, the others reckon, the number of jobs to be had by the ones that have to work all day, and may tend also to lower wages, since any partly subsidized worker can afford to take less than the girl who has to support herself out of her earnings. The latter has never heard of parasitic trades, and yet in her heart she knows there is something not quite right here, something that she blindly feels she would like to put an end to.

She is quite right in resisting any lowering of wages, but she will have to accept this inroad into the trades of these exceptionally placed married women. She will have to throw her efforts into another channel, using organization to raise the position of working-women generally into dignified industrial independence. For this still limited number of half-time married women workers are but the leaf on the stream, showing the direction events are taking. As specialization goes on, as the domestic industries are more and more taken out of our homes, as the gifted and trained teacher more and more shares in the life of the child, more and more will the woman after she marries continue to belong to the wage-earning class by being a part-time worker. To propose eliminating the present (sometimes unfair) competition of the married woman with the single girl, by excluding her from any or every trade is as futile as the resentment of men against all feminine rivals in industry.

We have been observing, so far, how the lives of women have been modified, often not for the better, by the industrial revolution. Let us glance now in passing at the old home industries themselves, and note what is still happening. One after another has been taken, not merely out of the home, where they all originated, but out of the hands of the sex who invented and developed them. Trade after trade has thus been taken over from the control of women, and appropriated and placed on a modern business basis by men. I make no criticism upon this transference beyond remarking that you hear no howl about it from the supplanted ones, as you never fail to do over the converse process, when male workers are driven out of occupations to make way for women, whose cheapness makes them so formidable an industrial competitor. But whichever way it works, sex discrimination usually bodes no good to the lasting interest of any of the workers. When a trade passes out of the status of a home industry, and takes on the dignity of an outside occupation, women are rarely in a position to take hold of it in its new guise. We find men following it, partly because they are more accustomed to think in terms of professional skill, and partly because they are in the business swim, and can more easily gain command of the capital necessary to start any new enterprise. Men then proceed to hire the original owners as employés, and women lose greatly in their economic status.

This is the general rule, though it is by no means wholly the sex line that divides the old-fashioned house-worker from the specialized professional, though this habitual difference in standing between groups of different sex does tend to blur fundamental issues. The economic struggle in its bare elements would be easy to follow compared with the complex and perpetually changing forms in which it is presented to us.

But the home industries are not yet fully accounted for and disposed of. Some of the household occupations, essential once to the comfort and well-being of the family, are shrinking in importance, prior to vanishing before our eyes, because now they do not for the most part represent an economical expenditure of energy. Meanwhile, however, they linger on, a survival in culture, and in millions of homes today the patient housewife is striving with belated tools to keep her family fed and clothed and her house spotless.

Take the cleaning process, for example, and watch what is happening. Dr. Helen Sumner draws attention to the fact that we ourselves are witnessing its rapid transformation. It is being taken out of the hands of the individual houseworker, who is wont to scrub, sweep and dust in the intervals between marketing, cooking, laundry-work or sewing, and by whom it is performed well or ill, but always according to the standards of the individual household, which means that there are no accepted standards in sweeping, scrubbing and dusting. House-cleaning is becoming a specialized, skilled trade, performed by the visiting expert and his staff of professionally trained employés. Even if as yet these skilled and paid workers enter an ordinary home only at long intervals, when the mystic process of spring cleaning seems to justify the expense, the day is plainly in sight when the usual weekly cleaning will be taken over by these same visitors. At present the abruptness of the change is broken for us by the introduction into the market, and the use by the house-mother of various hand-driven machines, a vast improvement upon the old-fashioned broom, and accustoming women to the idea of new and better methods of getting rid of dirt. Few realize the tremendous import of this comparatively insignificant invention, the atmospheric cleaner, or what a radical change it is bringing about in the thoughts of the housewife, whose ideas on the domestic occupations so far have been mostly as confused as those of the charwoman, who put up on her door the sign: "Scrubbing and Window-Cleaning Done Here." In the same way the innumerable electric appliances of today are simplifying the labors of the housewife; but their chief value is that through them she is becoming accustomed to the thought of change, and being led on to distinguish between the housework that can be simplified, and still done at home, and the much larger proportion which must sooner or later be relegated to the professional expert, either coming in at intervals or performing the task elsewhere. And this is true, fortunately, of women in the country as well as in the cities.

We have traveled a long way during the last hundred and fifty years or so, and in that time have witnessed the complete transference from home to factory of many home industries, notably spinning and weaving, and soap- and candle-making. Others like the preparation of food are still in process of transference. The factory industries are the direct and legitimate offspring of the primitive home industries, and their growth and development are entirely on the lines of a normal evolution.

But there is another form of industry that is a ghastly hybrid, the "home-work" that has been born of the union of advanced factory methods and primitive home ap-

Courtesy of The Pine Mountain Settlement
Primitive Industry. Kentucky mountain woman
at her spinning-wheel, 1915

Courtesy of The Chicago School of Civics and Philanthropy
Italian Woman Home Finisher

A CONTRAST

pliances. Such a combination could never have come into existence, had the working classes at the time of the inception of machine-driven industry possessed either an understanding of what was happening, or the power to prevent their own exploitation. The effects of this home-work are in every way deadly. There is not a single redeeming feature about the whole business. Like the spinner or the weaver of olden times, the sewing-machine operator or the shirt-finisher of the present day provides her own workroom, lighting and tools, but unlike her, she enjoys no freedom in their use, nor has she any control over the hours she works, the prices she asks or the class of work she undertakes.

With the home-worker hard-driven by her sister in poverty, and driving her in turn, helpless both in their ignorance under the modern Juggernaut that is destroying them, pushed ever more cruelly by relentless competition, the last stronghold, the poor little home itself, goes down. The mother has no time to care for her children, nor money wherewith to procure for them the care of others. In her frantic desire to keep them alive, she holds the whip over her own flesh and blood, who have to spend their very babyhood in tying feather-flues or pulling out bastings. Home-work, this unnatural product of nineteenth-century civilization, as an agency for summarily destroying the home is unparalleled. Nor do its blighting effects end with homes wrecked, and children neglected, stunted and slain. The proud edifice of modern industry itself, on whose account homes are turned into workshops, children into slaves, and mothers into slave-drivers, is undermined and degraded by this illegitimate competition, the most powerful of all factors in lowering wages, and preventing organization among regular factory hands. The matter lies in a nutshell. Industry which originated in the home could be safely carried on there only as long as it remained simple and the operations thereof such as one individual could complete. As soon as through the invention of power-driven machinery industry reached the stage of high specialization and division of labor, at once it became a danger to the home, and the home a degradation to it. It was at the call of specialized industry that the factory came into existence, and only in the factory can it be safely housed.

A similar and, if it were possible, a worse form of family and group slavery prevails outside of the cities in the poorer farming regions and in the cotton states. It is harder to reach and to handle, and there is cause to fear that it is increasing. Especially in the busy season when the corn has to be harvested or the cotton picked the mother is considered as a toiler first, and she is to have her babies and look after her poor little home and her children as a mere afterthought. The children are contributors to the family support from the time they can toddle and schooling comes a bad second in making the family arrangements. One reason for this growing evil is the threatening degradation and disappearance of the independent farmer class, who made up what would have been called in England formerly the yeomanry of this country, and their replacement by a poor peasantry degraded by the wretched terms upon which they are driven to snatch a bare existence from a patch of land to which they are tied by lease, by mortgage or by wages, and which they have neither the money nor the knowledge to cultivate to advantage.

The Federal Commission on Industrial Relations has brought to light some startling facts in this phase of our social life, as in many others. I can refer to the evidence of but one witness. She speaks for many thousands. This is as it is quoted in the daily press.

Picture for the moment the drama staged at Dallas. Mrs. J. Borden Harriman of New York is presiding over the commission. Mrs. Levi Stewart, the wife of a tenant farmer, is on the witness stand. Mrs. Stewart is a shrinking little woman with "faded eyes and broken body." She wears a blue sunbonnet. Her dress of checkered material has lost its color from long use. In a thin, nervous voice she answers the questions of the distinguished leader of two kinds of "society."

"Do you work in the fields?" Mrs. Harriman began.

"Yes, ma'am."

"How old were you when you married?"

"Fifteen."

"How old was your husband?"

"Eighteen."

"Did you work in the fields when you were a child?"

"Oh, yes'm, I picked and I chopped."

"Have you worked in the fields every year?"

"I do in pickin' and choppin' times."

"And you do the housework?'

"There ain't no one else to do it."

"And the sewing?"

"Yes, ma'am. I make all the clothes for the children and myself. I make everything I wear ever since I was married."

"Do you make your hats?"

"Yes, ma'am. I make my hats. I had only two since I was married."

"And how long have you been married?"

"Twenty years."

"Do you do the milking?"

"Most always when we can afford a cow."

"What time do you get up in the morning?"

"I usually gits up in time to have breakfast done by 4 o'clock in summer time. In the winter time we are through with breakfast by sun-up."

"Did you work in the fields while you were carrying your children?"

"Oh, yes, sometimes; sometimes almost nigh to birthin' time."

"Is this customary among the tenant farmers' wives you have known?"

The answer was an affirmative nod.

Let us now once more consider the home, and compare factory operations with the domestic arts. There is no doubt that in cooking, for instance, the housewife finds scope for a far higher range of qualifications than the factory girl exercises in preparing tomatoes in a cannery, or soldering the cans after they are filled with the cooked fruit. The housewife has first of all to market and next to prepare the food for cooking. She has to study the proper degree of heat, watch the length of time needed for boiling or baking in their several stages, perhaps make additions of flavorings, and serve daintily or can securely. There is scarcely any division of housework which does not call for resource and alertness. Unfortunately, however, although these qualities are indeed called for, they are not always called forth, because the house-worker is not permitted to concentrate her whole atten-tion and interest upon any one class of work, but must be constantly going from one thing to another. Hence women have indeed acquired marvelous versatility, but at what a heavy cost! The houseworker only rarely acquires perfect skill and deftness or any considerable speed in performing any one process. Her versatility is attained at the price of having no standards of com-parison established, and worse than all, at the price of working in isolation, and therefore gaining no training in team-work, and so never having an inkling of what organized effort means.

Our factory systems, on the other hand, go to the other extreme, being so arranged that the majority of

workers gain marvelous dexterity, and acquire a dizzy-
ing rate of speed, while they are apt to lose in both
resourcefulness and versatility. They do not, however,
suffer, to anything like the same degree, from isolation,
and factory life, even where the employers are opposed
to organization, does open a way to the recognition of
common difficulties and common advantages, and therefore leads eventually in the direction of organization.
In the factory trades the workers have to some extent
learnt to be vocal. It is possible for an outsider to learn
something of the inner workings of an establishment.
Upon the highly developed trades, the searchlight of
official investigation is every now and then turned. From
statistics we know the value of the output. We are
also learning a good deal about the workers, the environment that makes for health or invalidism, or risk
to life, and we are in a fair way to learn more. The
organized labor movement furnishes an expression, although still imperfect, of the workers' views, and keeps
before the public the interests of the workers, even of
the unorganized groups.

But with the domestic woman all this is reversed. In
spite of the fact that in numbers the home women far
exceed the wage-earners, the value of their output has
been ignored, and as to the conditions under which it
is produced, not even the most advanced and progressive
statisticians have been able to arrive at any estimate. Of
sentiment tons have been lavished upon the extreme importance of the work of the housewife in the home,
sometimes, methinks, with a lingering misgiving that
she might not be too well content, and might need a
little encouragement to be induced to remain there. What
adulation, too, has been expended upon the work of
even the domestic servant, with comparisons in plenty
unfavorable to the factory occupations into which girls

still persist in drifting. Yet in freedom and in social status, two of the tests by which to judge the relative desirability of occupations, the paid domestic employments take inferior ranks. Again, they offer little prospect of advance, for they lead nowhere.

Further, as noted in an earlier chapter in the census reports all women returning themselves as engaged in domestic duties (not being paid employés), were necessarily not listed as gainfully employed. Yet it is impossible to believe that compared with other ways of employing time and energy, the hours that women spend in cooking and cleaning for the family, even if on unavoidably primitive lines, have no value to the community. Or again, that the hours a mother spends in caring for her baby, later on in helping with the lessons, and fitting the children for manhood or womanhood, have no value in the nation's account book. I will be reminded that this is an unworthy way of reckoning up the inestimable labors of the wife and mother. Perhaps so. Yet personally, I should much prefer a system of social economics which could estimate the items at a fair, not excessive value, and credit them to the proper quarter.

A well-known woman publicist recently drew attention to the vast number of the women engaged in domestic life, and expressed regret that organizations like the National Women's Trade Union League confined their attention so exclusively to the women and girls employed in factories and stores, who, even today, fall so far short numerically of their sisters who are working in the home or on the farm. The point is an interesting one, but admits of a ready explanation. Every movement follows the line of least resistance, and a movement for the industrial organization of women must first approach those in the most advanced and highly organized industries. As I have shown, we really know very much more about the conditions of factory workers than of home-workers. The former have, in a degree, found their voice, and are able to give collective expression to their common interests.

The League recently urged upon the Secretary for Labor, the recognition, as an economic factor, of the work of women in the household trades; the classification of these occupations, whether paid or unpaid, on a par with other occupations, and lastly, that there be undertaken a government investigation of domestic service.

In this connection a long step forward has just been taken through the inquiries, which during the last two years, the Department of Agriculture has been making as to the real position of women on the farm, and has been making them of the women themselves. This came about through a letter addressed to the Secretary from Mr. Clarence Poe, Raleigh, North Carolina, under date of July 9, 1913, in which he said: "Have some bulletins for the farmer's wife, as well as for the farmer himself. The farm woman has been the most neglected factor in the rural problem, and she has been especially neglected by the National Department of Agriculture. Of course, a few such bulletins are printed, but not enough."

A letter was accordingly sent out from Washington to the housewives of the department's 55,000 volunteer crop correspondents, on the whole a group of picked women. They were invited to state both their personal views and the results of discussions with women neighbors, their church organization or any women's organization to which they might belong. To this letter 2,225 relevant replies were received, many of these transmitting the opinions of groups of women in the neighborhood.

The letter asked "how the United States Department

of Agriculture can better meet the needs of farm house-wives." Extracts from the replies with comments have been published in the form of four bulletins. Many of the letters make tragic reading: the want of any money of their own; the never-ending hours; the bad roads and poor schools; neglect in girlhood and at times of childbirth. A great many thoughtless husbands will certainly be awakened to a sense of neglected oppor-tunities, as well as to many sins of commission.

The bulletins contain appendices of suggestions how farm women can help one another, and how they may gain much help from the certainly now thoroughly converted Department of Agriculture, through farmer's institutes for women, through demonstrations and other extension work under the Smith-Lever Act of 1914, and through the formation of women's and girls' clubs.

It is of the utmost importance to society, as well as to herself, that the whole economic status of the married woman, performing domestic duties, should be placed upon a sounder basis. It is not as if the unsatisfactory position of the average wife and mother could confine its results to herself. Compared with other occupations, hers fulfills none of the conditions that the self-respecting wage-earner demands. The twenty-four-hour day, the seven-day week, no legal claim for remuneration, these are her common working conditions. Other claims which a husband can and usually does make upon her I leave unnoticed; also the unquestioned claim of her children upon her time and strength. Marital duties, as they are evasively termed, could not be exacted from any wage servant. Moreover, the very existence of children whom the married pair have called into being is but an argu-ment, on the one hand, for the father taking a larger share in their care, and on the other, for the lightening of the mother's multifarious burden by the better organization of all household work, as well as everything that belongs to child culture and care.

The poor working conditions she suffers under, and the uncertainty of her position, reduce many a woman's share in the married partnership to that of an employé in a sweated trade. This kind of marriage, therefore, like all other sweated trades tends to lower the general market value of women's work. This is casting no reflection upon the hundreds of thousands of husbands who do their part fairly, who share and share alike whatever they have or earn with their wives. How many a workingman regularly hands over to his wife for the support of the home the whole of his earnings with perhaps the barest deduction, a dollar or two, or sometimes only a few cents, for small personal expenditures. Many wives enjoy complete power over the family purse. Or the married pair decide together as to how much they can afford to spend on rent and food and clothing, and when sickness or want of work face them, they meet the difficulty together. The decisions made, it is the wife who has the whole responsibility for the actual spending.

But though so often a man does fulfill in spirit as in letter his promise to support, as well as to love and honor the girl he has married, there is very little in the laws of any country to compel him. And because the man can slip the collar more easily than the woman can, the woman's position is rendered still more uncertain. If she were an ordinary wage-worker, we should say of her that her occupation was an unstandardized one, and that individually she was too dependent upon the personal goodwill of another. Therefore, like all other unstandardized callings, marriage, considered as an occupation, tends to lower the general market value of woman's work. Conversely, Cicely Hamilton in "Marriage as a Trade," points out that the improvements in the economic position of the married woman, which have come about in recent years, are partly at least due to the successful efforts of single women to make themselves independent and self-supporting.

But during the process of transition, and while single women are forging farther and farther ahead, many a married woman is finding herself between the upper and the nether millstone. And unfortunately precisely in the degree that the paid domestic worker is able to make better arrangements in return for her services, whether as resident or as visiting employé, many housemothers are likely for a time to find conditions press yet more severely upon themselves. They will soon have no one left upon whom they can shift their own burdens of overwork, as they have so frequently done in the past. Sooner or later they will be driven to take counsel with their fellows, and will then assuredly plan some method of organizing housewives for mutual help and coöperation, and for securing from society some fairer recognition of the true value of the contribution of the domestic woman to the wealth of the community.

It is not strange that she with whom industry had its rise and upon whom all society rests should be the last to benefit by the forces of reorganization which are spiritually regenerating the race and elevating it to a level never before reached. The very function of sex, whose exercise enters into her relation with her husband, has complicated what could otherwise have been a simple partnership. The helplessness of her children and their utter dependence upon her, which should have furnished her with an additional claim for consideration, have only tied her more closely and have prevented her from obtaining that meed of justice from society which a less valuable servant had long ago won.   But in the sistership of womanhood, now for the first time admitted and hopefully accepted, fortunate and unfortunate clasp hands, and go forward to aid in making that future the whole world awaits today.

XII

THE WORKING WOMAN AND THE VOTE

Olive Schreiner, in "Woman and Labor," lays it down as almost axiomatic that "the women of no race or class will ever rise in revolt or attempt to bring about a revolutionary readjustment of their relation to society, however intense their suffering, and however clear their perception of it, while the welfare and persistence of society requires their submission; that whenever there is a general attempt on the part of the women of any society to readjust their position in it, a close analysis will always show that the changed or changing conditions of society have made women's acquiescence no longer necessary or desirable."

If this be so, it can only be accepted as the application to women of a statement which could be made equally of all the down-trodden races and classes of humanity. The one reason that makes me hesitate about accepting it as a complete explanation of the age-long submission of the oppressed is that we are all rather too ready to accept an explanation that explains away (shall I say?) or at least justifies the suffering of others. The explanation fits so well. Does it not fit too well? Probably Olive Schreiner did not intend it to cover the whole ground.

In one detail, in any case, I take exception to it. An oppressed class or race or sex may often suffer intensely and go on suffering and submitting, but not *after* they have gained a clear perception of the intensity

244

of those sufferings, for then the first stage of rebellion has already begun. Not one of us who has grown to middle age but can remember, looking back to her own girlhood, how meekly and as a matter of course women of all classes accepted every sort of suffering. as part of the lot of woman, especially of the married woman, whether it was excessive child-bearing, pain in child-birth, physical overwork, or the mental suffering arising out of a penniless and dependent condition, with the consequent absolute right of the husband to the custody and control of the children of the union. And in all nations and classes where this state of affairs still continues, the women have as yet no clear intellectual perception of the keenness and unfairness of their suffering. They still try to console themselves with believing and allowing others to suppose that after all, things are not so bad; they might be worse. These poor women actually hypnotize themselves into such a belief.

Have you not heard a mother urge a daughter or a friend to submit uncomplainingly to the most outrageous domestic tyranny, for is not hers after all the common fate of woman?

No clear perception there!

This argument in no way touches the exceptional woman or man, belonging to an oppressed class. Such a woman, for instance, as the Kaffir woman spoken of by Olive Schreiner in this passage, is the rare exception.

But so far Olive Schreiner is undoubtedly right. When the revolt at length takes place it is in answer to an immediate and pressing need of the whole community. When the restrictions upon a class have become hurtful to the whole, when their removal is called for because society is in need of the energies thus set free, then takes place a more or less general uprising of the oppressed and restricted ones, apparently entirely spontaneous and voluntary, in reality having its origin partly at least in the claim which society is making upon the hitherto restricted class to take up fuller social responsibilities.

When observing then the modern change of attitude among women, towards life, we can therefore only conclude that such an immediate and pressing need is felt by society today, a claim neither to be ignored nor denied.

On this reasoning, then, and observing the eager demand of women everywhere for increased freedom and independence, we can only draw the conclusion that the whole world is dimly recognizing an immediate and pressing need for the higher services of women, services which they cannot render unless freed legally, politically and sexually. It is this immense and universal social claim which has been responded to by the whole organized movement among women, industrial as well as educational and political.

In order to understand the relation of the organized suffrage movement to the question of improving women's industrial and economic conditions and status, we have to consider the changed conditions of society under which we live, and we will have to recognize that the demand for the vote in different countries and at different times may or may not coincide with the same social content. Psychologically, indeed, as well as practically, the vote connotes all sorts of different implications to the women of today, contemporaries though they are.

It was with an appreciation of these complexities that Professor W. I. Thomas has pointed out that in his opinion suffragists often place too great stress upon primitive woman's political power, and ignore the fact that women held an even more important relation to the occupational than to the political life of those early days, and that in her occupational value is to be traced the true source of her power and therefore her real influence in any age.

While agreeing with Professor Thomas that some suffrage arguments do on the surface appear inconsistent with historical facts, I believe the inconsistency to be more formal than real.

As the centuries pass a larger and still larger proportion of human affairs passes away from individual management and comes under social and community control. As this process goes on, more and more does the individual, whether man or woman, need the power to control socially the conditions that affect his or her individual welfare. In our day political power rightly used, gives a socialized control of social conditions, and for the individual it is embodied in and is expressed by the vote.

To go back only one hundred years. The great bulk of men and women were industrially much more nearly on a level than they are today. A poor level, I grant you, for with the exception of the privileged classes, few and small were the political powers and therefore the social control of even men. But every extension of political power as granted to class after class of men has, as far as women are concerned, had the fatal effect of increasing the political inequality between men and women, thus placing women, though not apparently, yet relatively and actually upon a lower level.

Again, the status of woman has been crushingly affected by the contemporaneous and parallel change which has passed over her special occupations; so that the conditions under which she works today are decidedly less than ever before by purely personal relationships and more by such impersonal factors as the trade supply of labor, and interstate and international competition. This change has affected woman in an immeasurably greater degree than man. The conditions of industrial life are in our day in some degree controllable by political power so that at this point woman again finds herself civilly and industrially at greater disadvantage than when her status in all these respects depended principally upon her individual capacity to handle efficiently problems arising within an area limited by purely personal relationships. To alter so radically the conditions of daily life and industry, and not merely to leave its control in the hands of the old body of voters, but to give over into the hands of an enlarged and fresh body of voters, and these voters inevitably the men of her own class who are her industrial competitors, that degree of control represented by the vote and to refuse it to women is to place women (though not apparently, yet actually and relatively) upon a distinctly lowered level.

So that what suffragists are asking for is in reality not so much a novel power, as it is liberty to possess and use the same new instrument of social control as has been already accorded to men. Without that instrument it is no mere case of her standing still. She is in very truth retrogressing, as far as effective control over the conditions under which she lives her life, whether inside the home or outside of it. In this instinctive desire not to lose ground, to keep up both with altered social claims of society upon women and with the improved political equipment of their brothers, is to be found the economic crux of women's demand for the vote in every country and in every succeeding decade.

In the course of human development, the gradual process of the readjustment of human beings to changed social and economic conditions is marked at intervals by crises wherein the struggle always going on beneath the surface between the new forces and existing conditions wells up to the surface and takes on the nature of a duel between contending champions. If this is true of one class or of one people, how much more is it true when the change is one that affects an entire sex.

There have been occasions in history and there occur still today instances when economic conditions being such that their labor was urgently needed and therefore desired, it was easy for newcomers to enter a fresh field of industry, and give to a whole class or even to a whole sex in one locality an additional occupation. Such very evidently was the case with the first girls who went into the New England cotton mills. Men's occupations at that time in America lay for the most part out of doors, and there was therefore no sense of rivalry experienced, when the girls who used to spin at home began to spin on a large scale and in great numbers in a factory.

It is far different where women have been forced by the economic forces driving them from behind to make their slow and painful way into a trade already in the possession of men. Of course the wise thing for the men to do in such a case is to bow to the logic of events, and through their own advantageous position as first in the field and through whatever organizations they may possess use all their power to place their new women rivals on an equal footing with themselves and so make it impossible for the women to become a weakening and disintegrating force in the trade. The women being thus more or less protected by the men from the exploitation of their own weakness it is then for them to accept the position, as far as they are able, stand loyally by the men, meet factory conditions as they find them, being the latest comers, and proceed afterwards to bring about such modifications and improvements as may seem to them desirable.

Unfortunately this in a general way may stand for a description of everything that has not taken place. The bitter and often true complaints made by workmen that women have stolen their trade, that having learnt it, well or ill, they are scabs all the time in their acceptance of lower wages and worse conditions, relatively much worse conditions, and that they are often strike-breakers when difficulties arise, form a sad commentary upon the men's own short-sighted conduct. To women, driven by need to earn their living in unaccustomed ways, men have all too often opened no front gate through which they could make an honest daylight entrance into a trade, but have left only side-alleys and back-doors through which the guiltless intruders could slip in. Organized labor today, however, is on record as standing for the broader policy, however apathetic the individual unions and the individual trade unionists may often be.

A dramatic presentation of one of these very complicated situations is found in the experience of Miss Susan B. Anthony in the printers' strike in New York in 1869. By some this incident has been interpreted to show a wide difference of outlook between those women who were chiefly intent on opening up fresh occupational possibilities for women, and those who, coming daily face to face with the general industrial difficulties of women already in the trades, recognized the urgent need of trade organization for women if the whole standard of the trades wherein they were already employed was not to be permanently lowered.

While there is no such general inference to be drawn, the occurrence does place in a very strong light the extreme complexity of the question and the need that then existed, the need that still exists for closer co-operation between workers approaching the problem of the independence of the wage-earning woman from different sides.

The files of the *Revolution,* which Miss Anthony, in conjunction with Mrs. Stanton and Mr. Parker Pillsbury, published from 1868 to 1870, are full of the industrial question. Though primarily the paper stood for the suffrage movement, the editors were on the best of terms with labor organizations and they were constantly urging working-women to organize and cooperate with men trade unionists, and in especial to maintain constantly their claim to equal pay for equal work.

But just about the time of our story, in the beginning of 1869, Miss Anthony seems to have been especially impressed with the need of trade-schools for girls, that they might indeed be qualified to deserve equal pay, to earn it honestly if they were to ask for it; for we find her saying:

"The one great need of the hour is to qualify women workers to *really earn* equal wages with men. We must have *training-schools for women* in all the industrial avocations. Who will help the women will help ways and means to establish them."

Just then a printers' strike occurred and Miss Anthony thought she saw in the need of labor on the part of the employers an opportunity to get the employers to start training-schools to teach the printing trade to girls, in her enthusiasm for this end entirely oblivious of the fact that it was an unfortunate time to choose for making such a beginning. She attended an employers' meeting held at the Astor House and laid her proposal before them.

The printers felt that they were being betrayed, and by one, too, whom they had always considered their friend. On behalf of organized labor Mr. John J. Vincent, secretary of the National Labor Union, made public protest.

Miss Anthony's reply to Mr. Vincent, under date

February 3, 1869, published in the New York *Sun,* and reprinted in the *Revolution,* is very touching, showing clearly enough that in her eagerness to supply the needed thorough trade-training for young girls, she had for the moment forgotten what was likely to be the outcome for the girls themselves of training, however good, obtained in such a fashion. She had also forgotten how essential it was that she should work in harmony with the men's organizations as long as they were willing to work with her. Though not saying so in so many words, the letter is a shocked avowal that, acting impulsively, she had not comprehended the drift of her action, and it amounts to a withdrawal from her first position. She writes:

Sir: You fail to see my motive in appealing to the Astor House meeting of employers, for aid to establish a training school for girls. It was to open the way for a thorough drill to the hundreds of poor girls, to fit them to earn equal wages with men everywhere and not to undermine "Typographical No. 6." I did not mean to convey the impression that "women, already good compositors should work for a cent less per thousand ems than men," and I rejoice most heartily that Typographical Union No. 6 stands so nobly by the Women's Typographical Union No. 1 and demands the admission of women to all offices under its control, and I rejoice also that the Women's Union No. 1 stands so nobly and generously by Typographical Union No. 6 in refusing most advantageous offers to defeat its demands.

My advice to all the women compositors of the city, is now, as it has ever been since last autumn, to join the women's union, for in union alone there is strength, in union alone there is protection.

Every one should scorn to allow herself to be made a tool to undermine the just prices of men workers; and to avoid this union is necessary. Hence I say, girls, stand by each other, and by the men, when they stand by you.

With this the incident seems to have closed, for nothing more is heard of the employers' training-school.[1]

---

[1] This illustrates well the cruel alternative perpetually placed before the working-woman and the working-woman's friends. She is afforded little opportunity to learn a trade thoroughly, and yet, if she does not stand by her fellow men workers, she is false to working class loyalty.

That the women printers of New York were between the devil and the deep sea is evidenced by the whole story told in Chapter XXI of "New York Typographical Union No. 6," by George Stevens. In that is related how about this time was formed a women printers' union, styled "Women's Typographical No. 1," through the exertions of a number of women compositors with Augusta Lewis at their head. Miss Lewis voiced the enthusiastic thanks of the women when, a few months later, the union received its charter from the International Typographical Union at its next convention in June, 1869. A different, and a sadder note runs through Miss Lewis's report to the convention in Baltimore in 1871, in describing the difficulties the women labored under.

"A year ago last January, Typographical Union No. 6 passed a resolution admitting union girls in offices under the control of No. 6. Since that time we have never obtained a situation that we could not have obtained if we had never heard of a union. We refuse to take the men's situations when they are on strike, and when there is no strike, if we ask for work in union offices we are told by union foremen 'that there are no conveniences for us.' We are ostracized in many offices because we are members of the union; and though the principle is right, the disadvantages are so many that we cannot much longer hold together. . . . No. 1 is indebted to No. 6 for great assistance, but as long as we are refused work because of sex we are at the mercy of our employers, and I can see no way out of our difficulties."

In 1878 the International enacted a law that no further charter be granted to women's unions, although it was not supposed to take effect against any already in existence. Women's Typographical No. 1, already on the downward grade, on this dissolved. But not till 1883 did the women printers in New York begin to join the men's union, and there have been a few women members in it ever since. But how few in proportion may be

I have given large space to this incident, because it is the only one of the kind I have come across in Miss Anthony's long career. Page after page of the *Revolution* is full of long reports of workingmen's conventions which she or Mrs. Stanton attended.[1] At these they were either received as delegates or heard as speakers, advocating the cause of labor and showing how closely the success of that cause was bound up with juster treatment towards the working-woman. Many indeed must have been the labor men, who gained a broader outlook upon their own problems and difficulties through listening to such unwearied champions of their all but voiceless sex.

To the more conservative among the workingmen the uncompromising views of these women's advocates must have been very upsetting sometimes, and always very unconventional. We find that in a workingmen's assembly in Albany, New York, when one radical delegate moved to insert the words "and working-women" into the first article of the Constitution, he felt bound to explain to his fellow-delegates that it was not his intention to offer anything that would reflect discredit upon the body. He simply wanted the females to have the benefit of their trades and he thought by denying them this right a great injustice was done to them. The speaker

---

judged from the figures on September 30, 1911. Total membership 6,969, of whom 192 were women. I believe this to be typical of the position of the woman compositor in other cities.

[1] Mrs. Stanton's first speech before the New York legislature, made in 1854, was a demand that married working-women should have the right to collect their own wages. She and the workers with her succeeded in having the law amended. Up till then a married woman might wash all day at the washtub, and at night the law required that her employer should, upon demand, hand over her hard-earned money to her husband, however dissolute he might be.

who followed opposed the discussion of the question. "Let the women organize for themselves." The radicals, however, rose to the occasion.

Mr. Graham in a long speech said it was a shame and a disgrace for this body, pretending to ask the elevation of labor to neglect or refuse to help this large, deserving, but down-trodden class.

Mr. Topp said he would be ashamed to go home and say he had attended this assembly if it overlooked the claims of the female organizations.

The resolution to include the women was carried with applause.

At the National Labor Congress held in Germania Hall, New York, the *Revolution* of October 1, 1868, had noted the admission of four women delegates as marking a new era in workingmen's conventions. These were: Katherine Mullaney, president of the Collar Laundry Union of Troy, N. Y.; Mrs. Mary Kellogg Putnam, representing Working Women's Association No. 2 of New York City; Miss Anthony herself, delegate from Working Women's Association No. 1, New York City; and Mary A. Macdonald, from the Working Women's Protective Labor Union, Mount Vernon, New York.

Mrs. Stanton, after a long and exciting debate, was declared a delegate, but the next day, to please the malcontents, the National Labor Congress made clear by resolution that it did not regard itself as endorsing her peculiar ideas or committing itself to the question of female suffrage, but simply regarded her as a representative from an organization having for its object "the amelioration of the condition of those who labor for a living." "Worthy of Talleyrand" is Miss Anthony's sole comment.

The connection between the woman movement and the labor movement is indeed close and fundamental, but that must not be taken to imply that the workingman and the woman of whatever class have not their own separate problems to handle and to solve as each sees best. The marriage relation between two individuals has often been wrecked by assuming as the basis of their common life that man and wife are one and that the husband is that one. And so the parallel assumption that all the working-woman's wrongs will naturally be righted by redress if their righting is left in the hands of her working brother for many years led to a very curious and unfortunate neglect of suffrage propaganda among working-women, and on the part of working-women and to a no less unfortunate ignorance of industrial problems, also, on the part of many suffragists, whether those affecting workingmen and women alike or the women only.

It was not so in the early days. The instances given above show how close and friendly were the relations between labor leaders and suffrage pioneers. What has been said of Miss Anthony applied equally to the other great women who carried the suffrage banner amid opprobrium and difficulty.

The change came that comes so often in the development of a great movement. One of the main objects which the pioneers had had in view somehow slipped out of the sight of their successors. The earliest move of the advanced women of America had been for equal rights of education, and there success has been greatest and most complete and thorough. But it was almost exclusively the women who were able to enter the professions who gained the benefits of this campaign for equal educational and consequently equal professional opportunities.

The next aim of the leaders in the woman movement of the last century had been to accord to woman equality before the law. This affecting primarily and chiefly woman in her sex relations, had its permanent results in reference to the legal status of the married woman and the mother, bearing at the same time secondarily upon the safety and welfare of the child; hence in the different states a long series of married women's property acts, equal guardianship acts, modifications of the gross inequalities of the divorce law, and the steady raising of the age of protection for girls.

At least that was the position ten years ago. But today the tide has turned. Partly is this due to the growth of industrial organization among women, a development that has followed the ever-increasing need of mutual protection. Trade unionism has helped to train the working-woman to listen to the suffrage gospel, though therein she has often been slower than the workingman, her better educated brother. On the other hand a great many influences have combined to wake up the suffragist of our day to the true meaning and value of what she was asking. Especially has the work of the National Women's Trade Union League and the campaign of publicity it has conducted on behalf of the working-woman, both within and without its membership, focused attention upon the woman in industry as a national responsibility. Then again the tremendous strikes in which such large numbers of women and girls have been involved were an education to others than the strikers—to none more than to the suffrage workers who coöperated with the ill-used girl strikers in New York, Boston, Philadelphia and Chicago.

An influence of even more universal appeal, if of less personal intensity, has been the suffrage movement in Great Britain. That movement has educated the public of this country, as they never would have been educated by any movement confined to this country alone. Inside

the ranks of enrolled suffragists it has been an inspiration, showering upon their cause a new baptism of
mingled tears and rejoicing. In calmer mood we have
learned from our British sisters much regarding policies
adapted to modern situations, and they have assuredly
shown us all sorts of new and original methods of organization and education. The immense and nation-
wide publicity given by the press of the United States
to the more striking and sensational aspects of the British
movement and all the subsequent talk and writing in
other quarters has roused to sex-consciousness thousands
of American women of all classes who had not been
previously interested in the movement for obtaining full
citizenship for themselves and their daughters. These
women also aroused, and men, too, have furnished the
huge audiences which have everywhere greeted such
speakers as Mrs. Pankhurst and Mrs. Philip Snowden,
when in person they have presented the mighty story of
the transatlantic struggle. There is no difficulty nowadays in gathering suffrage audiences anywhere, for the
man and the woman walking along the street supply them
to the open-air speaker in the large city and the little
country town as one by one city and town take up the
new methods.

Even more close to lasting work for all the issues that
affect the community through placing upon women an
ordered civic responsibility are the plans for the organizing under different names of woman suffrage parties
and civic leagues which blend the handling of local activities everywhere with a demand for the ballot in keeping with the needs of the modern community. No
clear-eyed woman can work long in this sort of atmosphere without realizing how unequally social burdens
press, how unequally social advantages are allotted,
whether the burdens come through hours of work, inad-

equate remuneration, sanitary conditions, whether in home or in factory, and whether the advantages are obtainable through public education, vocational training, medical care, or in the large field of recreation.

So important does work through organization appear to me that, remembering always that tendencies are more important than conditions, it would seem in some respects a more wholesome and hopeful situation for women to be organized and working for one of their common aims, even though that aim be for the time being merely winning of the vote, rather than to have the vote, and with it working merely as isolated individuals, and with neither the power that organization insures nor the training that it affords.

But with what we know nowadays there should be no need for any such unsatisfactory alternative. It would be much more in keeping with the modern situation if the object of suffrage organizations were to read, not "to obtain the vote" but "to obtain political, legal and social equality for women."

Then as each state, or as the whole country (we hope by and by) obtains the ballot, so might the organizations go on in a sense as if nothing had happened. And nothing would have happened, save that a great body of organized women would be more effective than ever. The members would individually be equipped with the most modern instrument of economic and social expression. The organizations themselves would have risen in public importance and esteem and therefore in influence. Moreover, and this is the most important point of all, they would be enrolled among those bodies, whose declared policy would naturally help in guiding the great bulk of new and untrained feminine voters.

In the early days of the woman movement, the leaders, I believe, desired as earnestly and as keenly saw the need for legal and social or economic equality as we today with all these years of experience behind us. But the unconscious assumption was all the time that given political equality every other sort of equality would readily and logically follow. Even John Stuart Mill seems to have taken this much for granted. Not indeed that he thought that with universal enfranchisement the millennium would arrive for either men or women. But even to his clear brain and in his loyal and chivalrous heart, political freedom for women did appear as one completed stage in development, an all-inclusive boon, as it were, in due time bringing along by irrefragable inference equality on every other plane, equality before the law and equality in all social and sexual relations.

Looking back now, we can see that whatever thinkers and statesmen fifty years ago may have argued for as best meeting the immediate needs of the hour, the organized suffrage movement in all the most advanced countries should long ago have broadened their platform, and explicitly set before their own members and the public as their objective not merely "the vote," but "the political, legal and social equality of women."

We are not abler, not any broader-minded nor more intellectually daring than those pioneers, but we have what they had not, the test of results. Let us briefly glance at what has been the course of events in those states and countries which were the earliest to obtain political freedom for their women.

In none of the four suffrage states first enfranchised in this country, Wyoming, Utah, Idaho and Colorado, in Australia or in New Zealand, did any large proportion of women ask for or desire their political freedom. In that there is nothing strange or exceptional. Those who see the need of any reform so clearly that they will work for it make up comparatively a small proportion of any nation or of any class. Women are no exception. Note Australia. As the suffrage societies there, as elsewhere, had been organized for this one purpose, "to obtain the vote," with the obtaining of the vote all reason for their continued existence ceased. The organizations at once and inevitably went to pieces. The vote, gained by the efforts of the few, was now in the hands of great masses of women, who had given little thought to the matter previously, who were absolutely unaware of the tremendous power of the new instrument placed in their hands. A whole sex burst into citizenship, leaderless and with no common policy upon the essential needs of their sex.

Except in Victoria, where the state franchise lagged behind till 1909, the women of Australia have been enfranchised for over twelve years, and yet it is only recently that they are beginning to get together as sister women. Those leaders who all along believed in continuous and organized work by women for the complete freeing of the sex from all artificial shackles and unequal burdens are now justified of their belief. New young leaders are beginning to arise, and there are signs that the rank and file are beginning to march under these leaders towards far-off ends that are gradually being defined more clearly from the mists of these years. But they have much ground to make up. Only so lately as 1910 there were leading women in one of the large labor conferences who protested against women entering the legislature, using against that very simple and normal step in advance the very same moss-grown arguments as we hear used in this country against the conferring of the franchise itself.

Nowadays, it is true, no quite similar result is likely to happen in any state or country which from now on receives enfranchisement, for the reason that there are now other organizations, such as the General Federation of Women's Clubs here, and the active women's trade unions, and suffrage societies on a broad basis and these are every day coming in closer touch with one another and with the organized suffrage movement. But neither women's trade unions nor women's clubs can afford to neglect any means of strengthening their forces, and a sort of universal association having some simple broad aim such as I have tried to outline would be an ally which would bring them into communication with women outside the ranks of any of the great organizations, for it alone would be elastic enough to include all women, as its appeal would necessarily be made to all women.

The universal reasons for equipping women with the vote as with a tool adapted to her present day needs, and the claims made upon her by the modern community, the reasons, in short why women want and are asking for the vote, the universal reasons why men, even good men, cannot be trusted to take care of women's interests, were never better or more tersely summed up than in a story told by Philip Snowden in the debate in the British House of Commons on the Woman Suffrage Bill of 1910, known as the Conciliation Bill. He said that after listening to the objections urged by the opponents of the measure, he was reminded of a man who, traveling with his wife in very rough country, came late at night to a very poor house of accommodation. When the meal was served there was nothing on the table but one small mutton chop. "What," said the man in a shocked tone, "have you nothing at all for my wife?"

XIII

TRADE UNION IDEALS AND POLICIES

Trade unionism does not embrace the whole of industrial democracy, even for organized labor and even were the whole of labor organized, as we hope one of these days it will be, but it does form one of the elements in any form of industrial democracy as well as affording one of the pathways thither.

The most advanced trade unionists are those men and women who recognize the limitations of industrial organization, but who value it for its flexibility, for the ease with which it can be transformed into a training-school, a workers' university, while all the while it is providing a fortified stronghold from behind whose shelter the industrial struggle can be successfully carried on, and carried forward into other fields.

If we believe, as all, even non-socialists, must to some extent admit, that economic environment is one of the elemental forces moulding character and deciding conduct, then surely the coming together of those who earn their bread in the same occupation is one of the most natural methods of grouping that human beings can adopt.

There are still in the movement in all countries those of such a conservative type that they look to trade organization as we know it today as practically the sole factor in solving the industrial problem.

In order to fulfill its important functions of protecting the workers, giving to them adequate control over their working conditions, and the power of bargaining for the disposal of their labor power through recognized representatives, trade-union organization must be world-wide. Organizations of capital are so, or are becoming so, and in order that the workers may bargain upon an equal footing, they must be in an equally strong position. Now is the first time in the history of the world that such a plan could be even dreamt of. Rapid means of communication and easy methods of transport have made it possible for machine-controlled industry to attract workers from all over the world to particular centers, and in especial to the United States, and this has taken place without any regard as to where there was the best opening for workers of different occupations or as to what might be the effects upon the standards of living of the workers of artificially fostered migrations, and haphazard distribution of the newcomers.

It is sadly true of the labor movement, as of all other movements for social advance, that it lags behind the movements organized for material success and private profit. It lags behind because it lacks money, money which would keep more trained workers in the field, which would procure needed information, which would prevent that bitterest of defeats, losing a strike because the strikers could no longer hold out against starvation. The labor movement lacks money, partly because money is so scarce among the workers; they have no surplus from which to build up the treasury as capital does so readily, and partly because so many of them do not as yet understand that alone they are lost, in organization they have strength. While they need the labor movement, just as much does the labor movement need them.

More and more, however, are the workers acknowledging their own weakness, at the same time that they remember their own strength. As they do so, more and more will they adopt capital's own magnificent methods of organization to overcome capital's despotism, and be able to stand out on a footing of equality, as man before man.

One tendency, long too much in evidence in the labor movement generally, and one which has still to be guarded against, is to take overmuch satisfaction in the unionizing of certain skilled trades or sections of trades, and to neglect the vast bulk of those already handicapped by want of special skill or training, by sex or by race. I have heard discussions among labor men which illustrate this. The platform of the Federation of Labor is explicit, speaking out on this point in no doubtful tone, but there are plenty of labor men, and labor women who make their own particular exceptions to a rule that should know of none.

I have heard men in the well-paid, highly skilled, splendidly organized trades speak even contemptuously of the prospect of organizing the nomad laborers of the land, recognizing no moral claim laid upon themselves by the very advantages enjoyed by themselves in their own trade, advantages in which they took so much pride. That is discouraging enough, but more discouraging still was it to gather one day from the speech of one who urged convincingly that while both for self-defense and for righteousness' sake, the skilled organized workers must take up and make their own the cause of the unskilled and exploited wanderers, that he too drew his line, and that he drew it at the organization of the Chinese.[1]

---

[1] I am not here discussing the unrestricted admission of Orientals under present economic conditions. I merely use the illustration to press the point, that organized labor should include in

Others again, while they do not openly assert that they disapprove of the bringing of women into the trade unions, not only give no active assistance towards that end, but in their blindness even advocate the exclusion of women from the trades, and especially from their own particular trade. The arguments which they put forward are mostly of these types: "Girls oughtn't to be in our trade, it isn't fit for girls"; or, "Married women oughtn't to work"; or, "Women folks should stay at home," and if the speaker is a humane and kindly disposed man, he will add, "and that's where they'll all be one of these days, when we've got things straightened out again." As instances of this attitude on the part of trade-union men who ought to know better, and its results, the pressmen in the printing shops of our great cities are well organized, and the girls who feed the presses, and stand beside the men and work with them, are mostly outside the protection of the union. Some of the glass-blowers are seriously arguing against the suggestion of organizing the girls who are coming into the trade in numbers. "Organization won't settle it. That's no sort of a solution," say the men; "they're nice girls and would be much better off in some other trade." Just as if girls went into hard and trying occupations from mere contrariness! It is too late in the day, again, to shut the door on the women who are going in as core-makers in the iron industry, but the men in the foundries think they can do it. Men who act and talk like this have yet much to learn of the true meaning and purposes of labor organization.

Wherever, then, we find this spirit of exclusion manifested, whether actively as in some of the instances I

its ranks all workers already in the United States. A number of the miners in British Columbia are advocates of the organization of the Chinese miners in that province.

have cited, or passively in apathetic indifference to the welfare of the down-trodden worker, man or woman, American or foreign, white or colored, there is no true spirit of working-class solidarity, only a self-seeking acceptance of a limited and antiquated form of labor organization, quite out of keeping with twentieth-century conditions and needs. This does not make for advance ultimately in any branch of labor, but is one of the worst retarding influences to the whole movement. In former ages the principles of democracy could only extend within one class after another. The democracy of our day is feeling after a larger solution; the democracy of the future cannot know limits or it will be no democracy at all.

It has been pointed out many times that the rich are rich, not so much in virtue of what they possess, but in virtue of what others do not possess. The ratio of the difference between the full pocket and many empty pockets represents the degree in which the one rich man or woman is able to command the services of many poor men and women. We all recognize these crude differences and regret the results to society. But after all is the case so very much bettered when for rich and poor, we read skilled and unskilled, when we have on the one hand a trade whose members have attained their high standing through the benefits of years of training, a strong union, high initiation fees, perhaps limitation of apprentices? I am neither praising nor criticizing any methods of trade protection. All of them are probably highly beneficial to those within the charmed circle of the highly organized trades. But if, in the very midst of the general state of industrial anarchy and oppression which the unskilled workers have to accept, it is possible to find trades in which organization has been so successful in maintaining good conditions, this is partly because the number of such artisans, so skilled and so protected, has always been limited. And let us ask ourselves what are the effects of these limitations upon those outside the circle, whether those excluded from the trade or from the organization because of the demands exacted, or those debarred by poverty or other circumstances from learning any skilled trade at all. Unquestionably the advantages of the highly protected ones are not won solely from the employers. Some part of their industrial wealth is contributed by the despised and ignored outsiders. Some proportion of their high wages is snatched from the poor recompense of the unskilled. Women are doubly sufferers, underpaid both as women and as unskilled workers. It is not necessary to subscribe to the old discredited wage-fund theory, in order to agree with this.

Just here lies the chief danger of the craft form of organization as a final objective. If the trade-union movement is ever to be wholly effective and adequate to fulfill its lofty aims, it must cease to look upon craft organization as a final aim. The present forms of craft organization are useful, only so long as they are thought of as a step to something higher, only in so far as the craft is regarded as a part of the whole. Were this end ever borne in mind, we should hear less of jurisdictional fights, and there would be more of sincere endeavor and more of active effort among the better organized workers to share the benefits of organization with all of the laboring world. The more helpless and exploited the group, the keener would be the campaign, the more unsparing the effort on the part of the more fortunate sons of toil.

Against such a narrow conservatism, however, there are other forces at work, both within and without the regularly organized labor movement, one of them aiming at such reorganization of the present unions as shall gradually merge the many craft unions into fewer and larger bodies.[1] This process is evolutionary, and constructive, but slow, and meanwhile the exploited workers cry in their many tongues, "O Lord, how long!" or else submit in voiceless despair.

Is it any wonder that under these conditions of industrial anarchy and imperfect organization of labor power a new voice is heard in the land, a voice which will not be stilled, revolutionary, imperious, aiming frankly at the speedy abolition of organized governments, and of the present industrial system? This is the movement known in Europe as syndicalism, and on this continent represented by the Industrial Workers of the World, usually termed the I. W. W.

Their program stands for the one big union of all the workers, the general strike and the gaining possession and the conducting of the industries by the workers engaged in them. They deprecate the making of agreements with employers, and acknowledge no duty in the keeping of agreements.

The year 1911 will be remembered among word-historians as the year when the word "syndicalism" became an everyday English word. It had its origin in the French word "syndicalisme," which is French for trade unionism, just as French and Belgian trade unions are "syndicats." But because for reasons that cannot be gone into here so many of the French trade unionists profess this peculiarly revolutionary philosophy, there has grown up out of and around the word "syndicalisme" a whole literature with writers like George Sorel and Gustave Hervé as the prophets and exponents of the new movement. So the word "syndicalism," thus anglicized, has

---

[1] The United Mine Workers are essentially on an industrial basis; they take in all men and boys working in and about the mine.

come to signify this latest form of trade-union organization and action.

Although sabotage, interfering with output, clogging machinery, blocking transportation and so forth have been advocated and practiced by extreme syndicalists, such do not seem to me to form an essential and lasting element in syndicalist activity, any more than we find the wholesale destruction of machinery as carried on by displaced workmen a hundred years ago, has remained an accepted method of trade-union action, although such acts may easily form incidents in the progress of the industrial warfare to which syndicalists are pledged. Neither at Lawrence, Massachusetts, nor later at Paterson, New Jersey, did the Industrial Workers of the World, or the large bodies of strikers whom they led set any of these destructive practices in operation.

Syndicalism is the latest despairing cry of the industrially vanquished and down-trodden, and is not to be suppressed by force of argument, whether the argument comes from the side of the employer or the fellow-workman. Only with the removal of the causes can we expect this philosophy of despair to vanish, for it is the courage of despair that we witness in its converts. The spirit they display lies outside the field of blame from those who have never known what it means to lose wife and children in the slow starvation of the strike or husband and sons in the death-pit of a mine, and themselves to be cheated life-long of the joys that ought to fall to the lot of the normal, happiness-seeking human being, from birth to death.

The syndicalists will have done their work if they rouse the rest of us to a keener sense of our responsibilities. When the day comes that every worker receives the full product of his toil, the reasons for existence of this form of revolutionary activity will have passed away.

Of one thing the present writer is convinced. That this newest form of the industrial struggle, however crude it may appear, however blind and futile in some of its manifestations, is destined to affect profoundly the course of the more orthodox trade-union movement. The daring assumptions that labor is the supreme force, that loyalty to the working world is the supreme virtue, and failure in that loyalty the one unpardonable sin, has stirred to the very depths organized labor of the conservative type, has roused to self-questioning many and many a self-satisfied orthodox trade unionist, inspiring him with loftier and more exacting ideals. He has been thrilled, as he had never been thrilled before with a realization of the dire need of the submerged and unorganized millions, and of the claims that they have upon him. Verily, in the face of such revelations, satisfaction in the fine organization of his own particular trade receives a check. The good of his own union as his highest aim sinks into insignificance, though regarding it as a means to an end, he may well go back to his workshop and his union card, intending to do for his fellow-craftsmen in his shop and in his trade more than ever before.

The very activities of the I. W. W. during the last two or three years, side by side with the representatives of the American Federation of Labor on the same strike fields, and often carrying out opposition tactics, have for the first time in their lives given many furiously to think out policies and plans of campaign. From such shocks and stimuli are born thinkers and original tacticians, especially among the younger men and women.

Wherever syndicalists have actively taken part in labor struggles, there has been the bitterest antagonism between them and the regular labor bodies. The latter ever bear in mind the risks of a divided front, and they have just reason to dread the "dual" organization as the most completely disruptive influence that can weaken labor's forces, and play into the employers' hands. Of this experience there have been too many instances in the United States.

Syndicalists condemn agreements as a device of the enemy. It is true that agreements may be so managed as to prove a very weak reed for the workers to depend on in time of trouble. We have had many instances within the last few years of the disintegrating effect on the labor movement of agreements made between the employers and sections of their employés, which while protecting these particular sections leave other employés of the same firms out in the cold, either because the latter have no agreement at all, or because it is worded differently, or, most common defect of all, because it terminates upon a different date, three months, say, or a year later. It was on this rock that the printing pressmen struck during the huge newspaper fight in Chicago which lasted the whole summer of 1912, ending in a defeat costly to the conqueror, as well as to the conquered and whose echoes are still to be heard in discussions between representatives of the organizations and the sub-organizations involved. Though the fight was lost by the pressmen, the dispute between the unions involved is not settled yet, and the two principles at stake, loyalty to the interest of their fellow-workers and the duty of keeping a pledge made to employers, are as far as ever from being reconciled. The solution ahead is surely the strengthening of organizations so that failing a common agreement one branch or one craft will be in a position to refuse to sign one of these non-concurrent agreements, or any sort of agreement, which will leave other workers at a palpable disadvantage.

The demand for the speedy taking over of the direct

control of industries by the workers appears to me to ignore alike human limitations and what we know of the evolution of society. But great hope is to be placed in the coöperative movement, with the gradual establishment of factories and stores by organizations of the workers themselves.

The condemnation of political activity, too, is, as I see it, out of line with the tendencies of social evolution, which demands organization and specialized skill in managing the affairs of the largest community as of the smallest factory.

The strength and value of syndicalism is rather in criticism than in constructive results. In almost every paragraph in the platform we can detect a criticism of some weak point in the labor movement, in political socialism, or in the existing social framework we are consenting to accept and live under.

So far in every country where it has risen into notice syndicalism has been more of a free-lance body than a regular army, and it may be that that is what syndicalists will remain. Up to the present they have shown no particular constructive ability. But they may develop great leaders, and with development work out plans to meet the new problems that will crowd upon them. Even if they should not, and should pass away as similar revolutionary groups have passed before, they will have hastened tremendously the closer knitting together of all groups of trade unionists. On the one hand they have already stirred up socialists to a better understanding and more candid admission of their own shortcomings in the political field, and on the other, they have already made labor more fearless and aggressive, and therefore more venturesome in the claims it makes, and more ready and resourceful in its adaptation of new methods to solve modern difficulties.

Before leaving the syndicalists, I would call attention to a change that is coming over the spirit of some of their leaders, as regards immediate plans of action. From a recent number of *La Guerre Sociale,* edited by Gustave Hervé, the *Labour Leader* (England), quotes an article attributed to Hervé himself, in which the writer says:

"Because it would be a mistake to expect to achieve everything by means of the ballot-box, it does not follow that we can achieve nothing thereby."

Another syndicalist of influence has been advocating the establishment of training-schools for the workers, in preparation for the day when they are to take over the industries. Vocational instruction this upon the great scale!

Ramsay McDonald, by no means an indulgent critic of syndicalism, does not believe that Sorel really anticipates the general strike as the inauguration of the new order, but as a myth, which will lead the people on to the fulfillment of the ideal that lies beyond and on the other side of all anticipated revolutionary action.

It is time now to consider the tendencies towards growth and adaptation to modern needs that have been, and are at work, within the American Federation of Labor, and among those large outside organizations on the outer edge of the Federation, as it were, such as the brotherhoods of railroad trainmen. These tendencies, are, speaking generally, towards such reorganization as will convert many small unions into fewer, larger, and therefore stronger bodies, and towards the long-delayed but inevitable organization of the workers on the political field. Such reorganization is not always smooth sailing, but the process is an education in itself.

The combination or the federation of existing organizations is but the natural response of the workers to the ever-growing complexity of modern industrial life. Ever closer organization on the part of the employers, the welding together of twenty businesses into one corporation, of five corporations into one trust, of all the trusts in the country into one combine, have to be balanced by correspondingly complete organization on the part of the workers. There is this difference of structure, however, between the organization of employers and that of the employed. The first is comparatively simple, and is ever making for greater simplicity. Without going into the disputed question of how far the concentration of business can be carried, and of whether or not the small business man is to be finally pushed out of existence, it is beyond question that every huge business, for example, each one of our gigantic department stores, includes and represents an army of small concerns, which it has replaced, which have either been bought up or driven to the wall. In either case the same amount of trade, which it once took hundreds of separate small shopkeepers to handle, is now handled by the one firm, under the one management. Such welding together makes for the economy in running expenses which is its first aim. But it also makes for simplicity in organization. It is evidently far easier for the heads of a few immense businesses to come together than it was for the proprietors of the vast agglomeration of tiny factories, stores and offices which once covered the same trade area, or to be quite accurate, a much smaller trade area, to do so.

But if, at the one end of the modern process of production and distribution, we find this tendency towards a magnificent simplicity, at the other, the workers' end, we have the very same aim of economy of effort and the cheapening of production resulting in an enormously increased complexity. The actual work performed by each worker is simplified. But the variety of processes and the consequent allotting of the workers into un-related groups make for social complexity; render it not easier, but much harder for the workers to come together and to see and make others see through and in spite of all this apparent unlikeness of occupation, common interests and a common need for coöperative action.

Again, take a factory, such as a cotton mill. The one firm, before marketing its product, will have employed in its preparation and final disposal till it reaches the consumer, groups engaged in very different occupations, spinners, weavers, porters, stenographers, salesmen, and so on. The industry which furnished employment to one, or at most, to two groups, has been cut up into a hundred subdivisions, but the workers have still many interests in common, and they need to cling together or suffer from all the disadvantages of unorganized or semi-organized occupations.

The first unions were naturally craft unions. The men working in the same shop, and at the same processes got together, and said: "We who do this work must get to know the fellows in the other shops; we must just stick together, make common demands and support one another."

As industry became more highly specialized, there slipped in, especially during the last fifty years or so, a disintegrating tendency. The workers in what had been one occupation, found themselves now practicing but a small fraction of what had been their trade. They were performing new processes, handling novel tools and machinery unheard of before. The organizations became divided up into what were nominally craft unions, in reality only process unions. Or if a new organization was formed, it was but a mere clipping off the whole body of operatives. And these unions, too, would probably have their international organization, to which they could turn to come in touch with brother workers, similarly qualified and employed.   There is necessarily involved an element of weakness in any organization, however extensive, built up upon so limited a foundation, unless the membership has other local and occupational affiliations as well.   So, to meet this defect, there have been formed all sorts of loose aggregations of unions, and almost every day sees fresh combinations formed to meet new needs as these arise.   Within the wide bounds of the American Federation itself exist the state federations, also city federations, which may include the unions in adjoining cities, even though these are in different states, such as the Tri-City Federation, covering Davenport, Iowa, and Moline and Rock Island, Illinois.   The district councils, again, are formed from representatives of allied trades or from widely different branches of the same trade, such as the councils of the building trades, and the allied printing trades.   There are the international unions (more properly styled continental) covering the United States and the Dominion of Canada.   With these are affiliated the local unions of a trade or of a whole industry, sometimes, from all over the continent of North America.   Among these the most catholic in membership are such broadly organized occupations as the united mine-workers, the garment-workers, the ladies' garment-workers, the iron, steel and tin-plate workers.   An international union composed of separate unions of the one trade, or a state or a city federation of local unions of many trades, bears the same relation to the component single unions as does the union itself to the individual workers; so we find that all these various and often changing expressions of the trade-union principle are accepted and approved of to-day.

Even more significant are other groupings which may be observed forming among the rank and file of the union men and women themselves.

Sometimes these groups combine with the full approval of the union leaders, local and international. Sometimes they are more in the nature of an insurgent body, either desiring greater liberty of self-government for themselves, or questioning the methods of the organization's leaders, and desiring to introduce freer, more democratic and more modern methods into the management of the parent organization. This may take the form of a district council, and in at least one noteworthy instance, the employés of one large corporation send their representatives to a joint board, for purposes of collective bargaining.

The railway unions within the American Federation of Labor, one of the largest and most powerful bodies of union men in the United States feel the need of some method of grouping which shall link together the men's locals and the internationals into which the locals are combined. This is seen in the demand made by the men for the acknowledgment by the railways of the "system federation." The reason some of the more radical men were not found supporting the proposal was not that they objected to a broader form of organization, but because they considered the particular plan outlined as too complicated to be effective.

There is one problem pressing for decisive solution before very long, and it concerns equally organized labor, governments and public bodies and the community as a whole. That is, the relations that are to exist between governing bodies in their function as employer, and the workers employed by them. So far all parties to this momentous bargain are content to drift, instead of thinking out the principles upon which a peaceful and permanent solution can be found for a condition of affairs, new with this generation, and planning in concert such arrangements as shall insure even-handed justice to all three parties.

It is true that governments have always been employers of servants, ever since the days when they ceased to be masters of slaves, but till now only on a limited scale. But even on this limited scale no entirely satisfactory scheme of civil-service administration has anywhere been worked out. Of late years more and more have the autocratic powers of public bodies as employers been considerably clipped, but on the other hand, the iron-clad rules which make change of occupation, whether for promotion or otherwise, necessary discipline and even deserved dismissal, so difficult to bring about, have prejudiced the outside community whom they serve against the just claims of an industrious and faithful body of men and women. And the very last of these just claims, which either governing bodies or communities are willing to grant, is liberty to give collective expression to their common desires.

The question cannot be burked much longer. Every year sees public bodies, in the United States as everywhere else, entering upon new fields of activity. In this country, municipal bodies, state governments, and even the Federal Government, are in this way perpetually increasing the number of those directly in their employ. The establishment of the parcel post alone must have added considerably to the total of the employés in the Postal Department. It cannot be very many years before some of the leading monopolies, such as the telegraph and the telephone, will pass over to national management, with again an enormous increase in the number of employés. Schools are already under public control, and one city after another is taking up, if not manufacture or production, at least distribution as in the case of water, lighting, ice, milk or coal.

This is no theoretical question as to whether governmental bodies, large and small, local and national, should or should not take over these additional functions of supplying community demands. The fact is before us now. They are doing it, and in the main, doing it successfully. But what they are not doing, what these very employés are not doing, what organized labor is not doing, what the community is not doing, is to plan intelligently some proper method of representation, by which the claims, the wishes and the suggestions of employés may receive consideration, and through which, on the other hand, the governing body as board of management, and the public, as in the long last the real employer, shall also have their respective rights defined and upheld.

The present position is exactly as if a sovereign power had conquered a territory, and proposed to govern it, not temporarily, but permanently, as a subject province. We know that this is not the modern ideal in politics, and it ought not to be assumed as the right ideal when the territory acquired is not a geographical district, but a new function. In this connection, moreover, the criticisms of our candid friends the syndicalists are not to be slighted. Their solution of the problem, that the workers should come into actual, literal possession and management of the industries, whether publicly or privately owned, may appear to us hopelessly foolish and impractical, but their misgivings regarding an ever-increasing bureaucratic control over a large proportion of the workers, who are thus made economically dependent upon an employer, because that employer chances also to hold the reins of government, have already ample justification. The people have the vote, you will say? At least the men have. Proposals to deprive public employés of the vote have been innumerable, and in not a few instances have been enacted into law. There are whole bodies of public employés in many countries today who have no vote.

The late Colonel Waring was far-sighted beyond his day and generation. When he took over the Street Cleaning Department of New York, which was in an utterly demoralized condition, he saw that reasonable self-government among his army of employés was going to help and not to hinder his great plans, and it was not only with his full consent, but at his suggestion and under his direction, that an organization was formed among them, which gave to the dissatisfied a channel of expression, and to the constructive minds opportunity to improve the work of the department, as well as continually to raise the status of the employé.

All such organizations to be successful permanently and to be placed on a solid basis must join their fortunes with the labor movement, and this is the last pill that either a conservative governing body or the public themselves are willing to swallow. They use exactly the same argument that private employers used universally at one time, but which we hear less of today—the right of the employer to run his own business in his own way.

Very many people, who see nothing wicked in a strike against a private employer, consider that no despotic conduct on the part of superiors, no unfairness, no possible combination of circumstances, can ever justify a strike of workers who are paid out of the public purse. Much also is made of the fact that most of such functions which governments have hitherto undertaken are directly associated with pressing needs, such as street-car and railroad service, water and lighting supplies, and the same line of reasoning will apply, perhaps in even a higher degree, to future publicly owned and controlled enterprises. This helps yet further to strengthen the idea that rebellion, however sorely provoked, is on the part of public employés a sort of high treason, the reasons for which neither deserve nor admit of discussion. The greatest confusion of thought prevails, and no distinction is drawn between the government as the expression and embodiment of the forces of law, order and protection to all, as truly the voice of the people, and the government, through its departments, whether legislative, judicial or administrative, as just a plain common employer, needing checks and control like all other employers.

The problem of the public ownership of industries in relation to employés might well be regarded in a far different light. It holds indeed a proud and honorable position in social evolution. It is the latest and most complex development of industry, and as such the heads of such enterprises should be eager to study the development of the earlier and simpler forms of industry in relation to the labor problem, and to study them just as conscientiously and gladly as they study and adopt scientific and mechanical improvements in their various departments.

But no. We are all of us just drifting. Every now and then the question comes before us, unfortunately rarely as a matter for cool and sane discussion, but usually arising out of some dispute. Both sides are then in an embittered mood. There may be a strike on. The employés may be in the wrong, but any points on which they may yield are merely concessions wrung from them by force of superior strength, for the employing body unfailingly assumes rights and privileges beyond those of the ordinary employer. In particular, discontented employés are invariably charged with disloyalty, and lectured upon their duty to the public. As if the public owed nothing to them!

More democratic methods of expressing the popular will, giving us legislation, and in consequence administration more in harmony with the interests of the workers as a whole, and therefore in the end reacting for the advantage of the community at large, will assuredly do much to remove some of these difficulties. This is one reason why direct legislation and such "effective voting" as proportional representation should be earnestly advocated and supported by organized labor on all possible occasions. But that we may make full and wise use of such additional powers of democratic expression in placing public employment upon a sounder footing, it is necessary that we should give the subject the closest attention and consideration both in its general principles, and in details as they present themselves. If not, satisfaction in the growth of publicly controlled industry may be marred through the sense that the public are being served at an unfair cost to an important section of the workers.

All of these problems touch women as well as men; and if they are to be solved on a just as well as a broad basis women must do their share towards the solving. Needless to say, women in industry suffer as much or more than their brothers from whatever makes for reaction in the labor movement. It is therefore fortunate for the increasing numbers of wage-earning women that progressive forces are at work, too. From one angle, the very activity of Women's Trade Union Leagues in the cities where they are established is to be regarded as one expression of the widespread and growing tendency towards such complete organization of the workers as shall correspond to modern industrial conditions.

Mrs. Gilman is never tired of reiterating that we live in a man-made world, and that the feminine side in either man or woman will never have a chance for development until this is a human-made world. And before this can come about woman must be free from the economic handicap that shackles her today.

The organization of labor is one of the most important means to achieve this result. It is not only in facing the world outside, and in relation to the employer and the consumer that woman organized is stronger and in every way more effective than woman unorganized. The relation in which she stands to her brother worker is very different, when she has behind her the protection and with her the united strength of her union, and the better a union man he is himself the more readily and cheerfully will he appreciate this, even if he has occasionally to make sacrifices to maintain unbroken a bargain in which both are gainers.

But at first, in the same way as the average workingman is apt to have an uncomfortable feeling about the woman entering his trade, even apart from the most important reason of all, that she is wont to be a wage-cutter, the average trade-union man retains a somewhat uneasy apprehension when he finds women entering the union. As they become active, women introduce a new element. They may not say very much, but it is gradually discovered that they do not enjoy meeting over saloons, at the head of two or three flights of grimy backstairs, or where the street has earned a bad name.

Woman makes demands. Leaders that even the decenter sort of men would passively accept, because they are put forward, since they are such smart fellows, or have pull in trade-union politics, she will have none of, and will quietly work against them. The women leaders have an uncomfortable knack of reminding the union that women are on the map, as it were.

It is at a psychological moment that she is making herself felt in the councils of organized labor. Just as the labor movement is itself being reorganized, with the modern development of the union and of union activity; just as woman herself is coming into her own; just as we are passing through the transition period from one form of society to another; and just as we catch a glimpse of a distant future in which the world will become, for the first time, one.

From the very fact that they are women, women trade unionists have their own distinct contribution to make to the movement. The feminine, and especially the maternal qualities that man appreciates so in the home, he is learning (some men have learnt already) to appreciate in the larger home of the union.

In speaking thus, I freely, if regretfully, admit that the rank and file of both sexes are far indeed from playing their full part. We have still to depend more largely than is quite fitting or democratic upon the leaders as standard-bearers. It is also true that there are women who are willing to accept low ideals in unionism as in everything else. Their influence is bound to pass. If women are to make their own peculiar contribution to the labor movement, it will be by working in glad coöperation with the higher idealism of the men leaders.

And when the day comes (may its coming be hastened!) that women are even only as extensively organized as men are today, the organization of men will indeed proceed by leaps and bounds. It will not be by arithmetical, but by geometrical progression, that the union will count their increases, for it is the masses of unskilled, unorganized, ill-paid women and girl workers today, who in so many trades today increase the difficulties of the men tenfold. That dead weight removed, they could make better terms for themselves and enroll far more men into their ranks. What increase of power, what new and untried forces women may bring with them into the common store, just what these may be, and the manner of their working out, it is too early to say.

But the future was never so full of hope as today, not because conditions are not cruelly hard, and problems not baffling, but, because, over against these conditions, and helping to solve these problems, are ranged the great forces of evolution, ever on the side of the workers, slowly building up the democracy of the future.

APPENDIX I

This document, which is the contract under which a union waitress works, is typical.

AGREEMENT

Between the Hotel and Restaurant Employés' International Alliance Affiliated with the American and the Chicago Federation of Labor.

This contract made and entered into this 10th day of April, 1914, by and between the H. R. E. I. A. affiliated with the American and Chicago Federation of Labor of the City of Chicago, County of Cook and State of Illinois, party of the first part,
and:

Chicago,
Illinois, party of the second part.

Party of the first part agrees to furnish good, competent and honest craftsmen, and does hereby agree to stand responsible for all loss incurred by any act of their respective members in good standing while in line of duty.

The Business Agents of the allied crafts shall have the privilege of visiting and interviewing the employés while on duty, their visits to be timed to such hours when employés are not overly busy.

The second party agrees to employ only members in good standing in their respective unions, of cooks, and waitresses, except when the unions are unable to furnish help to the satisfaction of the   which choice shall be at the discretion of the above company. Then the employer may employ any one he desires, provided the employé makes application to become a member of the union within three days after employment.

Chefs, and Head Waitresses must be members of their respective craft organizations.

WAITRESSES

RESTAURANTS

Steady Waitresses, 6 days, 60 hours........$8.00 per week
Lunch and Supper Waitresses, 7 days, 42
    hours or less............................ 6.50 per week
Dinner Waitresses, 6 days, 3 hours......... 4.00 per week
Extra Supper Waitresses, 6 days, 3 hours.... 4.00 per week
Night Waitresses, 6 days, 60 hours.......... 9.00 per week
Extra Girls, 10 hours a day................. 1.50 per day
Extra Girls, Sundays and Holidays........ 2.00 per day
Head Waitresses, 6 days, 60 hours..........10.00 per week
Ushers, 6 days, 60 hours or less............ 9.00 per week
Ushers, dinner, 6 days, 6 hours or less....... 5.00 per week
Dog watch Waitresses, 6 days, 60 hours...... 9.00 per week

BANQUETS

Three (3) hours or less, $1.50.

Any waitress working extra after midnight serving a banquet, dinner, etc., shall receive 50 cents per hour or fraction of an hour, except the steady night and dog watch waitresses.

Waitresses shall do no porter work.

Overtime shall be charged at the rate of 25 cents per hour or fraction of an hour.

Waitresses shall not be reprimanded in the presence of guests.

Waitresses walking out during meals shall be fined $1.00.

Waitresses after being hired and failing to report for duty shall be fined $1.00.

Employés shall be furnished with proper quarters to change their clothing and there shall be no charge for same.

No profane language shall be used to employés.

There shall be only one split in a ten-hour watch in restaurants.

If employers desire special uniforms they must furnish same free of charge.

Employer shall pay for the laundry of all working linen and furnish same for waitresses.

No member shall be permitted to leave the place of employment during working hours except in case of sickness when a substitute shall be furnished at the earliest possible moment.

Employés shall report for duty at least 15 minutes before the hour called for. They shall be furnished with good, wholesome food.

All hours shall be the maximum.

Head Waitresses and Head Waiters are required to give business agent a list of employés the first week of each month.

Members must wear their working buttons. There shall be no charge for breakage unless breaking is wilful or gross carelessness.

It is agreed that waitresses shall clean silverware once a day.

THIS CONTRACT shall remain in effect until May 1, 1916, unless there is a violation of trade union principles.

ARBITRATION

During the term of this contract, should any differences arise between parties of the first and second part of any causes which cannot be adjusted between them, it shall be submitted to an Arbitration Committee of five, two selected by the party of the first part and two by the party of the second part, and the fifth by the four members of said committee, and while this matter is pending before said committee for adjustment, there shall be no lockout or strike, and the decision of the committee on adjustment shall be final and shall supplement or modify the agreement.

This CONTRACT shall remain in effect until May 1, 1916.

—SIGNED—

PARTY OF THE FIRST PART   PARTY OF THE SECOND PART

....

....

....

....

[NOTE. The dog watch waitress has part day and part night work. She is on duty usually from 11 a. m. till 2 p. m., and again from 5 p. m. till midnight, in some non-union restaurants till one o'clock in the morning. The above agreement calls for not more than one split in a ten-hour watch, otherwise a waitress might be at call practically all day long and yet be only ten hours at work. A. H.]

APPENDIX II

[The following brief abstract covers the essential points in the successive agreements between Hart, Schaffner and Marx, clothing manufacturers, of Chicago, and their employés, and is taken from the pamphlet compiled by Earl Dean Howard, chief deputy for the firm, and Sidney Hillman, chief deputy for the garment workers.]

The conditions upon which the strikers returned to work, as defined in the agreement dated January 14, 1911, summed up, were:

1. All former employés to be taken back within ten days.
2. No discrimination of any kind because of being members, or not being members, of the United Garment Workers of America.
3. An Arbitration Committee of three members to be appointed; one from each side to be chosen within three days; these two then to select the third.
4. Subject to the provisions of this agreement, said Arbitration Committee to take up, consider and adjust grievances, if any, and to fix a method for settlement of grievances (if any) in the future. The finding of the said Committee, or a majority thereof, to be binding upon both parties.

The Arbitration Committee, or Board, consisted of Mr. Carl Meyer, representing the firm, and Clarence Dar-

row, representing the employés. The office of chairman
was not filled until December, 1912, when Mr. J. E. Williams was chosen. The Board settled the questions
around which the dispute had arisen, and an agreement
for two years between the firm and the workers was
signed. For some time the Board continued to handle
fresh complaints, but it gradually became apparent that
the Board, composed of busy men, could not hear all the
minor grievances. The result of a conference was the
organization of a permanent body, the Trade Board, to
deal with all such matters, as these arose, or before they
arose, reserving to both parties the right of appeal to
the Arbitration Board. The plan can be judged from the
following clauses in the constitution of the Trade Board:

TRADE BOARD

The Trade Board shall consist of eleven members who
shall, if possible, be practical men in the trade; all of whom,
excepting the chairman, shall be employés of said corporation; five members thereof shall be appointed by the corporation, and five members by the employés. The members appointed by the corporation shall be certified in writing by the corporation to the chairman of the board, and
the members appointed by the employés shall be likewise
certified in writing by the joint board of garment workers
of Hart Schaffner & Marx to said chairman. Any of said
members of said board, except the chairman, may be removed and replaced by the power appointing him, such new
appointee to be certified to the chairman in the same manner as above provided for.

DEPUTIES

The representatives of each of the parties of the Trade
Board shall have the power to appoint deputies for each
branch of the trade, that is to say, for cutters, coat makers,
trouser makers and vest makers.

APPEAL TO ARBITRATION BOARD

In case either party should desire to appeal from any decision of the Trade Board, or from any change of these rules by the Trade Board, to the Board of Arbitration, they shall have the right to do so upon filing a notice in writing with the Trade Board of such intention within thirty days from the date of the decision, and the said Trade Board shall then certify said matter to the Board of Arbitration, where the same shall be given an early hearing by a full Board of three members.

The Trade Board was accordingly organized, with Mr. James Mullenbach, Acting Superintendent of the United Charities of Chicago, as chairman.

When the time approached for the renewal of the agreement, the closed or open shop was the point around which all discussions turned. Eventually, neither was established, but instead the system of preference to unionists was adopted. It was thus expressed:

1. That the firm agrees to this principle of preference, namely, that they will agree to prefer union men in the hiring of new employés, subject to reasonable restrictions, and also to prefer union men in dismissal on account of slack work, subject to a reasonable preference to older employés, to be arranged by the Board of Arbitration, it being understood that all who have worked for the firm six months shall be considered old employés.

2. All other matters shall be deliberated on and discussed by the parties in interest, and if they are unable to reach an agreement, the matter in dispute shall be submitted to the Arbitration Board for its final decision.

Until an agreement can be reached by negotiation by the parties in interest, or in case of their failure to agree, and a decision is announced by the Arbitration Board, the old agreement shall be considered as being in full force and effect.

This came in force May 1, 1913.

The chairman of the Arbitration Board, making a statement, three months later, in August, 1913, after defining the principle to be "such preference as will make an efficient organization for the workers, also an efficient, productive administration for the company," went on:

In handing down the foregoing decisions relating to preference which grew out of a three months' consideration of the subject, and after hearing it discussed at great length and from every angle, the Board is acutely conscious that it is still largely an experiment, and that the test of actual practice may reveal imperfections, foreseen and unforeseen, which cannot be otherwise demonstrated than by test.

It therefore regards them as tentative and subject to revision whenever the test of experiment shall make it seem advisable.

The Board also feels that unless both parties coöperate in good faith and in the right spirit to make the experiment a success, no mechanism of preferential organization, however cunningly contrived, will survive the jar and clash of hostile feeling or warring interests. It hands down and publishes these decisions therefore in the hope that with the needed coöperation they may help to give the workers a strong, loyal, constructive organization, and the Company a period of peaceful, harmonious and efficient administration and production which will compensate for any disadvantage which the preferential experiment may impose.

The published pamphlet, under date January 28, 1914, concludes:

There have been no cases appealed from the Trade Board to the Board of Arbitration since January, 1913. During the last six months of 1913 there were not more than a dozen Trade Board cases. So many principles have been laid down, and precedents established by both of these bodies, that the chief deputies are in all cases able to reach

an agreement without appeal to a higher authority. A gradual change has taken place in the method of dealing with
questions which present new principles, or which represent
questions never before decided. The Board of Arbitration
has appointed Mr. Williams as a committee to investigate
and report, with the understanding that if an agreement
can be reached by both parties without arbitrators, or, if
the parties are willing to accept the decision of the Chairman, then no further meeting of the Board of Arbitration
will be required. This method has proved to be exceedingly
satisfactory to both sides and has resulted in a form of
government which has gradually taken the place of formal
arbitration. In most cases, the Chairman is able by thorough sifting of the evidence on each side, to suggest a
method of conciliation which is acceptable to both parties.

A further experience of the System up till July, 1915,
only confirms the above statement.

BIBLIOGRAPHY

LIST OF BOOKS AND REPORTS AND PERIODICAL LITERATURE SUGGESTED FOR READING AND REFERENCE

ABBOTT, EDITH. Women in Industry. New York, 1909.

ADAMS, T. H., and SUMNER, H. L. Labor Problems. New York, 1909.

ADDAMS, JANE. The Spirit of Youth in City Streets. New York, 1909.

ANDREWS, JOHN B. A Practical Plan for the Prevention of Unemployment in America. New York, 1914.

—— and BLISS, W. P. D. History of Women in Trade Unions in the United States. Vol. X of the United States Report on the Condition of Women and Child Wage Earners.

BEBEL, AUGUST. Woman in the Past, Present and Future (Trans.). New York, 1885.

BOWEN, LOUISE DE KOVEN. Safeguards for City Youth at Work and at Play. New York, 1915.

BRANDEIS, L. D. *Curt Miller* v. *The State of Oregon.* Brief for defendants. Supreme Court of the United States. New York, 1908.

—— *Frank C. Stettler and others* v. *The Industrial Welfare Commission of the State of Oregon.* Brief and arguments for the defendants in the Supreme Court of the State of Oregon. Consumers' League, New York, 1915.

—— and GOLDMARK, JOSEPHINE. Brief and Arguments for appellants in the Supreme Court of the State of Illinois. National Consumers' League, New York, 1909.

BRECKINRIDGE, SOPHONISBA P. Legislative Control of Women's Work. *Journal of Political Economy.* XIV. 107-109.

298 BIBLIOGRAPHY

BROOKS, JOHN GRAHAM. The Social Unrest. New York, 1903.

BROWN, ROME G. The Minimum Wage. Minneapolis, 1914.

BUSBEY. Women's Trade Union Movement in Great Britain. U. S. Department of Labor. Bul. No. 83.

BUTLER, ELIZABETH B. Saleswomen in Mercantile Stores. New York, 1913.

—— Women in the Trades. New York, 1909.

CANADA. Department of Labor. Report of Royal Commission on Strike of Telephone Operators. Ottawa, 1907.

CLARK, SUE AINSLIE, and WYATT, EDITH. Making Both Ends Meet. New York, 1911.

CLARK, VICTOR S. The Labor Movement in Australia. New York, 1907.

COMMONS, JOHN R. Races and Immigrants in America. New York, 1907.

—— ANDREWS, JOHN B., SUMNER, HELEN L., and OTHERS. Documentary History of American Industrial Society. Cleveland, 1910.

—— and OTHERS. Trade Unionism and Labor Problems. Boston, 1905.

COMMONWEALTH OF AUSTRALIA. Legislative Regulation of Wages. Year Book, No. 5, 1901-1911. pp. 1065-1069.

COOLEY, E. G. See publications of Commercial Club of Chicago on vocational education.

DEVINE, EDWARD T. Social Forces. New York.

DEWEY, JOHN. Schools of Tomorrow. New York, 1915.

—— The School and Society.

DORR, RHETA CHILDE. What Eight Million Women Want. Boston, 1910.

ELY, RICHARD T. The Labor Movement in America. New York, 1905.

GILMAN, CHARLOTTE P. Concerning Children. Boston, 1900.

—— Women and Economics. New York, 1905.

HAMILTON, CICELY. Marriage as a Trade.

HARD, WILLIAM. The Women of Tomorrow. New York, 1911.

HENDERSON, CHARLES RICHMOND. Citizens in Industry. New York, 1915.

HERRON, BELVA M. Progress of Labor Organization Among Women. University of Illinois studies, Vol. 1, No. 10. Urbana, 1908.

HILLMAN, SIDNEY, and HOWARD, EARL DEAN. Hart, Schaffner and Marx Labor Agreements. Chicago, 1914.

HOBSON, JOHN A. Evolution of Modern Capitalism. London, 1904.

—— Problems of Poverty, London, 1906.

HOURWICH, ISAAC A. Immigration and Labor. New York, 1912.

HUMPHREY, J. R. Proportional Representation. London, 1911.

ILLINOIS STATE FEDERATION OF LABOR. Report of Committee on Vocational Education, 1914.

JACOBI, ABRAHAM. Physical Cost of Women's Work. New York, 1907.

KELLEY, FLORENCE. Modern Industry in Relation to the Family. New York, 1915.

—— Some Ethical Gains Through Legislation. New York, 1906.

KELLOR, FRANCES A. Out of Work. New York, 1915 ed.

KERCHENSTEINER, G. M. A. Idea of the Industrial School (Trans.). New York, 1913.

—— Schools and the Nation (Trans.). London, 1914.

KEY, ELLEN. The Woman Movement (Trans.). New York, 1912.

KIRKUP, THOMAS. History of Socialism. London, 1906.

LAGERLÖF, SELMA. Home and the State (Trans.). New York, 1912.

Leavitt, Frank M.   Examples of Industrial Education.
    Boston, 1912.
Levine, Louis.   Syndicalism in France.   New York, 1914.

MacLean, Annie Marion.   Wage Earning Women.   New
    York, 1910.
Marot, Helen.   American Labor Unions.   New York, 1914.
Mason, Otis T.   Woman's Share in Primitive Culture.   1894.
Massachusetts Commission on Industrial Education.
    Reports, 1909.
Matthews, Lillian R.   Women in Trade Unions in San
    Francisco.   University of California, 1913.
Mitchell, John.   Organized Labor.   Philadelphia, 1903.

National Association of Manufacturers.   Preliminary
    report on the Minimum Wage.   New York.
Nearing, Scott.   Wages in the United States, 1908 to 1910.
    New York, 1911.

Oliver, Thomas.   Dangerous Trades.   London, 1902.

Patten, Simon N.   The New Basis of Civilization.   New
    York, 1907.
Peixotto, Jessica B.   Women of California as Trade Union-
    ists.   *Association of Collegiate Alumnæ,* Dec., 1908.
Prescott and Hall.   Immigration and Its Effects.   New
    York, 1900.
Putnam, Emily James.   The Lady.   New York, 1910.

Rauschenbusch, Walter.   Christianity and the Social
    Crisis.   New York, 1907.
——   Christianizing the Social Order.   New York, 1912.
Rhinelander, W. S.   Life and Letters of Josephine Shaw
    Lowell.   New York, 1911.
Richardson, Dorothy.   The Long Day.   New York, 1905.
Rogers, J. E. Thorold.   Six Centuries of Work and Wages.
Roman, F. W.   Industrial and Commercial Schools of the
    United States and Germany.   New York, 1915.
Ross, Edward Alsworth.   Sin and Society.   Boston, 1907.

RUSSELL, CHARLES EDWARD. Why I Am a Socialist. New York, 1910.

RYAN, JOHN A. A Living Wage in Its Ethical and Economic Aspects. New York, 1906.

SALMON, LUCY M. Progress in the Household. Boston, 1906.

SCHREINER, OLIVE. Woman and Labour. London and New York, 1911.

SIMONS, A. M. Social Forces in American History.

SNEDDEN, DAVID M. Problems of Educational Readjustment. New York, 1913.

—— The Problem of Vocational Education. Boston, 1910.

SNOWDEN, PHILIP. The Living Wage. London and New York, 1912.

SOMBART, WERNER. Socialism and the Social Movement (Trans.). New York, 1909.

SPARGO, JOHN. Socialism. New York, 1909.

Syndicalism, Industrial Unionism and Socialism. New York, 1913.

—— and ARNER, G. B. L. Elements of Socialism. New York, 1912.

SPENCER, ANNA GARLIN. Woman and Social Culture. New York, 1913.

SUMNER, HELEN L. History of Women in Industry in the United States. Vol. IX of the United States Report on the Condition of Women and Child Wage Earners. 1910.

THOMAS, W. I. Sex and Society. University of Chicago Press, 1907.

VAN KLEECK, MARY. Artificial Flówer Making. Women in the Bookbinding Trade. Russell Sage Foundation publications, 1912.

VAN VORST, BESSIE and MARIE. The Woman Who Toils. New York, 1903.

WARD, LESTER F. Pure Sociology (especially Chapter XIV). New York.

WEBB, SIDNEY. Economic Theory of a Legal Minimum

Wage. *Journal of Political Economy*, Vol. 20, No. 12., Dec., 1912.

—— and BEATRICE. History of Trade Unionism. London, 1907.

WELLS, H. G. New Worlds for Old. New York, 1909.

WEYL, WALTER E. The New Democracy. New York, 1910.

WILLETT, M. H. Employment of Women in the Clothing Trades. Columbia University. New York, 1902.

WILSON, JENNIE L. Legal and Political Status of Women in the United States.

WINSLOW, CHARLES H., Editor. Twenty-fifth Annual Report of the United States Bureau of Labor. Industrial Training.

WOLFE, F. E. Admission to Labor Unions. Johns Hopkins University Press.

MINIMUM WAGE, THE CASE FOR.
By Louis D. Brandeis, M. B. Hammond, John A. Hobson, Florence Kelley, Esther Packard, Elizabeth C. Watson, Howard B. Woolston. *The Survey*, Feb. 6, 1915.

Periodicals and Reports

American Federationist, A. F. of L. Newsletter, and other publications of the American Federation of Labor. Washington, D. C.

American Legislation Review and other publications of the American Association for Labor Legislation. New York.

Annals of the American Academy of Political Science. Philadelphia.

Child Labor Bulletin, The (National), and other publications of the National Child Labor Committee, New York.

Commercial Club of Chicago. Publications on Vocational Training.

Crisis, The. New York.

Economic Review.

Forerunner, The. New York.

Immigrant in America Review, The. New York.

Journal of Political Economy, The. University of Chicago Press.

Journal of Sociology, The. University of Chicago Press.

Labour Leader, The. Manchester, England.

Labour Woman, The, and other publications of the National Women's Labour League. London.

Life and Labor, and other publications of the National Women's Trade Union League of America. Chicago; and of the local leagues in Boston, Chicago, New York and elsewhere.

Masses, The. New York.

National Consumers' League, Publications of. New York.

National Society for the Promotion of Industrial Education, Publications of. New York.

New Republic, The. New York.

New York State Factory Investigation Commission, Reports. New York.

New York Sunday Call, The. New York.

Political Science Quarterly. Columbia University.

Public, The. Chicago.

Quarterly Journal of Economics. Harvard University.

Survey, The. New York.

Union Labor Advocate. Woman's Department, up to Dec., 1910.

United States Bureau of Education. Bulletins on vocational education.

—— Census of 1910. Occupational statistics.

—— Children's Bureau. Bulletins.

—— Department of Agriculture. Bulletins for Women on the Farm.

—— Department of Labor, Bulletins.

—— Industrial Relations Commission Reports.

—— Women and Child Wage Earners, Report on Conditions of. 19 Volumes.

Woman's Industrial News, The. London.

Woman's Journal, The. Boston.

INDEX